# ARCHITECTURE 09
## RIBA BUILDINGS OF THE YEAR
### EDITED BY TONY CHAPMAN

RIBA 🏛 Trust

**MERRELL**
LONDON · NEW YORK

First published 2009 by

Merrell Publishers Limited
81 Southwark Street
London SE1 0HX

merrellpublishers.com

British Library Cataloguing-in-Publication Data:
Architecture 09 : RIBA buildings of the year.
1. Architecture – Awards – Great Britain –
    Periodicals.
2. Architecture – Awards – Europe – Periodicals.
I. Chapman, Tony, 1950– II. Royal Institute of
    British Architects.
720.7'941'05-dc22

ISBN 978-1-8589-4490-6


Produced by Merrell Publishers Limited
Picture research by Clemency Christopherson
Designed by Paul Arnot
Indexed by Vicki Robinson

Printed and bound in Slovenia

# INTRODUCTION: WHAT HAS THE RIBA EVER DONE FOR US?

**TONY CHAPMAN**

'Don't you know there's a recession on?' only one architect asked me in February, complaining about the cost of entering the RIBA Awards during hard times. I pointed out that perhaps it made even more sense to enter a meaningful awards programme right now, that an award might give winners a competitive edge. But I would say that, wouldn't I? Even though it's my day, night and weekend job to organize these and other awards, I really do believe in them and in what they can do to reward good practice and to promote the best practitioners to the wider world.

As you can see from the extra pages in this year's book, the RIBA does a lot more in this field besides running its own awards. The Housing Design Awards have been demonstrating the benefits of good design since 1947, when Nye Bevan – who, as Minister of Health, had responsibility for housing – approached the RIBA with the idea of such an awards programme. For more than sixty years these awards have rewarded the best and encouraged the not-so-good developers to do better. And by involving planners as well as housebuilders in the process, they have persuaded all parties to buy into the idea. The connection with the government and its agencies is as important today as ever it has been, the Homes and Communities Agency joining the Department of Communities and Local Government, the National House-Building Council, the Royal Town Planning Institute and the RIBA as sponsors of the awards. The unique selling point of the Housing Design Awards is that they reward the best as-yet-unbuilt projects, as well as completed schemes. The unbuilt schemes are all reconsidered when they are built, the best winning further awards, while those that disappointed are notable by their absence.

The Royal Gold Medal has been awarded annually since 1848. It is one of world architecture's premier prizes, although the upstart Pritzker attracts more press coverage, largely on account of its generous prize money (the Gold Medallist receives just a silver gilt medal). The Pritzker can afford to give away $100,000 out of an annual budget that is rumoured to be around $2,000,000.

Judging the Royal Gold Medal couldn't be more different from judging the RIBA Stirling Prize. The Stirling Prize involves more than seven hundred visits; the Gold Medal is determined by a handful of men and women sitting around a table. They look at images, pore over books and argue passionately and endlessly. You wouldn't expect it to be easy. These are architectural heavyweights going fifteen rounds: Kenneth Frampton vs Jeremy Dixon, Richard Rogers vs Terry Farrell – and that's just the judges. Egging them on are the backers of the various nominations, the crowd *in absentia*. Because these proceedings take place behind closed doors, there are no formal minutes. And no list of nominees is published: who would benefit from it being made known that *X* was unsuccessfully nominated *Y* times? There's always next year – unless the Grim Reaper steps in, which has been known.

Only the architectural press, keen to boost falling subscriptions and plummeting advertising revenues, might benefit from the juicy details of the Gold Medal judging being made available. However, while journalists fall over one another to get a scoop on the RIBA Awards and the Stirling Prize, with the Gold Medal all is decorum. It was not ever thus. We used to try to keep the winner secret for months until the medal was presented. We gave that up after Paul finch, then editor of *Building Design*, armed with a shortlist of nominees, rang round all the major London hotels the day before the presentation and asked to speak to whoever was his first guess. He rang back with another name and then another until the receptionist said, 'Signor Piano is not in his room.' Bingo! Hold the front page. That's what I call journalism. These days we wait only until the proposed recipient has accepted and Her Majesty has approved the name. (She's yet to refuse, even when the City of Barcelona won the medal in the midst of a bitter dispute between the United Kingdom and Spain over Gibraltar. Perhaps she was well advised that, given the choice, the Catalans would probably side with the Brits against the Madrileños.)

Things might be different with the next monarch. There was a suggestion this year – the RIBA's 175th anniversary – to invite HRH The Prince of Wales to revisit the topic of his speech of 1984, when he used the occasion of presenting Charles Correa with his Gold Medal to rebuke architects for their 'carbuncular' tendencies. Instead, HRH was invited to give the Annual Lecture, in which he delivered a not-dissimilar message, albeit in somewhat more conciliatory language. He also cleverly praised David Chipperfield's Neues Museum in Berlin, much to Chipperfield's embarrassment.

The RIBA recently commissioned some research about perceptions of the Gold Medal – and then sat on the findings it didn't like. Not that it was particularly surprising to learn that more people have heard of the Pritzker Prize than the Royal Gold Medal. Or that some architects would rather win the former than the latter. Really? You mean, not everyone would choose $100,000 over zilch pounds? Most people who were questioned felt that the judging process should be more transparent, with publication of the shortlist and minutes. The Gold Medal is the nearest the RIBA gets to papal white smoke, and I rather like that. The choices of Álvaro Siza, Toyo Ito, Le Corbusier or Oscar Niemeyer are scarcely exceptionable, so can't we just celebrate the winner? And if people consider a winner controversial, telling them that one out of seven jurors agrees will only encourage them. We elect governments on lower majorities.

A favourite architectural parlour game is to name your top five architects who have never won the Gold Medal. A&P Smithson would still win it if some had their way. I continue to be lobbied for a rule change that would allow dead architects to win. The more fruitful game would be to name five living greats who have never won the medal: Nicholas Grimshaw, of course, the most significant non-winning hi-tech architect; Günter Behnisch (we gave it to Frei Otto, his Munich Stadium collaborator); Glenn Murcutt; Zaha Hadid? Have they really never won it? Top of most people's list till this year, however, would have been Siza, the man who epitomizes half a century of Portuguese architecture.

It was one of the highlights of my architectural life – up there with meeting Niemeyer – to interview Siza (see pp. 214–15) and to film most of his buildings for a short movie to be shown at the Gold Medal presentation (architecture.com/Awards/RoyalGoldMedal/RoyalGoldMedal2009/RGM2009Videos). Siza was roguishly charming and extraordinarily generous with his time. He even managed not to smoke for most of our three-hour interview. (People who want to work with him have to sign a contract saying they won't object to his smoking; only one has ever done so.) 'My friends have all given up smoking, and they die', he told me, lighting up on the doorstep of a Porto restaurant to which he took me and his protégé, Eduardo Souto de Moura, one of this year's International Fellows. Siza is still very much alive and busier than ever. He gave one of the most gracious acceptance speeches ever, concluding with these words: 'The nomination has for me a special meaning, as it comes from an institution [that promotes] architecture as an art, as a big tree with roots that immerse deeply into the ground and with long branches that spread in all directions: the tree of life. I felt a tremble as I crossed the hall of this house and looked at the wall covered with engraved names, but here I am, as quiet as emotion allows. Thank you very much.'

RIBA Fellowships are a bit like the honorary degrees handed out by universities. Similarly, it is not unknown for the honour to mean more to the donor than it does to the recipient. These days there are two categories: Honorary Fellowships for non-architects, and International Fellowships for non-British architects. Formerly, recipients, including foreign Royal Gold Medallists, were all made Honorary Fellows, until the Architects Registration Board stamped on the hypothetical possibility of non-architects passing themselves off as architects. The present arrangement is probably tidier, although I rather liked the alphabetic serendipity of Henning Larsen and Lucinda Lambton or Renzo Piano and the late Monica Pidgeon. At the ceremony at which we celebrated Siza's Gold Medal we also welcomed the likes of Doreen Lawrence, mother of the murdered black teenager who aspired to be an architect, who since her son's death has run a trust in his name to encourage young people from minority backgrounds to train as architects; and Laura Lee, who runs the cancer-care charity Maggie's, named after the wife of Charles Jencks, whom she nursed, and who has commissioned a series of fine, small centres from the world's top architects, including this year's Stirling-shortlisted centre in Hammersmith by Rogers Stirk Harbour + Partners.

At the ceremony we also welcomed architects including Kengo Kuma from Japan, and Lacaton and Vassal from France. For these International Fellows, recognition is a passport to the RIBA Awards and the Lubetkin Prize, much to the chagrin of those members of the RIBA with a 'Little Britain' tendency. But I'm all for it; we are an international organization, after all. In fact, because of the history and prestige of the RIBA, because the Institute has led the world in architectural education, and because of its honours system, which makes members of architects from all over the world, the RIBA's awards are a bit like the Premier League, where British footballers are given the chance to compete against the best in the world week in, week out. And while we are arguing about whether the 'A' in RIBA stands for 'Architects' or 'Architecture', why don't we also discuss whether the 'B' stands for 'British' or 'Boundless'?

Then there are the President's Medals, given to students of architecture. These are the only major awards in the RIBA that I don't run; I'm more than happy to leave that to my expert colleagues in the Education Department, ably led by John-Paul Nunes. The three major prizes are all represented in this book (see pp. 234–41): the Dissertation Medal; the Bronze Medal, presented to the best Part 1 student; and the Silver Medal, given to the best Part 2 postgraduate student. Gold is, of course, reserved for the Royal Gold Medallist, and this neat and flattering hierarchy is celebrated every February, when the students are invited to present their work to be criticized by the Medallist. Language can be a problem; it certainly was for Toyo Ito, less so for Siza. But there may also be other failures of communication. Ted Cullinan, recipient of the Gold Medal in 2008, couldn't fathom how students who, unlike him, were born in an age of communications could find it so difficult to present what was, as he stressed, brilliant work. It was a painful lesson, but an ever-more important one in these recessionary times. There's a danger that, as in the late 1980s and early 1990s, we'll lose a whole generation of architects. This isn't altogether surprising. Some would say we're training too many architects, and architectural skills are highly transferable. But the students can't all become good clients or planners, curators or journalists. They can't all do my job.

Times are hard for the RIBA itself, dependent as it is on membership subscriptions, the profits of its trading arm, and sponsorship. It was thanks to the generosity of new sponsors – and happy accidents of geography – that we were able to continue to judge this year's Lubetkin Prize, the fourth, as rigorously as ever. This year we did a bit of gerrymandering. Two years ago we changed the rules of the Stirling Prize so that projects had to be either designed or built in Britain. This requirement disenfranchised non-British firms building in Europe. This year we've put that right, and have allowed such schemes to enter the International Awards, which means they are now eligible for the Lubetkin Prize. And this year, instead of two visiting judges, there were three, although they did not all go together. Sunand Prasad, in his presidential capacity, had already been to see the Chinese and Sri Lankan schemes, and I and Paul Monaghan, Chair of the Awards Group, dragged him off to see the shortlisted buildings in Ireland and Germany.

One victim of cost-cutting this year was the National Awards Dinner, which was scaled back to the presentation of the European Union and International Awards and the Lubetkin Prize, and from a dinner to a reception. The change of venue from the Hilton to the Durbar Court at the Foreign Office, however, felt more like an upgrade, in spite of the technical problems. We were there courtesy of UK Trade & Investment and Trade Minister Lord Davies.

Our final meeting to decide the Lubetkin winner had been as tough as any I've taken part in or witnessed. We viewed the five-minute movies I'd made about each visit, to remind those who had been there and to inform those who hadn't seen all the schemes: Alison Brooks (one of last year's Stirling winners) and journalist and broadcaster Tom Dyckhoff. The criteria are broadly the same for all our awards: we're looking for the most significant contribution to architecture; the best response to a challenging brief; a building that is sustainable in construction and in use. But criteria are better suited to whittling away at shortlists than to picking winners.

Sometimes the winner speaks – or shouts – for itself; more often, there are a couple of even contenders. The Lubetkin debate centred around what constitutes sustainability and how such factors should weigh against other architectural considerations. The quantity of steel in the National Stadium in Beijing counted against it, but this is a building that could be around for hundreds of years, so in terms of lifetime costing … And steel can be recycled, whereas concrete can't, and what about the double structure, and why is the concrete pretending to be steel? But consider the challenge, the degree of difficulty. They must come into play. And the stadium has proved itself in combat, so to speak, whereas the gallery in Munich has only just opened, although its environmental credentials are immaculate, using ground-source water to heat and cool the building. And the skin … Talking of skin, the Watercube has a skin to die for, but it's let down by the cost-cutting inside and the overdone graphics. And talking of combat, the British High Commission in Sri Lanka has seen real combat, with its glass window on the world standing up to mass demonstrations. And the way it builds on the local vernacular … but isn't that section a bit fussy? While we're on the subject of degree of difficulty, what about Beijing Airport? It's quite an achievement to build an airport in the time it took Heathrow's Terminal 5's planning inquiry to agree its terms of reference. But the roof is both its strength and its weakness; a thing of great beauty, but thrown away by unimaginative lighting at night, when the complexity of the space frame and the timber could have been enhanced by … so perhaps the Dublin community centre might be the one to come through the middle. It ticks more boxes than a voter in a by-election using the single transferable voting system: tough, rigorous, beautiful, a simple, effective plan and a social agenda to boot. But surely that tower was a mistake …

These were tough calls. We all agreed that four out of the six projects were probably their architects' best buildings. In the end we held our breath, and some even their noses, and we jumped. We employed the judgment-of-history argument (as did the Stirling jury in 2005, when it picked the Scottish Parliament). Even though history is notoriously hard to second-guess, this was perhaps one of those decisions that had to be. The losers were all magnanimous. After congratulating the winner, I always make a point of commiserating with the runners-up. It's just a pity we never got to hear Richard Murphy's winner's speech for the British High Commission; it sounded like a cracker. 'I knew I was going to win tonight', he re-rehearsed for me. 'As I was walking through Westminster to get here, every building site was festooned with signs saying Murphy.'

The Stirling Prize this year lacked the same big hitters as Lubetkin, but generated far more controversy. Ever since questions were raised about whether, in the light of reduced sponsorship, there could or should be a £20,000 prize, everyone has been having their say. I firmly believe that there should be prize money, just not at the risk of jeopardizing the thoroughness of the judging process. And in the end there was, thanks to ex-RIBA President Marco Goldschmied, and – just as he couples the Stephen Lawrence Prize money with a donation to a student bursary in Stephen's name – he matched it with a donation to Amnesty. We matched it by accepting a donation from the Chinese company Crystal, which created the amazing computer graphics for the opening ceremony of the Beijing Olympics in 2008, and will be doing something similar for London in 2012. More controversy was stirred up, not least by architects who are happy to work in China themselves but don't think their institute should take Chinese money. Why, others asked, didn't we take up an offer from a British company? Simple: because there was no firm offer on the table at the time.

Then there were the usual arguments over the Stirling shortlist. Many people seem to think it's a question of drawing names out of a hat, and that their six picks are as good as or better than the six that emerge from three levels of judging. I can deal rationally with arguments about the eligibility of masterplans (anyway, we were judging not just the masterplan but also its delivery), but the idea that we might put someone on the list – twice – because Prince Charles was horrid to him is simply risible. The Awards Group visited twenty-two projects across Europe, heard the presentations of their architects and clients and of the original visiting judges, watched videos of them all, and for a full day debated the issues arising before agreeing the final six. The Awards Group is sometimes accused of fixing the Stirling shortlist to make good television. We don't need to: good architecture makes good telly.

So these were the six projects we set out to see in early September. Four days of visits, not counting the travelling. The judges came from as far afield as the buildings were flung. John Tuomey from Dublin replaced Edward Jones in late July, when Ed was disbarred because he designed one-twenty-sixth of Liverpool One; as did Sam Jacob of FAT, replaced by Stephen Bates. See how scrupulous we are? Benedetta Tagliabue, who completed her late husband's designs for the Scottish Parliament, flew in from Barcelona. And then there were the non-architects: Sir John Sorrell, out-going Chair of the Commission for Architecture and the Built Environment, and designer Thomas Heatherwick. We gathered in Kentish Town to see the health centre designed by Paul Monaghan – a Finsbury Health Centre *de nos jours*. I had seen all six buildings before and had my say, so I was there only to keep the show on the road, to arbitrate and to make sure we kept to time and, of course, budget. No flights were missed, and we travelled economy class, even flying with a cut-price airline. We finished up with a fixed-price meal in Copenhagen harbour, arguing into the early hours without reaching any serious conclusion. That came when the judges emerged from five weeks of isolation and regrouped at Old Billingsgate on the afternoon of the presentation. And the winner was ...

# A YEAR IN
# ARCHITECTURE

**RUTH REED, RIBA PRESIDENT**

In 2009 the RIBA celebrates a significant birthday. It is 175 years since, in the words of a Report of Council of 1836, the Institute 'burst into life'. Earl de Grey, who remained President for twenty-five years – these days the term of office is restricted to two years – outlined in the objectives of the new Institute 'the advantages which Architecture, as a national art, would derive from its foundation'. Writing a century later in the official centenary history, past President J.A. Gotch speculated, 'Whether the noble President's expectations have been entirely fulfilled is perhaps doubtful. But this I think we may say – that the public do take a more intelligent interest in architecture than they did.' Today he would be even more convinced of the effective role that the RIBA plays in educating the public about architecture, thanks in no small part to the RIBA Stirling Prize, Channel 4 and Kevin McCloud.

The RIBA's Professional Services provides more practical support services and guidance for architects, with such initiatives as the Recession Survival Kit and the Value Toolkit, aimed at equipping members to deal better with the challenges of the economic climate. Other updated toolkits include those on climate change, which help members integrate the fast-evolving discipline of low-carbon design into their everyday practice.

The RIBA has put in place a series of measures to support and sustain its members in these challenging times. These include new member benefits; the promotion of Chartered Practices at such client exhibitions as *Cityscape Dubai* and *Grand Designs Live*; a new membership marketing department; changes to the membership classes, such as the new Associate Member class for the partly qualified; and new concession subscription rates. These measures will enable the RIBA to continue to fulfil the mission laid down in its Royal Charter: to 'advance architecture' by enabling architects and practices to produce good architecture and by promoting to clients, the public and the government the beneficial impact good design has on the way we all live.

The RIBA has its own charitable trust – the RIBA Trust – to do just that. It has been organizing lectures 'by men who were engaged in the practice of architecture to help students' (according to one annual report) since the 1860s. In 2009 it has offered platforms to speakers as distinguished and as diverse as Álvaro Siza, HRH The Prince of Wales, Peter Zumthor, Jonathon Porritt, Daniel Libeskind and Joseph Rykwert (the last two both part of the 'Open:Poland' series of talks and exhibitions). Not all speakers are architects, of course, because we believe that architecture is too important to be left entirely to architects.

The RIBA Trust is also the vehicle for extensive programmes of exhibitions and awards. The year 2009 has seen exhibitions at the RIBA of the work of Scottish architect Gareth Hoskins and of the Swiss architect Valerio Olgiati, while at the V&A + RIBA Architecture Gallery the major exhibition was *Europe and the English Baroque: Architecture in England 1660–1715*. However, by far the biggest exhibition the Trust has mounted to date took place in major venues away from Portland Place. *Le Corbusier – The Art of Architecture* attracted 25,000 people to the little-known Lutyens crypt of Liverpool's Metropolitan Cathedral. It formed the core of an ambitious programme of talks, displays, seminars, symposia and publications. The exhibition then moved to the Barbican in London, where a further 70,000 people saw it. For the RIBA, 'Corb' established new partnerships and a reputation on which to build future cultural projects.

The Royal Academy was the setting for the next of these collaborative exhibitions: *Andrea Palladio: His Life and Legacy*, the international touring exhibition to mark the quincentenary of Palladio's birth. As well as providing 70 per cent of the material for that exhibition, the British Architectural Library has been busy making its collections available electronically to all. A programme of digitization means that many of its images can now be seen online (ribapix.com) and in a series of online exhibitions on the RIBA's website (architecture.com), such as the one on the 162-year history of the Royal Gold Medal.

A series of other activities was organized to mark the RIBA's 175th anniversary. The Poet Laureate Andrew Motion was commissioned to write a poem that was more subtly allusive than commemorative, which then-President Sunand Prasad read out at the Royal Gold Medal Dinner, to the obvious pleasure of the highly literate Medallist. Her Majesty The Queen herself presented the medal to Álvaro Siza at Buckingham Palace, only the fourth occasion on which she had presented the award in person. And her heir was invited back for the first time in twenty-five years to give the Annual Lecture, in which he offered a kind of olive branch to the architectural profession, apologizing for the manner, if not the content, of the 'monstrous carbuncle' speech he gave at Hampton Court in 1984. There were other, somewhat lighter '175' events. Eastbourne College won a schools competition to design new parliament buildings with a radical scheme that relocated the national parliament to an old brownfield site in Ashford, Kent, and was commended for its consideration of sustainability issues.

As for the RIBA Awards proper, these are run by a surprisingly small team – considering the international renown and importance of their work – of just two people, backed up by an Events team of one. They support and are supported by a group of architects who advise on policy and criteria and who do most of the judging: the RIBA Awards Group. The results of those processes form the substance of this book.

The RIBA continues – in the words of the annual report of 1872 – 'to represent the interests of Architecture both as a Profession and as an Art'. At the end of 2008 the Planning Act received Royal Assent. RIBA lobbying on this bill and the Housing and Regeneration Bill helped ensure that local authorities and housing agencies now have a duty 'to take action on climate change in their development plans, and to have regard to the desirability of achieving good design'.

The RIBA's Building Futures launched a report on the prospects for universities and cities, which aimed to investigate synergies between 'town and gown'. Its client forums are designed to strengthen the relationship between architects and their clients working in such key industry sectors as housing, health, education, sport and leisure. Each forum co-ordinates its own programmes of workshops, exhibitions, best-practice guides and awards.

The Competitions Office, based in Leeds, organized a series of international architectural competitions for projects, including the extension of the Imperial War Museum North, a student centre at the London School of Economics, and an educational, conference and seed-production complex at the National Wildflower Centre in Knowsley. It also ran an ideas competition: London Bridge 800: Design an Inhabited Bridge.

The RIBA's Research and Development Department's interprofessional Knowledge Communities project provides a vehicle for advancing specialist areas of interest in architecture and the built environment by providing online forums and global collaborative tools to share and develop knowledge, in partnership with external stakeholders and organizations.

In 2009 the RIBA remained the world leader in setting standards for architectural education, responsible for validating forty-one schools of architecture and three examination centres in the

United Kingdom, and recognizing eighty-seven overseas schools of architecture (twenty-nine directly validated by the RIBA, twenty recognized via partnership with the Union Internationale des Architectes [UIA], and thirty-eight recognized via a mutuality agreement with the Commonwealth Association of Architects [CAA]). The RIBA is also responsible for the management of the UNESCO–UIA validation system, and acts as education consultant to the CAA.

As well as adding its voice to the campaign to raise the United Kingdom's 2050 carbon-emissions reductions target from 60 per cent to 80 per cent (on 1990 levels), a measure that has been adopted by the government, the RIBA continues to put its own house in order, switching to a 100 per cent sustainably sourced electricity supply at 66 Portland Place, which single action reduced our carbon footprint by 56 per cent, and implementing a zero waste-to-landfill policy. In 1934, in the midst of another major recession, the RIBA celebrated its centenary anniversary by opening its new headquarters. Today, in equally hard times, that fine building is an asset that is being heavily sweated – if that is the correct expression – with profits from the RIBA's venues business, which raises income for Institute activities and services from meetings, conferences and the cafe and restaurant at 66 Portland Place, holding up well.

So, what now? The Institute has to continue to address supporting operations with constraints on its finance but within a very clear policy remit of maintaining our public voice. The RIBA will be campaigning hard to maintain quality in the built environment in the face of financial pressures to cut back. Our position is strengthened by the public perception of the RIBA as the leading authority on architecture, so this too must be supported with exhibitions, lectures and media collaborations reinforcing the brand.

In practice, there must be a gear shift to speed up the implementation of low-carbon design, and the awards system is adapting to recognize this by making sustainability a prerequisite for success. In education, the new skill demands should be identified and delivered in order to maintain the key role of architects, while, in research and development, more work must be done towards the introduction of legislation on the ways our buildings perform. All of this needs to be clearly communicated to our members. A revitalized ethos of shared ownership of the challenges ahead will accelerate the response to the low-carbon agenda. This does not mean that we face a utilitarian response. Architects are good at converting constraints into drivers for excellence in design, and there are already plenty of examples of well-designed, high-performing buildings that demonstrate the way forward. The new stable of thoroughbred buildings in the awards of the future will be beautiful, lean, sustainable and very efficient – something to be anticipated with delight.

# THE RIBA STIRLING PRIZE

IN ASSOCIATION WITH THE *ARCHITECTS' JOURNAL*

The RIBA Stirling Prize, now in its fourteenth year, is sponsored for the ninth time by the *Architects' Journal*. It is awarded to the architects of the building thought to be the most significant of the year for the evolution of architecture and the built environment. It is the United Kingdom's richest and most prestigious architectural prize. A building is eligible for the Stirling Prize if it is in the UK or elsewhere in the European Union, and is designed by a practice whose principal office is in the UK. The shortlist for the RIBA Stirling Prize is selected from RIBA Award-winners. The winners receive a cheque for £20,000 and a trophy, which they hold for one year.

The prize is named after the architect Sir James Stirling (1926–1992), one of the most important British architects of his generation and a progressive thinker and designer throughout his career. He is best known for his Leicester University Engineering Building (1959–63), the Staatsgalerie in Stuttgart (1977–84) and his posthumous Number One Poultry building in London (1998). His former partner, Michael Wilford, won the Stirling Prize in 1997 for the jointly designed Stuttgart Music School, and in 2003 won an RIBA Award for the History Museum that completed Stirling's masterplan for the Stuttgart Staatsgalerie complex.

The first Stirling Prize winner, in 1996, was Hodder Associates, for the University of Salford. Subsequent winners have been Michael Wilford and Partners, for the Music School, Stuttgart, in 1997; Foster + Partners, for the American Air Museum, Duxford, in 1998, and 30 St Mary Axe, London, in 2004; Future Systems, for the NatWest Media Centre at Lord's, London, in 1999; Alsop & Störmer, for Peckham Library and Media Centre, London, in 2000; Wilkinson Eyre Architects, for Magna, Rotherham, in 2001, and Millennium Bridge, Gateshead, in 2002; Herzog & de Meuron, for Laban, London, in 2003; EMBT/RMJM for the Scottish Parliament, Edinburgh, in 2005; Richard Rogers Partnership with Estudio Lamela, for the New Area Terminal, Barajas Airport, Madrid, in 2006; David Chipperfield Architects, for the Museum of Modern Literature, Marbach am Neckar, Germany, in 2007; and Feilden Clegg Bradley Studios, Alison Brooks Architects and Maccreanor Lavington, for Accordia, Cambridge, in 2008.

## WINNER

MAGGIE'S LONDON
CHARING CROSS HOSPITAL,
FULHAM PALACE ROAD, LONDON W6
ROGERS STIRK HARBOUR + PARTNERS

## JUDGES

JOHN TUOMEY (CHAIR)
ARCHITECT

STEPHEN BATES
ARCHITECT

THOMAS HEATHERWICK
DESIGNER

SIR JOHN SORRELL
DESIGNER AND CHAIR OF CABE

BENEDETTA TAGLIABUE
ARCHITECT

## SHORTLIST

5 ALDERMANBURY SQUARE
LONDON EC2
ERIC PARRY ARCHITECTS

BODEGAS PROTOS
PEÑAFIEL, VALLADOLID, SPAIN
ROGERS STIRK HARBOUR + PARTNERS

FUGLSANG KUNSTMUSEUM
TOREBY, LOLLAND, DENMARK
TONY FRETTON ARCHITECTS

KENTISH TOWN HEALTH CENTRE
BARTHOLOMEW ROAD, LONDON NW5
ALLFORD HALL MONAGHAN MORRIS

LIVERPOOL ONE MASTERPLAN
LIVERPOOL
BDP

Maggie's London, Rogers Stirk Harbour + Partners

# MAGGIE'S LONDON
## CHARING CROSS HOSPITAL, FULHAM PALACE ROAD, LONDON W6
## ROGERS STIRK HARBOUR + PARTNERS

CLIENT **MAGGIE'S (LAURA LEE)**
LANDSCAPE ARCHITECT **DAN PEARSON STUDIO**
STRUCTURAL ENGINEER **ARUP**
SERVICES ENGINEER **TURNER & TOWNSEND**
LIGHTING CONSULTANT **SPEIRS AND MAJOR ASSOCIATES**
ACCESS CONSULTANT **VIN GOODWIN**
CONTRACTOR **ROK**
CONTRACT VALUE **£2,100,000**
DATE OF COMPLETION **APRIL 2008**
GROSS INTERNAL AREA **370 SQ. M**
IMAGES **RICHARD BRYANT – ARCAID**
**MAGGIE'S WAS JOINT WINNER OF THE RIBA CLIENT OF THE YEAR**

The latest in a line of Maggie's Centres designed by distinguished architects stands on a hectic corner on the Fulham Palace Road in Hammersmith. A deep-orange rendered wall puts a protective arm around the site, making it a place apart without denying it is a part of the city. This antithesis of a hospital provides an open

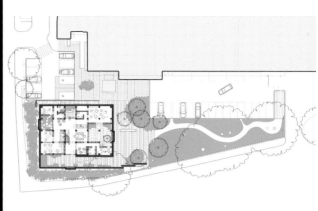

**FIRST-FLOOR PLAN**

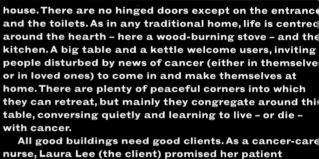

house. There are no hinged doors except on the entrance and the toilets. As in any traditional home, life is centred around the hearth – here a wood-burning stove – and the kitchen. A big table and a kettle welcome users, inviting people disturbed by news of cancer (either in themselves or in loved ones) to come in and make themselves at home. There are plenty of peaceful corners into which they can retreat, but mainly they congregate around this table, conversing quietly and learning to live – or die – with cancer.

All good buildings need good clients. As a cancer-care nurse, Laura Lee (the client) promised her patient Maggie Jencks that she would carry out her dying wish: to see cancer sufferers and their families and friends offered humane facilities in which they could learn about the illness and receive support. In just thirteen years since the first centre, designed by Richard Murphy, was opened in Edinburgh, five more, by some of the world's leading architects (including Frank Gehry and Zaha Hadid), have opened, with a further eight planned or under construction. For the latest, and the first in London, Charles Jencks turned to his old friend Richard Rogers, whose practice is just around the corner.

The centre was conceived as a two-storey pavilion, and its positive spirit is signalled by a bold roof canopy that hovers high above the walls to sail protectively over a series of intimate internal gardens, courtyards and roof terraces, all landscaped by Dan Pearson, as is the all-important approach. The architects, led by Ivan Harbour, considered placing the entrance on the street corner, but that would have denied the centre a proper approach. Passing along the garden wall to the centre's entrance, one notices a window seat, where one can stop, sit and contemplate. How many buildings provide their visitors with such simple luxury of time? One large opening in the façade provides a glimpse of a courtyard garden and the table beyond; it immediately speaks of simple human pleasures, and invites us in.

The building's domestic heart is washed in light and framed by concrete columns that were cast *in situ*. The column arrangement is based on a 4-metre grid, providing ideal proportions for the consultation and

treatment rooms, living-spaces and garden courtyards that all open off the kitchen. Privacy can be created by sliding screens, translucent glass panels, or bookshelves. These are built in a light timber, as is the furniture. The client suggested IKEA; the architects persuaded Maggie's to go for something closer to Aalto. And there is a Scandinavian air of well-being to the centre: this could be a private house in a Finnish forest instead of a health building on the Fulham Palace Road.

The first floor is given over largely to administration, but is informally arranged: staff work mainly at tables in corners, and users are free, even encouraged – by the presence of a library – to come up here. Balustrades at this level have been detailed as bookshelves and display surfaces – another example of the architects making every element of the building work in a multiplicity of modes, both beautiful and functional. This series of mezzanines, open to the floor below, feels like a tree house with views out on all four sides. A suntrap roof terrace, protected by the oversailing roof, frames an interesting view of the hospital tower.

This Maggie's Centre demonstrates architecture's power to shape our experience, and makes a fitting memorial to Maggie Keswick Jencks. Rogers Stirk Harbour has produced a timeless work of architecture

that not only distils the intentions of the brief, but also expresses, in built form, compassion, sensitivity and a deep sense of our common humanity.

The Stirling judges identified a fit between the sensibility of the practice and the achievement here. And they liked the way the practice is still experimenting, commenting: 'They have done something new, which would not be there without that crazy dream. This is Rogers in a bottle.' They concluded: 'The city has enough big icons. This is a little icon, a local hero, that gives something back to the local community.'

# 5 ALDERMANBURY SQUARE
## LONDON EC2
## ERIC PARRY ARCHITECTS

CLIENT **SCOTTISH WIDOWS**
STRUCTURAL ENGINEER **RAMBOLL WHITBYBIRD**
SERVICES ENGINEER **HILSON MORAN**
QUANTITY SURVEYOR **NORTHCROFT**
DEVELOPMENT MANAGER **HANOVER CUBE**
CONTRACTOR **BOVIS**
CONTRACT VALUE **£72,000,000**
DATE OF COMPLETION **OCTOBER 2007**
GROSS INTERNAL AREA **35,165 SQ. M**
IMAGES **HÉLÈNE BINET (TOP); MAX FENTON (CENTRE); NICK KANE – ARCAID (PP. 26–27; P. 27, BOTTOM 3 IMAGES); JAMES NEWTON (P. 26 TOP LEFT AND RIGHT); TIMOTHY SOAR (BOTTOM LEFT AND RIGHT; OPPOSITE; P. 26 BOTTOM; P. 27 TOP)**
SHORTLISTED FOR THE RIBA CABE PUBLIC SPACE AWARD

This 35,000-square-metre office project shares the same architect–client team as Parry's previous Stirling-shortlisted building, Finsbury Square. So pleased was Scottish Widows that when the opportunity arose to redevelop Royex House, an undistinguished 1960s office building by Richard Seifert, the company rang Eric Parry and said, 'We've got a new challenge for you.'

It certainly was a challenge: Scottish Widows wanted to double the floor space on the same footprint, while the planners wanted it to reduce the height. What's more, Parry's idea was to make the building look less massive by forming it of two staggered wings divided by a glazed belly that is cut back to admit light into the reception space and the new square, as well as stepping it back from the ninth floor to counter the looming perspective that makes any tall building appear to topple towards the bystander. Both these steps reduced the available floor space. The achievement of the brief therefore represents a kind of architectural magic.

The immediate context is provided by four buildings: the Guildhall, both ancient and modern; Wood Street Police Building by McMorran & Whitby (Whitby junior – Mark – was the engineer on this scheme); the massive 1980s Alban Gate project, which straddles London Wall; and Richard Rogers's 88 Wood Street, which dictates the triple height of Parry's entrance hall and was itself shortlisted for the Stirling Prize in 2000. And this is without mentioning the Foster and the Wren buildings next door. The area is, then, a kind of architectural zoo. This is the type of challenge on which Parry thrives. He believes in starting with the urban context and working his way in to the building,

rather than working out from the building and stitching it into a context. The important views of 5 Aldermanbury Square from the Guildhall were the first to be 'designed'. One thing that appealed to the City planners was that the new building exactly obscures views of Alban Gate from the Guildhall.

The entire structure of the building sits space-efficiently outside the floorplates. The 6-metre grid is defined by a Cor-Ten-steel frame filled with reinforced concrete for fire protection. The fact that the steel frame is already rusted is not for aesthetic reasons, which is why Cor-Ten is usually used (here it is nowhere to be seen), but because it prevents further deterioration of the frame. This is overclad with steel, a move that takes its inspiration from Skidmore, Owings & Merrill's Inland Steel Building (1955) in Chicago, although there the steel is brushed. Here it is shot-peened – a technique that entails blasting the surface of the steel with ceramic balls. Parry showed the Stirling judges a spoon designed by David Mellor, which he had taken to demonstrate to City Planning Officer Peter Rees the purity of finish that he guaranteed to deliver. The building is arranged in double- and, immediately above the base, triple-height bays, giving a strong sense of verticality to the elevations.

The scheme represents a clever balancing act between delivery of the office space Scottish Widows needed and also of the public space that the City desired. Linking the two entrances is a generous lobby with a sloping floor that

drops almost imperceptibly by a metre from west to east. Parry-designed bespoke furniture adds visual interest, as do woven enamelled-metal wall-hangings, designed with Parry's life-partner, over immaculately board-marked concrete, and carpets hand-knotted in Izmir, also designed by **EPA**.

Parry has created a square under and alongside his building. Granite, more board-marked concrete – its deep grain highlighted by sunshine – and a cascading rill add to the sense of place. Lookout benches of white Carrara marble and blue Kilkenny limestone, similar to life-sized Subbuteo players, result from a conversation with writer Iain Sinclair about the way people use the City. This used to be Addle Street, a route the City authorities, in exchange for these improvements to the urban realm, agreed to close. The work continues into Aldermanbury Square itself, a later addition to the brief, which has a quite different character, creating, improving and connecting public spaces in an area of the City notoriously difficult to resolve successfully as a result of the 1960s multi-level masterplan. The previous building was ramped round with now non-compliant inclines. The architects have neatly incorporated an up-to-date ramp in the London Wall façade to link with the Barbican High Walk.

This is intelligent, considered architecture: every move is thought through, every idea tested against history and context. Here, amid architectural mediocrity, Parry has created a masterpiece.

# BODEGAS PROTOS
## PEÑAFIEL, VALLADOLID, SPAIN
## ROGERS STIRK HARBOUR + PARTNERS

EXECUTIVE ARCHITECT **ALONSO BALAGUER Y ARQUITECTOS ASOCIADOS**
CLIENT **BODEGAS PROTOS**
STRUCTURAL ENGINEERS **ARUP; BOMA; AGROINDUS**
SERVICES ENGINEERS **BDSP PARTNERSHIP; GRUPO JG; AGROINDUS**
QUANTITY SURVEYORS **TÉCNICS G3; AGROINDUS; JOSÉ MARÍA GARRIDO**
CONTRACTOR **FOMENTO DE CONSTRUCCIONES Y CONTRATAS**
CONTRACT VALUE **£16,000,000**
DATE OF COMPLETION **SEPTEMBER 2008**
GROSS INTERNAL AREA **19,450 SQ. M**
IMAGES **BODEGAS PROTOS (P. 30 TOP); KATSUHISA KIDA (P. 31); PAUL
RAFTERY – VIEW (BOTTOM; OPPOSITE; P. 30 BOTTOM)**

This is a very memorable building that brilliantly succeeds
in fulfilling its purpose. Many of the great names are doing
or have already done wineries: Herzog & de Meuron, Frank
Gehry, Santiago Calatrava, even Foster + Partners just
up the road. But this is no starchitect showpiece; it is a
working shed that just happens also to be a landmark.

Bodegas Protos, the wine co-operative in the Ribera del
Duero, Peñafiel, near Valladolid in north-west Spain, chose
well when it selected Rogers Stirk Harbour + Partners,
a firm with a not-dissimilar philosophy of co-operation
leading to quality products, to give it wider international
recognition. In plan, the project, led by Graham Stirk,
marks a return to the thinking of the 1960s. The brief
called for three separate buildings, for production,
administration and as a visitor centre. In a move that
ended up doubling the budget but greatly improving the
complex's environmental credentials by reducing the
number of walls, the architects brought the three functions
together under one democratic roof, in the manner of
Team 4's Reliance Controls Building (1966) in Swindon.

And what a roof it is. The five parallel arches sit above a
stone plinth, providing a magnificently memorable image
of the Bodegas on its site overlooked by the fine medieval
castle of Peñafiel. From the castle, the visitor can see that
the building is triangular because so is the site that it
fills. There is no back to it. Everything is of the same high
quality. Up to four thousand of the monthly visitors to the
castle also come here to sample the excellent wines and
take a tour of the hi-tech production area and cellars,

where ten million bottles command a worth that is more than twice that of the building, making the £822-per-square-metre cost look even better value.

In its clear, legible section, the project carries forward ideas used in the practice's Welsh National Assembly (2005) in Cardiff, with entry at the upper level, and the functions laid out below for all to see. Visitors find themselves overlooking a double-height space, with the fermentation and storage vessels below them, at the level of the lower end of the site, where the loading bay penetrates the stone plinth. Descending the spiral steel-and-glass stair to the lower level, visitors gain sudden views of the castle through the glazed gable of the arches far above them. The grapes are deposited under the end bay of the roof, and are fed by gravity into the fermentation and storage vessels at the lower level. Yet the volume is deceptive: below the whole site is a double-height basement for the storage of wine in oak casks for four years, followed by bottling and further storage for up to three years. This vast area of storage uses thermal mass to provide steady environmental conditions analogous to the great caves that are ventilated by hobbit-house-like chimneys dotting the surrounding hillsides.

Everything was completed in sequence, so, as with traditional building methods, the trades never met. The handsome laminated timber trusses spring from the level of the plinth, while the terracotta-tile-covered roof is a ventilated insulating cavity, floating free of the purlins by means of steel arms. This is a building that uses traditional materials in a non-traditional way. As a structure it is – to borrow Stirk's word – nervous: boundaries were being pushed here.

This is also a working building, requiring strict temperature and humidity controls to protect the wine.

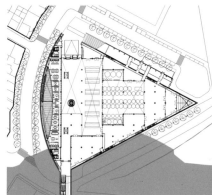

PRODUCTION-LEVEL (LEVEL 3) PLAN

BODEGAS PROTOS

The building form, its envelope and the use of proven construction systems are aimed at enhancing the environmental performance of the building. Energy-saving methods include high levels of insulation, designed-in sun-shading, natural ventilation and the efficient use of night-time cooling.

The plinth is of a raw-finish, top-sliced local stone, usually broken up for aggregate; the smoother stuff is used for internal walls and those of the elliptical sunken courtyard. This space provides another perfectly framed view of the castle, from which it takes its form (as well as its material). The courtyard also lets light into the offices and the tasting-room. Running and falling water relieves the summer heat, and a narrow curving stair provides a Staatsgalerie Stuttgart moment – not least for Stirling judge John Tuomey, who had the idea for the Stirling stairway. For him, Protos has all the emotional resonance, the poetry he looks for in a very good building. 'It makes my heart beat faster,' he said, 'and if I wasn't [one] already, it would make me want to be an architect.'

# FUGLSANG KUNSTMUSEUM
## TOREBY, LOLLAND, DENMARK
## TONY FRETTON ARCHITECTS

EXECUTIVE ARCHITECT **BBP ARKITEKTER**
CLIENT **BYGNINGSFONDEN**
LANDSCAPE ARCHITECT **SCHØNHERR LANDSKAB**
STRUCTURAL ENGINEER/SERVICES ENGINEER/QUANTITY SURVEYOR
**ALECTIA (FORMERLY BIRCH & KROGBOE)**
CONTRACTOR **C.C. BRUN ENTREPRISE**
CONTRACT VALUE **£6,500,000**
DATE OF COMPLETION **JANUARY 2008**
GROSS INTERNAL AREA **2500 SQ. M**
IMAGES **HÉLÈNE BINET**

This project, like so much of Tony Fretton's work, seems to be about the sublime in the context of the everyday. The countryside setting, while pretty, is gentle: a former landed estate in a rural part of the island of Lolland, just two hours from Copenhagen but, tucked in a geographic cul-de-sac, culturally a world away. The art gallery is part of a long-term programme – begun in 1890 – of relocating cultural facilities to rural areas; given the gallery's pre-eminent national collection of landscape paintings (1720–1970), it is an entirely appropriate move.

According to Fretton, all his successful public projects have been led by strong women. And in Anna Højer Petersen he also had one of the best informed. Funded by a Danish arts charity, she spent a year researching and working with a local architect to develop a brief that was very clear on some points but wide open on others – which is how a brief should be, otherwise there is no room for architecture. It called for an approachable, domestic-scale gallery that nonetheless had presence, and in which one could spend time with the art. Fretton's response was partially to enclose small 'pockets' off the main long gallery (really a broad corridor), just big enough for one or two people to look at one or two works. But Fretton disregarded one key element of the brief. It called for the

gap in the courtyard, which is made up of an eighteenth-
century manor and its ancillary buildings – including a
powerful long barn – to be closed off by the museum.
Instead, Fretton turned his gallery through 90 degrees,
leaving the view to the sea over meadowland. In this one
simple move, the project became outward-looking, thus
ulfilling the wider brief for the programme as a whole.

This brief Fretton fulfils hands-down. The building is
modest: low, clad in brick, with small, warm, homely
galleries inside, and entered through a 'kitchen-cafe' and
bookshop. There is more than a commercial imperative
at work here. The arrangement is also domestic and non-
threatening to an audience often unused to high art,
creating an art place, not an art space. The architects
wanted each room to have a different character, aiming
for juxtaposition and yet familiarity. Fretton believes that
the architecture should never dominate the art; that it
should encourage one to look at the paintings, but that
at the periphery one should be invigorated. Here, the

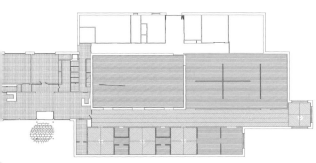

GROUND-FLOOR PLAN

architectural moves are subtle but persuasive: the arrangement of the top-lit galleries is circular, to encourage meandering, and their expressiveness is restrained to the extent that windows are almost entirely absent, so that the visitor's concentration focuses on the art, except for two rooms at the far end, which draw one through the building. After studying landscape art on the journey, one is then presented with the real thing, framed by architecture. The eye is refreshed by nature. The effect, after such architectural restraint, is mesmerizing.

Light is crucial. The flat light of this area and the plain-speaking nature of Fretton's architecture are not unconnected. Light draws people to it: to the centre of a top-lit room, or to the glazed edges of the plaster-cast collection room. Daylight gives true colour definition, but too much radiation is bad for works of art, so a balance has been struck between top and limited side light.

In Fuglsang, the body of art, the enclosure and the place all enhance one another. And this collection has been hugely enhanced by this project. Many visitors say they cannot recognize these as the same paintings, and the curators, as they unwrapped and hung them, said they fell in love with them all over again.

The design relies on a highly insulated envelope with minimal openings to reduce heat loss, and is heated from a biomass source.

Fretton describes his architecture as rear-guard rather than avant-garde; he is not afraid to be old-fashioned if that is what is appropriate. Like his Lisson Gallery in London, Fuglsang has similarities to found space. It is well constructed and detailed, and clearly erudite, with nods in its composition to architectural history. It feels, said one judge, almost as if it could have been built in any decade since the 1920s. That is quite a compliment. The Stirling judges thought it 'a celebration of a reflective architecture, by a man who is ambitious about what architecture can do; a soulful, serious building that will endure and change with time'.

# KENTISH TOWN HEALTH CENTRE
## BARTHOLOMEW ROAD, LONDON NW5
## ALLFORD HALL MONAGHAN MORRIS

CLIENT **CAMDEN & ISLINGTON COMMUNITY SOLUTIONS**
STRUCTURAL ENGINEER **ELLIOTT WOOD**
SERVICES ENGINEER **PETER DEER AND ASSOCIATES**
QUANTITY SURVEYOR/CONTRACTOR **MORGAN ASHURST**
GRAPHIC DESIGNER **STUDIO MYERSCOUGH**
CONTRACT VALUE **£10,100,000**
DATE OF COMPLETION **DECEMBER 2008**
GROSS INTERNAL AREA **2787 SQ. M**
IMAGES **ROB PARRISH** (OPPOSITE TOP; P. 38 CENTRE AND BOTTOM); **TIM SOAR**
(THIS PAGE; OPPOSITE, BOTTOM 3 IMAGES; P. 38 TOP; P. 39)
**CAMDEN & ISLINGTON COMMUNITY SOLUTIONS** WAS JOINT WINNER
OF THE **RIBA CLIENT OF THE YEAR**

Kentish Town Health Centre sets a new standard for the NHS. Dr Roy Macgregor has championed a building where new thinking on holistic health care, connectivity, flexibility and transparency were harnessed and worked on collaboratively by his team. Through its fusion of health practice, architecture and art, the resulting building is uplifting for both staff and patients. Architecturally and medically, this is a Finsbury Health Centre for the twenty-first century.

Composed both internally and externally of crisp-white rendered elements punctured by black-framed windows, the architecture derives its strength from the many visual cross-connections created by its internal and external voids, which the architects compare to a game of Jenga. Consulting rooms and stairs enjoy views into the triple-height central street and waiting-area around which the plan is organized, and this principle is extended to smaller light-wells on secondary circulation routes, which give access to small balconies.

The practice is known as the James Wigg Surgery, after the local Victorian doctor who unashamedly fleeced the rich to treat the poor for free. This is a similar public–private partnership for the present day. It is a **LIFT** (Local Improvement Finance Trust) project (60 per cent private, 40 per cent NHS), so it will be maintained by the private sector – a first for the NHS. **LIFT** is a notoriously difficult means by which to procure a health building, but this scheme shows the value that can be obtained when given a meticulous client working with a meticulous architect.

Macgregor's role included everything from strategic vision to micro-management. He had never written a brief before, but this one covered everything from the baby-changing tables (with raised edges so the babies won't roll off) to the magnetic rubberized nameplates for the doors and the small removable drawers for GPs' belongings, which allow for hot-desking throughout the building; and from the furniture to the lighting. (A lot of the furniture is bespoke, made by a Kentish Town cabinetmaker.) The brief asked for lots of daylight, for outdoor spaces directly accessible from the consulting rooms (these have helped with staff recruitment and retention) and for a flexible building that encourages the integration of all the services provided by the polyclinic. It also required the vast majority of the mature trees on the site to be retained.

Allford Hall Monaghan Morris won the competition because its interpretation of the brief was the most radical and adventurous. For instance, its scheme was the only one to include a street through the middle of the plan, following the line of what locals considered to be – although the law did not – a right of way. AHMM also proposed the most flexible design, inspired by the Jenga game, which allowed elements of the building to be slid forward or back, and broke down the scale of what was a big building on a very tight site, with three times the floor area of the health centre it replaced. The rhythm of the façades is broken up horizontally by square windows for the surgeries and linear windows for the open-plan areas, and vertically by the cantilevers, which are themselves responses to the surrounding trees, an effort to avoid root damage. The trees were so important to the locals that some of the latter chained themselves to them during planning.

The finished building is about as green as a health building can be: the stack effect is used in the open-plan areas, with rooflights opening automatically for night-time cooling, and solar wind-catchers drawing air through the cellular rooms. The only mechanical ventilation is in some internal rooms, where it is essential to prevent the spread of infections.

The signage is trademark AHMM. Studio Myerscough, originally briefed to do a letterhead, ended up creating everything from the large exterior graphic panel marking the entrance to the pictograms that guide people round the building. There is neither a conventional sign nor an NHS blue-and-white logo in sight, although the client has asked for one just to ensure that people do realize that this highly specced building really is part of our under-appreciated National Health Service.

As architect Paul Monaghan says, 'We proved at Westminster Academy last year and with Kentish Town this year that the problem is not money; it is having the right people in charge of decision-making.' It is very difficult in England today to create quality health buildings, so we need such symbols as Kentish Town as a stepping stone on the way to a better world. As the judges walked around, one asked: 'Why can't all health clinics be like this?'

**GROUND-FLOOR PLAN**

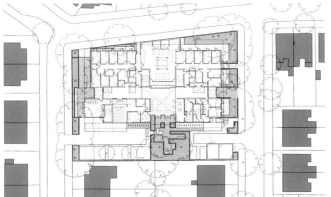

# LIVERPOOL ONE MASTERPLAN
## LIVERPOOL
## BDP

ARCHITECTS **AEDAS; ALLIES AND MORRISON ARCHITECTS; AUSTIN-SMITH:LORD; BDP; BROCK CARMICHAEL ARCHITECTS; CRAIG FOSTER ARCHITECTS; CZWG ARCHITECTS; DIXON JONES; FAT; GLENN HOWELLS ARCHITECTS; GREIG & STEPHENSON; GROSS MAX; GROUPE-SIX; HAWKINS\BROWN; HAWORTH TOMPKINS; JOHN MCASLAN + PARTNERS; LEACH RHODES WALKER; MARKS BARFIELD ARCHITECTS; OWEN ELLIS ARCHITECTS; PAGE\PARK; PELLI CLARKE PELLI ARCHITECTS; ROBERTS LIMBRICK; SQUIRE AND PARTNERS; STEPHENSON BELL ARCHITECTS; STUDIO THREE; WILKINSON EYRE ARCHITECTS**
CLIENT **GROSVENOR**
STRUCTURAL ENGINEER **WATERMAN PARTNERSHIP**
SERVICES ENGINEER **WSP**
QUANTITY SURVEYOR **DAVIS LANGDON**
ACCESS CONSULTANT **NIGHTINGALE ASSOCIATES**
CONTRACTORS **LAING O'ROURKE; BALFOUR BEATTY**
CONTRACT VALUE **£900,000,000+**
DATE OF OCCUPATION **OCTOBER 2008**
GROSS INTERNAL AREA **170,000 SQ. M**
IMAGES **DAVID BARBOUR (BOTTOM LEFT); GROSVENOR (OPPOSITE TOP AND CENTRE); PAUL MCMULLIN (BOTTOM RIGHT; OPPOSITE BOTTOM; P. 42; P. 43 TOP LEFT AND CENTRE); DAVID MILLINGTON (P. 43 TOP RIGHT AND BOTTOM)**
**SHORTLISTED FOR THE RIBA CABE PUBLIC SPACE AWARD**
**GROSVENOR WAS JOINT WINNER OF THE RIBA CLIENT OF THE YEAR**

The Liverpool One Masterplan has single-handedly reversed the fortunes of the city by bringing a new social and economic vibrancy to this previously derelict area at its heart – the result of Second World War bomb damage and subsequent poor-quality redevelopment. At more than £900 million, the investment has established a benchmark approach to development, and this masterplan is recognized as one of the most significant city-regeneration projects in Europe. That one project has been able to deliver sufficient critical mass to regenerate a city of such importance is the result of an outstanding client with vision and commitment to delivering design excellence and urban coherence.

Rod Holmes, aided and succeeded by Guy Butler, has led Grosvenor's drive for quality and guided all aspects of the design and construction process. To engage three major architects might be deemed brave, to employ twenty-six is sheer but brilliantly successful madness. The result is a vibrant and economically successful retail, leisure and mixed-use quarter – an entirely revitalized city centre that now connects properly with the docks.

The greatest danger was to create monoculture. Instead, egged on by BDP, Grosvenor took the radical decision to base the plan of its new shopping centre not on the mall but on the original grain of the old city streets. It engaged the city in the shape of former Liberal Democrat City Council Leader Mike Storey (now Lord Mayor) and the people of Liverpool. This was an approach that Holmes had developed when working in The Hague. Grosvenor then went a brave step further by commissioning twenty-six different architectural

practices to deliver BDP's masterplan. The practices ranged from such major national and international companies as Allies and Morrison, CZWG, Dixon Jones and Wilkinson Eyre, via such mid-size practices as Glenn Howells, Haworth Tompkins and Marks Barfield, to local firms ranging in size from Austin-Smith:Lord to Studio Three. Working alongside Cesar Pelli, who sited and redesigned Chavasse Park above a car park and also designed a new apartment block as one of the edge-buildings, BDP created a masterplan that set down generous public-space networks and rigorous yet flexible design briefs. Throughout the development it worked in close collaboration with the other architects to evolve the plan continually and to deliver buildings of a very high quality. This robust rubbing of edges makes the scheme look as if it has developed over at least twenty-five years rather than the mere ten it has actually taken. Another advantage of this apparently piecemeal development is that parts of it can be replaced at the end of their natural lives, rather than the whole thing needing to be comprehensively redeveloped.

Masterplanning must draw a fine line between being prescriptive and being permissive. Bizarrely, perhaps, there are five 'quarters' to this scheme, each with a subtly different character. The masterplan allows for exceptions to its few rules, and lets individual buildings stand out and draw attention to themselves. As a consequence, the area still feels like Liverpool.

At the heart of the plan, Allies and Morrison has created a building – more of an articulated urban block – clad in prefabricated panels of a German limestone with a

hammered finish. It gives a sense of permanence – of history even – and will no doubt come to be thought of as being as important as the nearby trio of grand buildings overlooking the Mersey. This, far more so than the new Museum of Liverpool, is the city's Fourth Grace. It links Paradise Street with Chavasse Park via a playful zigzag stair and escalators leading to a memorable semi-sheltered public space – called a 'galleria' by the architects – overlooking the Mersey. Just as impressive are Dixon Jones's elegant, bronze-clad covered arcade that plays tricks with perspective; Marks Barfield's coffee shop adorned with brightly coloured, striped pipes, as if it were a fairground organ designed by Paul Smith; and Haworth Tompkins's housing, which is every bit as characterful as that on the South Bank in London.

The overall result is that the masterplan has triumphantly co-ordinated and managed the development of 170,000 square metres of run-down land and building stock that includes buildings and streets of historic interest. Of course it has to wash its face, and of course Grosvenor won't be doing it again in a hurry in the current economic climate, but the successful implementation of the project in less than ten years is a triumph of skill and commitment by all the developers and design teams involved.

# THE RIBA
# LUBETKIN PRIZE
SPONSORED BY COSENTINO

The RIBA Lubetkin Prize, sponsored by Cosentino, is given to the architects of the best RIBA International Award-winning building. Buildings eligible for RIBA International Awards are those outside the European Union or those built in the EU (with the exception of the United Kingdom) that are designed by a practice based outside the UK.

The prize is named after Berthold Lubetkin (1901–1990), the architect from Georgia who immigrated to Britain in the 1930s and went on to establish the radical architecture group Tecton. He is best known for the two Highpoint buildings in Highgate, London (1933–38), and for the Penguin Pool at London Zoo (1934). The pool provided the inspiration for a cast-concrete plaque designed and made by the artist Petr Weigl. The plaque was presented to the winner of the Lubetkin Prize at the RIBA International Awards Dinner in June by Lubetkin's daughter Sasha.

The winner of the inaugural prize in 2006 was Noero Wolff Architects, for the Red Location Museum of the People's Struggle, New Brighton, South Africa. In 2007 the winner was Grimshaw (working within the Grimshaw Jackson Joint Venture), for Southern Cross Station, Melbourne, Australia. In 2008 the winner was Casa Kike, Cahuita, Costa Rica, by Gianni Botsford Architects.

## WINNER

THE NATIONAL STADIUM
BEICHEN EAST ROAD, CHAOYANG
DISTRICT, BEIJING, CHINA
HERZOG & DE MEURON

## VISITING JUDGES

PAUL MONAGHAN
CHAIR OF THE RIBA AWARDS GROUP

TONY CHAPMAN
RIBA HEAD OF AWARDS

## FULL JURY

SUNAND PRASAD
ARCHITECT AND RIBA PRESIDENT

ALISON BROOKS
ARCHITECT

TOM DYCKHOFF
ARCHITECTURE CRITIC

## SHORTLIST

BRITISH HIGH COMMISSION
BAUDDHALOKA MAWATHA,
COLOMBO, SRI LANKA
RICHARD MURPHY ARCHITECTS

MUSEUM BRANDHORST
THERESIENSTRASSE,
MUNICH, GERMANY
SAUERBRUCH HUTTON

SEAN O'CASEY COMMUNITY CENTRE
ST MARY'S ROAD, EAST WALL,
DUBLIN, IRELAND
O'DONNELL + TUOMEY

TERMINAL 3, BEIJING CAPITAL
INTERNATIONAL AIRPORT
CHAOYANG DISTRICT, BEIJING, CHINA
FOSTER + PARTNERS

WATERCUBE, THE NATIONAL
AQUATICS CENTER
NORTH 4TH RING ROAD,
BEIJING OLYMPIC
VILLAGE, CHINA
PTW ARCHITECTS

The National Stadium, Herzog & de Meuron

# THE NATIONAL STADIUM
## BEICHEN EAST ROAD, CHAOYANG DISTRICT, BEIJING, CHINA
## HERZOG & DE MEURON

EXECUTIVE ARCHITECTS **CHINA ARCHITECTURE DESIGN & RESEARCH GROUP; ARUP SPORT; OVE ARUP & PARTNERS HONG KONG**
CLIENT **ZHEJIANG JOYON REAL ESTATE COMPANY**
ARTISTIC ADVISER **AI WEIWEI**
LANDSCAPE ARCHITECT **HERZOG & DE MEURON**
STRUCTURAL/SERVICES ENGINEER **CHINA ARCHITECTURE DESIGN & RESEARCH GROUP**
CONTRACTOR **CHINA STATE CONSTRUCTION ENGINEERING CORPORATION (CSCEC)**
CONTRACT VALUE **£217,000,000**
DATE OF COMPLETION **MAY 2008**
GROSS INTERNAL AREA **258,000 SQ. M**
IMAGES **IWAN BAAN**

Few buildings that have received the worldwide attention that this stadium has attracted can live up to the hype; this one assuredly can. What may appear to be overly complicated in two dimensions becomes a thing of great subtlety in three dimensions. It is the result of a complex but hugely successful collaboration between Herzog & de Meuron, the China Architecture Design & Research Group, Arup Sport, Ove Arup & Partners' Hong Kong office and the artist Ai Weiwei, who played a key role in the initial concept.

The sports stadium is one of the oldest building types known to mankind and, on the surface at least, one of the simplest. And yet the ability to match the power of the spectacle is as hard as it is apparently simple. This building, the main stadium for the 2008 Beijing Olympics, has already earned its place as one of the most iconic of its type anywhere. If the trend in seminal modern stadia design was to break down the apparent separation of the perimeter exterior from the playing field inside – as seen memorably in Renzo Piano's Bari stadium of the late 1980s, via the act of cutting gaps into the encircling form – here the trick is subtler, the skin still more porous. Internally, the continuity of the bowl is maintained, whereas the entire perimeter skin dissolves into an irregular and seemingly random lattice of steel beams. By day the building appears as a bird's nest – famed for making exotic Chinese soup – while at night its inner bowl glows out in hot-red colours.

Form does not always follow function: the concrete inner lattice supporting the bowl is clad in steel, to match the outer steel frame, which supports the roof, but

**GROUND-FLOOR PLAN**

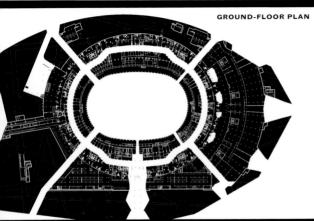

**ELEVATION**

here are aesthetic justifications aplenty for this. The structure also sets up constantly changing views both into and out of the stadium. And for all the environmental cost of the steel, elsewhere the sustainable credentials of the stadium are good. There are arrays of solar panels above the entrance, and the natural ventilation, which draws air through the building via the stack effect, works well, with the stands and the corridors connecting them pleasantly cool on the very hot day the judges visited. Most of the seats are effectively shaded by the ETFE/PTFE roof.

Much anticipated ever since the initial design images were published, the finished stadium is breathtaking. Symbolizing China's desire to reach cultural parity with developed Western nations, as part of the process of globalization, the use of such talented Swiss architects

ably supported by local architects and by Arup's specialist stadium architects and engineers, has paid off handsomely. As seen on millions of television screens around the world during 2008's Olympic ceremonies, the building deploys the representational power of architecture to show how sporting activities can memorably be framed. Interestingly, the owners are now making more money from the 30,000 visitors who come to wander through the stadium every day than they did from spectators during the Olympics. As is the case with the Watercube (pp. 68–71), these visitors are the legacy of the Olympics for the time being; there have been only two events at the building in the first post-Olympic year. At one level, the National Stadium in Beijing is like every other stadium, and yet it remains defiantly unique.

Unsurprisingly perhaps, the stadium produced a lively debate among the final judges. Olympic projects are very much one-offs: for some, they are a chance to push out the architectural boat; to show, literally, to the world what architects can do – in much the same way Frei Otto and Günter Behnisch did with their Munich Stadium in 1972. For others, they are a platform from which to demonstrate the social and environmental responsibilities of architects. Whichever line you take, this is still one of the most captivating and moving buildings of its generation, one that will inspire future generations of architects.

In the end the judges decided to award the National Stadium the Lubetkin Prize for what it is, rather than deny it the prize for what it is not. The building is a triumphant and compelling work of the imagination, and its delivery a feat of determination on the part of both architects and engineers. This is a Coliseum for the twenty-first century, and it could be around for just as long as that Roman landmark. As such, and in terms of lifetime costing, it may well prove to be good value indeed.

# BRITISH HIGH COMMISSION
## BAUDDHALOKA MAWATHA, COLOMBO, SRI LANKA
## RICHARD MURPHY ARCHITECTS

LOCAL ARCHITECT **MILROY PERERA ASSOCIATES**
CLIENT **FOREIGN & COMMONWEALTH OFFICE**
LANDSCAPE ARCHITECT **GROSS MAX**
STRUCTURAL ENGINEER **SKM ANTHONY HUNT**
SERVICES ENGINEER **FULCRUM CONSULTING**
CONTRACTOR **GIBS**
CONTRACT VALUE **£7,500,000**
DATE OF COMPLETION **MAY 2008**
GROSS INTERNAL AREA **3400 SQ. M**
IMAGES **WARUNA GOMIS (OPPOSITE TOP); RICHARD MURPHY ARCHITECTS (THIS PAGE; OPPOSITE BOTTOM; PP. 54–55)**

This project was a dream job for Richard Murphy – the chance to build in the home of Geoffrey Bawa, one of his two architectural masters (the other being Carlo Scarpa). The influence of Bawa, who designed the Sri Lankan Parliament, is direct: Murphy invited two former Bawa employees to join him in developing the competition entry. The winning result is a single-storey building that uses natural stack ventilation and a degree of natural top-lighting, arranged around a series of courtyards. There are nine partly enclosed courts, landscaped by Gross Max, adjacent to the central spine, and seven more around the edge.

Inevitably in a country torn by civil war, not to mention in the context of wider post-9/11 security demands, the whole is surrounded by a blast-wall. One generous window in the wall allows passers-by a glimpse of British democracy at work – a neat PR touch. Within the perimeter the buildings press up against the envelope. This is a tiny site for a high commission, chosen to replace the one on the Galle Road largely because it is next door to the High Commissioner's residence, thus reducing the need for many entertainment spaces in the new building.

Office workers are able, indeed encouraged, to turn off the air conditioning and open the windows to the courtyards, allowing in a breeze induced by a thermal chimney above each arm of the design. The section shows this arrangement, and the departments of trade, aid, visas, the consulate and so on are organized in a series of fingers radiating off the spine.

With structural engineer SKM Anthony Hunt, the architects have designed the necessary defensive structures, despite the rustic appearance of the project: the clay-tile roof, the timber, the rough granite walls, the reinforced-concrete throughout the entire building. And with services engineer Fulcrum Consulting they have produced a design that is as energy-efficient and naturally ventilated as possible.

High Commissioner Peter Hayes took up his post too late to influence the design, but he believes he has a commission that both encourages his staff to be 'flexible and fleet of foot' and allows them to hot-desk in any part of the building.

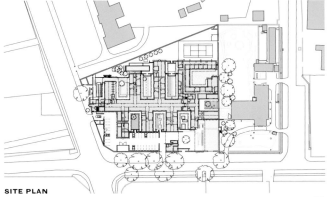

SITE PLAN

# MUSEUM BRANDHORST
## THERESIENSTRASSE, MUNICH, GERMANY
## SAUERBRUCH HUTTON

CLIENT **STAATLICHES BAUAMT MÜNCHEN 1**
LANDSCAPE ARCHITECT **ADELHEID GRÄFIN SCHÖNBORN**
STRUCTURAL ENGINEER **INGENIEURBÜRO REINHARD FINK**
SERVICES ENGINEER **OTTITSCH**
ACOUSTIC ENGINEER **AKUSTIK-INGENIEURBÜRO MOLL**
LIGHTING ENGINEER **ARUP LIGHTING**
CONTRACTOR **ALL TRADES INDIVIDUALLY CONTRACTED**
CONTRACT VALUE **€48,150,000**
DATE OF COMPLETION **OCTOBER 2008**
GROSS INTERNAL AREA **12,000 SQ. M**
IMAGES **ANNETTE KISLING (TOP; BOTTOM; OPPOSITE TOP; P. 58 TOP LEFT AND RIGHT; P. 59); HAYDAR KOYUPINAR (OPPOSITE BOTTOM); NOSHE (P. 58 BOTTOM)**

What is even more striking than the polychromatic skin of this project is the way in which the architects have captured, filtered and distributed light – both the friend and enemy of works of art – throughout the deep-plan building. The galleries on the top floor are naturally lit with ceiling panels of Barrisol, a stretch-fabric material that produces a soft, even light. On the ground floor, a complex system of reflectors and louvres collects and filters light, producing perfect illumination for the superb collection of modern art. On the lower ground floor, by off-setting the plan, the architects have achieved not dissimilar lux levels. The environmental strategy has led to a mechanical system of blinds and louvres that responds to the changing light conditions throughout the day, somewhat noisily disturbing the peace of these otherwise tranquil galleries. But it works: by mixing natural and artificial light in this way, each room has its own character, and one that changes with the movement of the sun.

A slow system of cooling of these spaces is achieved by means of ground water pumped up through the walls, ceilings and floors before being returned to source. The success of the system and its earlier adoption by other museum and university buildings in the vicinity have led to an increase in subterranean temperatures, but – for

the time being, at least – 50 per cent of thermal energy is being saved, as is 26 per cent of electrical energy through this and other systems. Overall $CO_2$ emissions are calculated to be reduced by 365 tons per annum.

The outside of the building is a work of art in its own right. Internal conditions required for the art allow few windows. To compensate and to give something back in urbanistic terms, the architects have produced a skin that, as well as working supremely well environmentally, is a thing of great and subtle beauty. Some 36,000 hand-crafted ceramic rods in twenty-three different colours, grouped in tonal families, produce an impression that the whole building is oscillating, almost dematerializing.

Museum Brandhorst is the culmination of Sauerbruch Hutton's career-long experimentation with colour and texture. It is the work of architects at the top of their game.

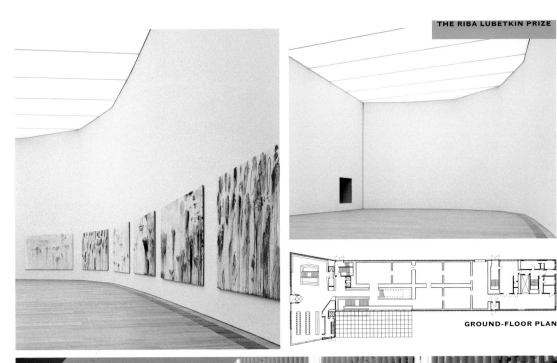

**GROUND-FLOOR PLAN**

# SEAN O'CASEY COMMUNITY CENTRE
## ST MARY'S ROAD, EAST WALL, DUBLIN, IRELAND
## O'DONNELL + TUOMEY

CLIENT **SEAN O'CASEY COMMUNITY CENTRE**
STRUCTURAL ENGINEER **CASEY O'ROURKE ASSOCIATES**
SERVICES ENGINEER **RPS GROUP**
QUANTITY SURVEYOR **CYRIL SWEETT**
LANDSCAPE CONSULTANT **HOWBERT & MAYS**
CONTRACTOR **P.J. HEGARTY & SONS**
CONTRACT VALUE **€6,800,000**
DATE OF COMPLETION **FEBRUARY 2009**
GROSS INTERNAL AREA **2223 SQ. M**
IMAGES **DENNIS GILBERT – VIEW (TOP; OPPOSITE TOP RIGHT; P. 62 TOP LEFT AND RIGHT); MICHAEL MORAN (BOTTOM; OPPOSITE TOP LEFT; PP. 62–63; P. 63)**

The community wanted their new building to be both resource and symbol; they wanted a solid building that would stand the test of time. The centre provides a theatre as well as day-care, educational and recreational facilities for all ages, arranged mainly at ground-floor level, with a five-storey 'learning tower'. The ground-floor accommodation is neatly arranged around four densely

planted courtyards, a lyrical reference to paradise in a tough urban streetscape.

The carefully considered plan creates a hierarchy between public and private, street and garden. The main entrance is accessed through the first courtyard, set back from the street behind a tall timber fence, which meets the need for security while maintaining the openness and transparency that define the building. A second courtyard garden separates the main reception area from the community sports hall. A third courtyard brings light and greenery into the canteen, which in turn opens out on to the entrance courtyard. A much larger fourth courtyard separates the public functions from the private day-care facilities, which are surrounded by greenery.

The Sean O'Casey Community Centre is the result of a clear vision and a strong concept that has been rigorously adhered to at every stage of the project. Materials have been chosen to co-exist harmoniously; brick paving used both inside and out reinforces the connection between interior and exterior. There are refreshing details: no attempt has been made to match the structural steel columns to the strong vertical rhythm of the timber glazing to the courtyards, and internal corners are single-glazed and frameless in order to reduce their material impact.

The dominant external material is off-shutter concrete, expertly formed on corrugated iron shutters. The use of circular windows, arranged in what initially appears to be a random way, defines the external façades. The architects describe the rationale behind the window pattern as that of a ball bouncing against a wall.

The idiosyncratic balance between delicacy and solidity in the Sean O'Casey Community Centre has been created by skilled architects who have exercised their craft in a manner appropriate to the scale and significance of this delightful and uplifting building.

GROUND-FLOOR PLAN

# TERMINAL 3, BEIJING CAPITAL INTERNATIONAL AIRPORT
## CHAOYANG DISTRICT, BEIJING, CHINA
## FOSTER + PARTNERS

EXECUTIVE ARCHITECTS **NACO; ARUP; BEIJING INSTITUTE OF ARCHITECTURAL DESIGN**
CLIENT **BEIJING CAPITAL INTERNATIONAL AIRPORT COMPANY**
LANDSCAPE ARCHITECT **MICHEL DESVIGNE**
STRUCTURAL/SERVICES ENGINEER **ARUP**
QUANTITY SURVEYOR **DAVIS LANGDON**
LIGHTING CONSULTANT **SPEIRS AND MAJOR ASSOCIATES**
CONTRACTOR **BEIJING CITY CONSTRUCTION COMPANY**
CONTRACT VALUE **£602,000,000**
DATE OF COMPLETION **AUGUST 2008**
GROSS INTERNAL AREA **1,300,000 SQ. M**
IMAGES **NIGEL YOUNG – FOSTER + PARTNERS**

The building is vast: 1.3 million square metres. Indeed, it is one of the largest, most complicated buildings ever constructed. It was also commissioned, designed and built in just five years – less time than it took for Heathrow's Terminal 5 to obtain planning permission. It is a testimony to its success that Foster + Partners has managed, despite the scale of the project and the infamous complexity of airport buildings, to make this one both look and feel like one of the simplest.

This is essentially the same 'shed' design that Foster reinvented at Stansted, nodding to the simpler origins of air-travel architecture, with terminals as tents. Here, the sheds are two Y-shaped main spaces – T3A for domestic flights, T3B for international – 3.25 kilometres apart, joined at their ends. An overground train whisks passengers from departures to their gates. The length maximizes perimeter space for docking planes and makes navigation simple.

Departures and arrivals are situated one above the other, housed in an internal structure independent of the external envelope. Throughout, visual and circulatory clarity is maintained, and natural light and visual connection to the outside world are maximized.

The roof is a delight and helps with orientation, the white power-coated steel slats above the orange space frame subtly pointing passengers towards their point of departure. A vast glass bubble – a Canary Wharf canopy on acid – shelters the Ground Transportation Complex. As is the case throughout Beijing, everything that was designed for the Olympic Games and the economic miracle they should have engendered has been done on a vast scale. This place is future-proofed for decades to come.

This is Foster at his best: making the complex simple and enjoyable. Terminal 3 may not be a radical reinvention of the airport. It may not give the building type a shot in the arm, but it does both vastly expand and refine it to make the terminal the most architecturally and technologically advanced in the world.

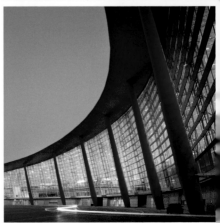

**TERMINAL 3, BEIJING CAPITAL INTERNATIONAL AIRPORT**

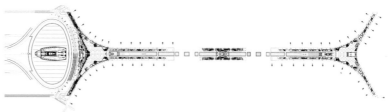

LEVEL-ONE PLAN

TERMINAL 3, BEIJING CAPITAL INTERNATIONAL AIRPORT

# WATERCUBE, THE NATIONAL AQUATICS CENTER
## NORTH 4TH RING ROAD, BEIJING OLYMPIC VILLAGE, CHINA
## PTW ARCHITECTS

EXECUTIVE ARCHITECTS **CHINA STATE CONSTRUCTION ENGINEERING CORPORATION (CSCEC); CHINA STATE CONSTRUCTION DESIGN INTERNATIONAL (CCDI); ARUP**
CLIENT **PEOPLE'S GOVERNMENT OF BEIJING MUNICIPALITY, BEIJING STATE-OWNED ASSETS MANAGEMENT COMPANY**
STRUCTURAL/ENVIRONMENTAL ENGINEER **ARUP**
CONTRACTOR **CHINA STATE CONSTRUCTION ENGINEERING CORPORATION (CSCEC)**
CONTRACT VALUE **AUS $140,000,000**
DATE OF COMPLETION **JANUARY 2008**
GROSS INTERNAL AREA **80,000 SQ. M**
IMAGES **BEN MCMILLAN (BOTTOM; OPPOSITE BOTTOM; PP. 70–71); PTW ARCHITECTS (OPPOSITE TOP LEFT AND RIGHT); MICHAEL YIP (TOP)**

At the competition stage the architects played around with organic forms, but – not least because of what they knew Herzog & de Meuron might be up to across the way with the National Stadium – they decided to go orthogonal instead. The square is an important symbol in Chinese culture (as is the bird's nest, of course), so the understated

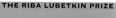

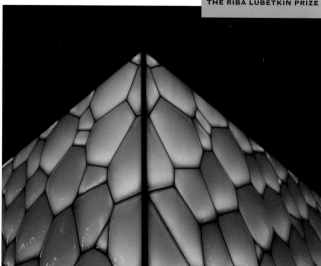

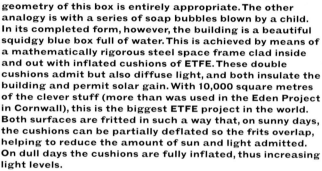

geometry of this box is entirely appropriate. The other analogy is with a series of soap bubbles blown by a child. In its completed form, however, the building is a beautiful squidgy blue box full of water. This is achieved by means of a mathematically rigorous steel space frame clad inside and out with inflated cushions of ETFE. These double cushions admit but also diffuse light, and both insulate the building and permit solar gain. With 10,000 square metres of the clever stuff (more than was used in the Eden Project in Cornwall), this is the biggest ETFE project in the world. Both surfaces are fritted in such a way that, on sunny days, the cushions can be partially deflated so the frits overlap, helping to reduce the amount of sun and light admitted. On dull days the cushions are fully inflated, thus increasing light levels.

Fabricated off-site, the ETFE cushions were fixed and inflated according to a programme that obviated the need for cranes and scaffolding (balloons and cranes do not mix well together). The other great thing about the material is its acoustic properties, a factor that would be much appreciated by any parent who has witnessed the deafening cacophony of a school swimming gala in a conventional pool. It took some time to convince the local authorities of the fire-resistant qualities of ETFE. Arup admitted that the material burns, but pointed out that, as it does so, it shrinks into itself, self-venting to allow the smoke to escape.

The Watercube proved to be a popular and exciting Olympic venue, both for locals and a vast television audience, and – once the visitor numbers have declined from the current 30,000 a day – it will be the legacy project par excellence, working as a swimming pool, an ice rink and a leisure centre with retail attached. This building symbolizes the new Beijing.

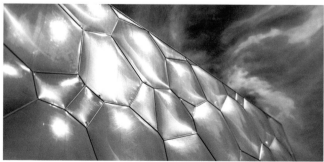

WATERCUBE, THE NATIONAL AQUATICS CENTER

WATERCUBE, THE NATIONAL AQUATICS CENTER

# THE RIBA
# SPECIAL AWARDS

The RIBA Special Awards are chosen from RIBA Award-winners. Panels that include specialist judges in the various fields assess the projects, and panel members pay follow-up visits to the shortlisted buildings. This year the RIBA decided to discontinue the Sustainability Award. The decision, taken in consultation with the Homes and Communities Agency (as past sponsors of the award), reflects the fact that the issue can no longer be considered 'special'. Instead, the RIBA has strengthened the requirement that the fulfilment of rigorous sustainability criteria is a prerequisite for the winning of an RIBA Award.

The following six awards reflect the diversity of architecture and reward the wide variety of specialist skills involved in delivering good buildings.

# THE CROWN ESTATE
# CONSERVATION AWARD

# THE MANSER MEDAL
**IN ASSOCIATION WITH THE ROOFLIGHT COMPANY**

# THE RIBA CLIENT
# OF THE YEAR

# THE RIBA CABE
# PUBLIC SPACE AWARD

# THE RIBA SORRELL
# FOUNDATION
# SCHOOLS AWARD

# THE STEPHEN
# LAWRENCE PRIZE
**IN ASSOCIATION WITH THE MARCO
GOLDSCHMIED FOUNDATION**

# THE CROWN ESTATE
# CONSERVATION AWARD

The Crown Estate Conservation Award is made to the
architects of the work that best demonstrates successful
restoration and/or adaptation of an architecturally
significant building. It carries a prize of £5000. Previous
winners have been Peter Inskip + Peter Jenkins, for the
Temple of Concord and Victory, Stowe, in 1998; Foster +
Partners, for the Reichstag, Berlin, in 1999, and JC Decaux
UK Headquarters, Brentford, in 2000; Rick Mather
Architects, for the Dulwich Picture Gallery, London, in
2001; Richard Murphy Architects with Simpson Brown
Architects, for the Stirling Tolbooth, Scotland, in 2002;
LDN Architects, for Newhailes House, Musselburgh, in
2003; HOK International, for the King's Library at the
British Museum, London, in 2004; Avanti Architects, for the
Isokon (Lawn Road) Apartments, London, in 2005; Dixon
Jones with Purcell Miller Tritton, for the National Gallery
East Wing and Central Portico, London, in 2006; Alec
French Architects, for SS *Great Britain* and Historic
Dockyard, Bristol, in 2007; and Alastair Lansley (for Union
Railways), for St Pancras International, London, in 2008.
    The Crown Estate manages a large and uniquely
diverse portfolio of land and buildings across the United
Kingdom. One of its primary concerns is to demonstrate
that conservation is not a dry, academic discipline but a
practical art, making yesterday's buildings work for
people today.

## WINNER

**THE MIDLAND HOTEL**
MARINE ROAD WEST, MORECAMBE
UNION NORTH

## JUDGES

**RICHARD GRIFFITHS**
CONSERVATION ARCHITECT

**PAUL VELLUET**
CONSERVATION ARCHITECT, HOK

**ROGER BRIGHT**
CHIEF EXECUTIVE OF THE
CROWN ESTATE

**TONY CHAPMAN**
RIBA HEAD OF AWARDS

## SHORTLIST

**14 LINCOLN'S INN FIELDS**
LONDON WC2
JULIAN HARRAP ARCHITECTS

**BOFORS TOWER**
DUNKIRK, CANTERBURY
ROBERT MAXWELL, ALLIES AND
MORRISON ARCHITECTS

**ST MARTIN-IN-THE-FIELDS**
TRAFALGAR SQUARE, LONDON WC2
ERIC PARRY ARCHITECTS WITH
CONSERVATION ARCHITECT CAROE &
PARTNERS ARCHITECTS

**TYNESIDE CINEMA**
PILGRIM STREET, NEWCASTLE
UPON TYNE
FLETCHER PRIEST ARCHITECTS WITH
CONSERVATION ARCHITECT
CYRIL WINSKELL

# THE MIDLAND HOTEL
## MARINE ROAD WEST, MORECAMBE
## UNION NORTH

CLIENT **URBAN SPLASH**
STRUCTURAL ENGINEER **RAMBOLL WHITBYBIRD**
SERVICES ENGINEER **ABACUS CONSULT**
QUANTITY SURVEYOR **SIMON FENTON PARTNERSHIP**
ACCESS CONSULTANT **HCD GROUP**
CONTRACTOR **URBAN SPLASH BUILD**
CONTRACT VALUE **£11,000,000**
DATE OF OCCUPATION **JUNE 2008**
GROSS INTERNAL AREA **5008 SQ. M**
IMAGES **SIMON WEBB**

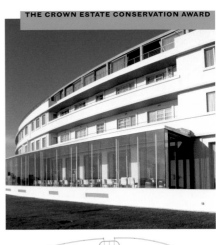

In its Midland Hotel renovation Union North has restored the glory of an original design by Oliver Hill and added a layer of lively contemporary design. Its trademark approach has resurrected and made relevant a derelict regional landmark.

The project has carefully upgraded and repaired the existing fabric, preserving important historic features, most notably the wall panels by Eric Gill. The reorganization of the interior of the hotel and the addition of discrete extensions have provided a modern, efficient and functional hotel environment without losing the character of the existing building. Interior spaces have been developed with flair and originality to create a range of remarkable public spaces, as well as stylish contemporary bedrooms. The spiral staircase has been meticulously reworked to make it compliant with current building regulations.

The specialist conservation judges were particularly impressed by the adoption of a creative and intelligent approach to the conservation of a major Modernist building, reflected in the retention and reinstatement of the most

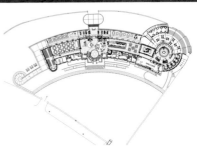

GROUND-FLOOR PLAN

significant qualities and features of the original building. They also applauded the introduction of explicitly new work that is sympathetic to the particular character of Hill's architecture; the use of sympathetic polymer render incorporating three types of glass to make it sparkle in the sun; and the wit of using Marion Dorn's seahorse motif in the stainless-steel grilles in the showers as well in the floor mosaic in the entrance lounge and on the stair banister.

The Midland Hotel represents a reinterpretation of the original architect's intentions in the light of the commercial requirements of the client and the regeneration needs of a depressed seaside town. Two new additions are beautifully judged: a replacement sun room with floor-to-ceiling glazing, which forms the dining-room, replacing a crude extension from 1979; and a glazed rooftop extension in place of an unused sun terrace. Much of the interior design is done with an unashamedly broad brush – both contemporary and populist. The result – after a wait of seven-and-a-half years – is a hotel that is bucking the recessionary trend and packing in both returning and new visitors to the hotel and to the town.

# THE MANSER MEDAL

IN ASSOCIATION WITH THE ROOFLIGHT COMPANY

The Manser Medal is awarded for the best one-off house or housing designed by an architect in the United Kingdom. Previous winners have been Cezary Bednarski, for Merthyr Terrace, London, in 2001; Burd Haward Marston Architects, for Brooke Coombes House, London, in 2002; Jamie Fobert Architects, for Anderson House, London, in 2003; Mole Architects, for Black House, Cambridgeshire, in 2004; Robert Dye Associates, for Stealth House, London, in 2005; Knox Bhavan Architects, for Holly Barn, Norfolk, in 2006; Alison Brooks Architects, for the Salt House, St Lawrence Bay, Essex, in 2007; and Oxley Woods, Milton Keynes, by Rogers Stirk Harbour + Partners in 2008.

The prize is named after Michael Manser, former President of the RIBA, who is well known for his own steel-and-glass house designs. These same materials are utilized in the Rooflight Company's products.

All the houses and housing schemes in the United Kingdom that received an RIBA Award in 2009 were considered for the Manser Medal.

## WINNER

GAP HOUSE
MONMOUTH ROAD, LONDON W2
**PITMAN TOZER ARCHITECTS**

## JUDGES

MICHAEL MANSER CBE
FORMER PRESIDENT OF THE RIBA

VALERIE KING
ROOFLIGHT COMPANY

IVAN HARBOUR
ROGERS STIRK HARBOUR + PARTNERS

TONY CHAPMAN
RIBA HEAD OF AWARDS

## SHORTLIST

BLOCK 3, TARLING REGENERATION
JAMES VOLLER WAY, LONDON E1
**S333 ARCHITECTURE + URBANISM;
STOCK | WOOLSTENCROFT**

HOUSE IN HIGHGATE CEMETERY
LONDON N6
**ELDRIDGE SMERIN**

HOUSE AT PIPER'S END
LETTY GREEN, HERTFORD
**NÍALL MCLAUGHLIN ARCHITECTS**

SLIDING HOUSE
HUNTINGFIELD, SUFFOLK
**DRMM**

# GAP HOUSE
## MONMOUTH ROAD, LONDON W2
## PITMAN TOZER ARCHITECTS

CLIENT **PRIVATE**
STRUCTURAL ENGINEER **RICHARD TANT ASSOCIATES**
SERVICES ENGINEER **RICHARD PEARCE ASSOCIATES**
CONTRACTOR **BROWNSTONE**
CONTRACT VALUE **£490,000**
DATE OF COMPLETION **AUGUST 2007**
GROSS INTERNAL AREA **185 SQ. M**
IMAGES **NICK KANE – ARCAID**

Once again the Manser Medal has been won by an intelligent, simple, practical, high-quality design that makes most of the house-building industry look inadequate.

The brief the architect set himself, as his own client, was to design a family house on a site reached through a 2.4-metre-wide gap between two white stucco villas on Monmouth Road, west London. The site widens out behind the villas and was previously occupied by a cottage that had become derelict. Although the existence of the cottage helped from a planning point of view, there were other problems, such as being in a conservation area with significant members of a powerful residents' association as close neighbours.

The design is one of impeccable detailing and simplicity in every respect. The narrow front elevation is an acme of understatement, and although frankly modern, at first glance it makes almost no impact on the street: it's just a narrow column of identical half-shuttered casement windows, above a basement-level entrance door, all in a background of white stucco to match the adjoining houses.

Once one is inside the narrow entrance hall, the plan soon widens, step by step, to a huge rectangular living space, one-quarter of which is an open court, separated only by full-height sliding and folding glass doors. The weight of the upper four floors, also stepped back as they rise, is borne by a single, slender bright-yellow steel column. At the back top corner of this space is a small first-floor office, which overlooks the open and covered living area.

The house has a ground-sourced heat pump (which required a deep bore hole, a special drill and an ingenious delivery method), high levels of insulation and a rainwater collection system.

Overall, the most impressive aspect of the design is its level of skill, imagination and practicality, which has created a series of apparently generous spaces. Despite encountering numerous problems – constraints of overlooking, conservation policies, initially hostile neighbours, difficulties of access for all trades and activities, and the need to maximize light penetration, all within a tight set of planning and legal constraints – the architect has produced a comfortable home in a great piece of architecture.

GROUND-FLOOR PLAN

# THE RIBA CLIENT OF THE YEAR

Since 1998 the RIBA has been recognizing the role good clients play in the delivery of fine architecture with its Client of the Year award.

Architecture is a team effort, and previous winners have amply demonstrated that: Roland Paoletti, who received the first award in 1998, for the new Jubilee line stations; in 1999, the MCC, for commissioning a series of fine buildings at Lord's Cricket Ground, London; in 2000, the Foreign & Commonwealth Office, for pulling off a series of iconic embassies around the world; in 2001, the Molendinar Park Housing Association, Glasgow, for its campus of buildings by a variety of Scottish architects; in 2002, Urban Splash, for its commitment both to design quality and the regeneration of Manchester and Liverpool; in 2003, the City of Manchester, for transforming its public realm with a wide range of post-IRA-bomb projects; in 2004, the Peabody Trust, for its pioneering work in off-site construction, the realization of truly sustainable housing, and, in particular, its commissioning of RIBA Award-winning schemes (Raines Court, London, by Allford Hall Monaghan Morris; Murray Grove, London, by Cartwright Pickard; and BedZED, Wallington, by Bill Dunster Architects); in 2005, Gateshead Council, for commissioning a series of major art and architecture projects (The Sage, the Millennium Bridge, BALTIC Centre for Contemporary Art, and the Angel of the North), each of which has contributed to the regeneration of the town, and each of which resulted from well-run competitions; in 2006, the Royal Botanic Gardens, for commissioning a series of fine buildings at Kew and at its country cousin, Wakehurst Place; in 2007, Derwent London, for 28 Dorset Square, London; and in 2008, Coin Street Community Builders, for their commissioning of high-quality community buildings from top architects on London's South Bank.

## WINNER

IN THE LIGHT OF THE EXTRAORDINARILY HIGH STANDARD OF THIS YEAR'S SHORTLIST, AND IN ORDER TO RECOGNIZE THE DIFFERENT SKILLS INVOLVED IN ARCHITECTURAL PATRONAGE, THE RIBA AWARDS GROUP DECIDED TO ELECT ALL SIX CLIENTS AS 2009 RIBA CLIENTS OF THE YEAR.

## JUDGES

MEMBERS OF THE RIBA AWARDS GROUP

## SHORTLIST

KENTISH TOWN HEALTH CENTRE
CLIENT DR ROY MACGREGOR ON BEHALF OF CAMDEN & ISLINGTON COMMUNITY SOLUTIONS

KIELDER OBSERVATORY
CLIENT PETER SHARPE ON BEHALF OF KIELDER PARTNERSHIP

KINGS PLACE
CLIENT PETER MILLICAN ON BEHALF OF PARABOLA LAND

LIVERPOOOL ONE MASTERPLAN
CLIENT ROD HOLMES ON BEHALF OF GROSVENOR

MAGGIE'S LONDON
CLIENT LAURA LEE ON BEHALF OF MAGGIE'S

ST MARTIN-IN-THE-FIELDS
CLIENT REVD NICHOLAS HOLTAM ON BEHALF OF ST MARTIN-IN-THE-FIELDS

# KENTISH TOWN HEALTH CENTRE
## BARTHOLOMEW ROAD, LONDON NW5
### ALLFORD HALL MONAGHAN MORRIS

CLIENT DR ROY MACGREGOR ON BEHALF OF CAMDEN & ISLINGTON COMMUNITY SOLUTIONS

KTHC sets a new standard for the NHS. Dr Roy Macgregor has championed a building where new thinking on holistic health care, connectivity, flexibility and transparency were harnessed and worked on collaboratively by his team. Through its fusion of health practice, architecture and art, the resulting building is uplifting for both staff and patients.

For the full citation, see p. 36.

# KIELDER OBSERVATORY
## BLACKFELL, BEWSHAUGH, NORTHUMBERLAND
### CHARLES BARCLAY ARCHITECTS

CLIENT PETER SHARPE ON BEHALF OF KIELDER PARTNERSHIP

Led by curator Peter Sharpe, Kielder Partnership has a proven track record of finding little-known architects and artists and commissioning adventurous works of art and architecture, set in the unique landscape of Kielder Water & Forest Park. The recently completed observatory, by Charles Barclay Architects, is the latest in a long line that includes Softroom's Belvedere and James Turrell's Skyspace.

For the full citation, see p. 121.

## KINGS PLACE
### YORK WAY, LONDON N1
### DIXON JONES

CLIENT **PETER MILLICAN ON BEHALF OF PARABOLA LAND**

Kings Place fulfils the personal dream of Peter Millican, ophthalmologist-turned-client and now arts administrator. This is a genuinely mixed-use project that brings a vibrant public environment into the heart of the building. As well as a restaurant, bar, shops and gallery, there are two concert halls good enough to offer residencies to national orchestras.

For the full citation, see p. 187.

## LIVERPOOL ONE MASTERPLAN
### LIVERPOOL
### BDP + 25 OTHER ARCHITECTS

CLIENT **ROD HOLMES ON BEHALF OF GROSVENOR**

Costing more than £900 million, Liverpool One is recognized as one of the most significant city-regeneration projects in Europe. Rod Holmes, aided and succeeded by Guy Butler, has led Grosvenor's drive for quality and guided all aspects of the design and construction process. To engage three major architects might be deemed brave; to employ twenty-six is sheer but brilliantly successful madness.

For the full citation, see p. 40.

# MAGGIE'S LONDON
## CHARING CROSS HOSPITAL, FULHAM PALACE ROAD, LONDON W6
## ROGERS STIRK HARBOUR + PARTNERS

CLIENT **LAURA LEE ON BEHALF OF MAGGIE'S**

As a cancer-care nurse, Laura Lee promised her patient Maggie Jencks that she would carry out her dying wish: to see cancer sufferers and their families and friends offered humane facilities in which they could learn about the illness and receive support. Six centres by some of the world's leading architects are now open, with eight more planned or under construction.

For the full citation, see p. 18.

**THE RIBA CLIENT OF THE YEAR**

# ST MARTIN-IN-THE-FIELDS
## TRAFALGAR SQUARE, LONDON WC2
## ERIC PARRY ARCHITECTS

CONSERVATION ARCHITECT **CAROE & PARTNERS ARCHITECTS**
CLIENT **REVD NICHOLAS HOLTAM ON BEHALF OF ST MARTIN-IN-THE-FIELDS**

Eric Parry Architects' design for St Martin-in-the-Fields has breathed new life into this landmark London church. It has been painstakingly delivered with great consideration and sensitivity at all levels of design, from masterplan to detail, all completely endorsed and supported by an enlightened client – the vicar, Revd Nicholas Holtam – supported by Chief Executive Hugh Player.

For the full citation, see p. 192.

# THE RIBA CABE
# PUBLIC SPACE AWARD

This award is sponsored by the Commission for Architecture and the Built Environment (CABE), the government's adviser on architecture, urban design and public space. The prize is presented to the architects and landscape architects of the best RIBA Award-winning public space in the United Kingdom, and recognizes the valuable contribution that a well-designed public realm makes to the quality of the built environment and of our daily lives.

In 2008, the first year of the award, the winner was Old Market Square, Nottingham, by Gustafson Porter.

## WINNER

CASTLEFORD BRIDGE
CASTLEFORD
MCDOWELL + BENEDETTI ARCHITECTS

## JUDGES

SARAH GAVENTA
DIRECTOR OF CABE SPACE

NEIL PORTER
ARCHITECT AND LANDSCAPE
ARCHITECT, GUSTAFSON PORTER

TONY CHAPMAN
RIBA HEAD OF AWARDS

## SHORTLIST

5 ALDERMANBURY SQUARE
LONDON EC2
ERIC PARRY ARCHITECTS

LIVERPOOL ONE MASTERPLAN
LIVERPOOL
BDP WITH LANDSCAPE ARCHITECTS
PELLI CLARKE PELLI AND GROSS MAX

NEW STREET SQUARE
LONDON EC4
BENNETTS ASSOCIATES ARCHITECTS

# CASTLEFORD BRIDGE
## CASTLEFORD
## MCDOWELL + BENEDETTI ARCHITECTS

CLIENT WAKEFIELD METROPOLITAN DISTRICT COUNCIL
STRUCTURAL ENGINEER ALAN BAXTER & ASSOCIATES
CIVIL ENGINEER ARUP WATER
QUANTITY SURVEYOR PHILIP PANK PARTNERSHIP
LIGHTING CONSULTANT SUTTON VANE ASSOCIATES
TIMBER CONSULTANT EWP
CONTRACTOR COSTAIN
CONTRACT VALUE £3,200,000
DATE OF COMPLETION JULY 2008
GROSS INTERNAL AREA 524 SQ. M (BRIDGE SURFACE); 2210 SQ. M
INCLUDING BANKS
IMAGES MCDOWELL + BENEDETTI ARCHITECTS (TOP; BOTTOM); TIM SOAR
(CENTRE; P. 88; P. 89)

THE RIBA CABE PUBLIC SPACE AWARD

SITE PLAN

As a public space, the bridge over Castleford Bay is hugely impressive. It provides a leisurely meeting place for the local community, but also acts as a catalyst for optimism for the future by refocusing Castleford's previously unexploited relationship with the River Aire as a key natural asset. It shows that a bridge, if developed as an important space for interaction and communal unity, can be as successful as a street, public square or park in creating public space.

As is the case with so many of our towns and cities, during its industrial past Castleford turned its back on its river, seeing it simply as a source of power and a medium for movement. A heavily trafficked road bridge was the only connection between the town's fractured northern and southern communities. By removing derelict buildings and placing the bridge alongside the weir, the architects have enabled one to experience the rush and thunder of water as it approaches and passes under the bridge. Locals meet and sit on the pedestrian bridge as part of their daily routine, chatting and observing surrounding activity. The movement of water and the newly found riverside vista momentarily remove them from the ordinary, and provide a unique spectacle.

The bridge spans the river with a subtle S-bend set lightly on three V-shaped supports. The timber boardwalk has been elegantly detailed to align with the line of movement. Benches arc out of its surface, giving a range of seating-height options, and the balustrade provides a leaning rail to ease observation and encourage

**CASTLEFORD BRIDGE**

conversation. The architects' attention to the human scale makes the bridge accessible and much loved by the community. There are no signs of vandalism or ageing, and local pride in communal involvement and achievement in getting the bridge built should ensure that it will stand the test of time.

Channel 4 and Kevin McCloud devoted an hour of television to this scheme, the biggest undertaking in the Castleford Project, which aims to regenerate the whole town. It is a project devised and led by the community, and an inspiring example of a successful dialogue between local people and the architects based on mutual understanding, respect and support.

THE RIBA CABE PUBLIC SPACE AWARD

# THE RIBA SORRELL FOUNDATION SCHOOLS AWARD

The RIBA Sorrell Foundation Schools Award is presented to the architects of the best RIBA Award-winning school – primary or secondary – with the aim of raising the standards of design in all new school building. The Sorrell Foundation sets out to inspire creativity in young people and to improve quality of life through good design, connecting such public sectors as education and health with the United Kingdom's world-class design community. Previous winners of the RIBA Sorrell Foundation Schools Award have been the Marlowe Academy, Ramsgate, by Building Design Partnership, in 2007; and Westminster Academy at the Naim Dangoor Centre, London, by Allford Hall Monaghan Morris, in 2008.

## WINNER

THE MINSTER SCHOOL
NOTTINGHAM ROAD, SOUTHWELL
PENOYRE & PRASAD

## JUDGES

LADY FRANCES SORRELL
CO-FOUNDER OF THE SORRELL
FOUNDATION

M.J. LONG
LONG & KENTISH ARCHITECTS

RYAN HAWLEY
HEAD TEACHER AT GARIBALDI
COLLEGE, MANSFIELD

TONY CHAPMAN
RIBA HEAD OF AWARDS

## SHORTLIST

DESIGN & TECHNOLOGY STUDIO,
FALMOUTH SCHOOL
TRESCOBEAS ROAD, FALMOUTH
URBAN SALON

MERCHANTS' ACADEMY
WITHYWOOD, BRISTOL
PENOYRE & PRASAD

ST MARY MAGDALENE ACADEMY
LIVERPOOL ROAD, LONDON N7
FEILDEN CLEGG BRADLEY STUDIOS

# THE MINSTER SCHOOL
## NOTTINGHAM ROAD, SOUTHWELL
## PENOYRE & PRASAD

CLIENT **THE MINSTER SCHOOL**
STRUCTURAL/SERVICES ENGINEER **BURO HAPPOLD**
PROJECT MANAGER/QUANTITY SURVEYOR **GLEEDS**
CONTRACTOR **GALLIFORD TRY**
CONTRACT VALUE **£28,900,000**
DATE OF COMPLETION **SEPTEMBER 2007**
GROSS INTERNAL AREA **13,837 SQ. M**
IMAGES **HÉLÈNE BINET (BOTTOM; P. 92); DENNIS GILBERT – VIEW (TOP; CENTRE; P. 93)**

The highly functional design of the Minster School is the result of close consultation between the architects and the school, and is highly sympathetic to the local community.

In the design for this relocated secondary school for 1600 pupils, with high-quality performance spaces, the architects have created a facility that clearly inspires its users. Working with a brief that provided exceptional opportunities, and with a strong ethical drive generated by governors, staff and pupils alike, the architects have synthesized the elements of the building in a beautifully resolved manner. There is continuity and consistency throughout a design in which each element is thoughtfully incorporated into a coherent composition.

Familiar materials have been selected and subtly crafted into a magical mix of more than the sum of their individual parts. The building adopts a palette of materials (brick and timber), hard and soft surfaces, and colours that connects it to the scale and texture of both the town and the open countryside. The architecture has clear navigation, with interconnected and flexible spaces, strong linkage between inside and out, and appropriate orientation, creating light and airy spaces. Circulation spaces are rhythmical, with alternating use of low and high ceilings.

It is evident that the new building has created a sense of aspiration in the pupils. The design takes a thorough and robust approach to sustainability, incorporating natural

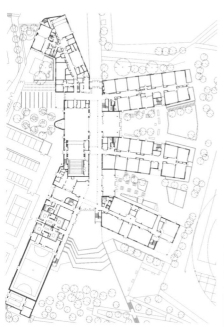

**GROUND-FLOOR PLAN**

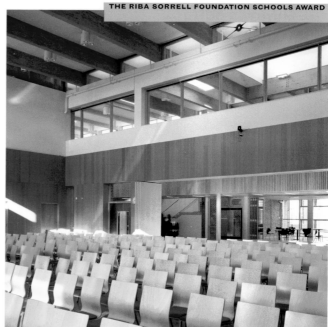

**THE MINSTER SCHOOL**

stack ventilation, high levels of insulation and underfloor heating with high-efficiency boilers, and uses rainwater recycling to reduce water consumption.

The RIBA Sorrell Foundation judges were particularly impressed by the deliberate flexibility of the project's spaces, pointing out that 'when a school goes through the journey of modernizing learning, it needs classrooms like these that are highly adaptable'. They thought that the beauty of the design lay in its detail. 'From the unique locker design to the wheelchair-height water fountains,' they said, 'it is clear that so much care has gone into it.' They added: 'The new school has a bright and interested pool of pupils to draw on, and they are clearly making good use of the opportunity, because the resulting anatomy works very convincingly.'

# THE STEPHEN LAWRENCE PRIZE

**IN ASSOCIATION WITH THE MARCO GOLDSCHMIED FOUNDATION**

The Stephen Lawrence Prize is funded by the Marco Goldschmied Foundation. The prize commemorates the teenager who was just setting out on the road to becoming an architect when he was murdered in 1993. It rewards projects with a construction budget of less than £1,000,000. In addition to the £5000 prize money, Marco Goldschmied donates £10,000 to fund the Stephen Lawrence Scholarship at the Architectural Association in London.

The Stephen Lawrence Prize was set up in 1998 to draw attention to the Stephen Lawrence Trust, which assists young black students in studying architecture, and to reward the creativity required for smaller projects with low budgets. Previous winners of the prize have been Ian Ritchie Architects, for Terrasson Cultural Greenhouse, France, in 1998; Munkenbeck + Marshall, for the Sculpture Gallery, Roche Court, near Salisbury, in 1999; Softroom Architects, for the Kielder Belvedere, Northumberland, in 2000; Richard Rose-Casemore, for Hatherley Studio, Winchester, in 2001; Cottrell + Vermeulen Architecture, for Cardboard Building, Westborough Primary School, Westcliffe-on-Sea, in 2002; Gumuchdjian Architects, for Think Tank, Skibbereen, in 2003; Simon Conder Associates, for Vista, Dungeness, in 2004; Níall McLaughlin Architects, for the House at Clonakilty, County Cork, in 2005; Alison Brooks Architects, for Wrap House, London, in 2006; David Sheppard Architects, for Wooda, Crackington Haven, in 2007; and John Pawson, for the Sackler Crossing, Royal Botanic Gardens, Kew, Richmond, in 2008.

## WINNER

**EL RAY**
DUNGENESS
SIMON CONDER ASSOCIATES

## JUDGES

**MARCO GOLDSCHMIED**
ARCHITECT

**DOREEN LAWRENCE, OBE**

## SHORTLIST

**DEAL PIER**
DEAL
NÍALL MCLAUGHLIN ARCHITECTS

**HIND HOUSE**
WARGAVE, READING
JOHN PARDEY ARCHITECTS

**HOUSE IN HIGHGATE CEMETERY**
LONDON N6
ELDRIDGE SMERIN

**STUDIO SPACE**
MAULDEN, BEDFORD
NICOLAS TYE ARCHITECTS

# EL RAY
## DUNGENESS
## SIMON CONDER ASSOCIATES

CLIENT **PRIVATE**
STRUCTURAL ENGINEER **FLUID STRUCTURES**
ENVIRONMENTAL ENGINEER **ZEF (UK)**
CONTRACTOR **ECOLIBRIUM SOLUTIONS**
CONTRACT VALUE **£215,000**
DATE OF COMPLETION **JULY 2008**
GROSS INTERNAL AREA **105 SQ. M**
IMAGES **CHRIS GASCOIGNE – VIEW (TOP; SECOND FROM BOTTOM; P. 96 TOP RIGHT AND BOTTOM; P. 97); PAUL SMOOTHY (SECOND FROM TOP; BOTTOM; P. 96 TOP LEFT AND CENTRE)**

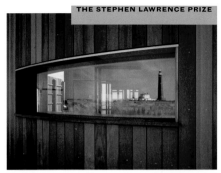

It is hard to believe that the white cliffs of Dover are only a few miles away from the big-sky flatlands of Dungeness. This area is more American prairie than Garden of England. The looming presence of Dungeness Power Station and its 33,000-volt tendrils spreading in all directions dominate the surreal landscape.

In this windswept setting, this small timber holiday house sits lightly on the shingle, with no foundations other than a raft. Insulated with 400-millimetre walls and roof, it is shaped to catch the sea breeze when balmy, and triple-glazed to deflect it when hostile. Requiring no energy from the nuclear monolith next door, the house mimics the self-sufficiency of a hermit crab.

The original 1870s timber railway carriage at the house's heart, unmoved since it was first placed on the shingle in the 1930s, evokes both the history of the ad-hoc settlement of Dungeness in the Great Depression and the owners' personal memories of it as the core of their family home.

It is a stroke of sensitive and humorous genius to leave the carriage in place, complete with scabrous, peeling, century-old paint. The carriage is both mad and perfect – and makes a very good galley kitchen, too. This is something that no amount of flashy kitchen fittings and plasma-screen wallpaper can buy.

The house also has two bedrooms, a bathroom and a large living/dining/kitchen area, which looks on to the sea. The room is elevated in section towards the window wall, which brings a private, framed beach landscape into the house. Each bedroom has its own private courtyard – a windbreak and place of shelter. The building sits perfectly in, and is another eccentric addition to, a landscape of reused and bespoke construction. The external timber (cedar), which is weathering naturally, and internal plywood both fit beautifully with the beach landscape and colours.

The house is simultaneously comfortable and comforting, the timber on all five elevations already settling into the landscape like driftwood. When it floats out to sea after the great floods of 2090, future marine archaeologists will puzzle over its origins and the hidden symbolic meaning of its wine-glass-shaped plan.

**SITE PLAN**

# THE RIBA INTERNATIONAL AWARDS

**SPONSORED BY COSENTINO**

The RIBA International Awards are sponsored by Cosentino.
Eligible buildings are those outside the European Union or
those built in the EU (with the exception of the United
Kingdom) that are designed by a practice based outside
the UK. The awards are judged by members of the Awards
Group, who carefully consider the entry material. A shortlist
for the Lubetkin Prize is then drawn up, and shortlisted
schemes are visited.

**JUDGES**

BOB ALLIES
GIANNI BOTSFORD
TONY CHAPMAN
PETER CLEGG
TOM DYCKHOFF
PAUL FINCH
MURRAY FRASER
RICHARD GRIFFITHS
RACHEL HAUGH
PAUL MONAGHAN
SHEILA O'DONNELL
DEBORAH SAUNT
BILL TAYLOR
CINDY WALTERS

# BEIJING SOUTH STATION
## KAIYANG ROAD, EAST DISTRICT, BEIJING
## TFP FARRELLS

DESIGN ARCHITECT/CLIENT **THIRD RAILWAY SURVEY AND DESIGN INSTITUTE GROUP CORPORATION (TSDI)**
STRUCTURAL/SERVICES ENGINEER **OVE ARUP & PARTNERS HONG KONG**
TRAFFIC ENGINEER **ATKINS CHINA**
CONTRACTOR **CHINA RAILWAY CONSTRUCTION ENGINEERING GROUP**
CONTRACT VALUE **£602,000,000**
DATE OF COMPLETION **AUGUST 2008**
GROSS INTERNAL AREA **226,000 SQ. M**
IMAGES **FU XING PHOTOGRAPHY (TOP RIGHT; SECOND FROM TOP); ZHOU RUOGU (TOP LEFT; SECOND FROM BOTTOM; BOTTOM)**

Designed to handle more than 80 million passenger movements annually, the building forms the focus of a masterplan for the surrounding city, and is one of the world's largest transport hubs.

By cleverly organizing all the functions concentrically and in section, the station plan is an excellent example of clarity and efficiency. Swooping above the rails and lengthy platforms, a series of wide-span canopies with integrated glazing creates an engine shed that is a worthy and striking addition to the lineage of this building type.

The passenger is put at the heart of the station, and the dramatic and generously daylit central concourse gives legible access to the trains beneath. This is an apt celebration of the journey just completed or begun.

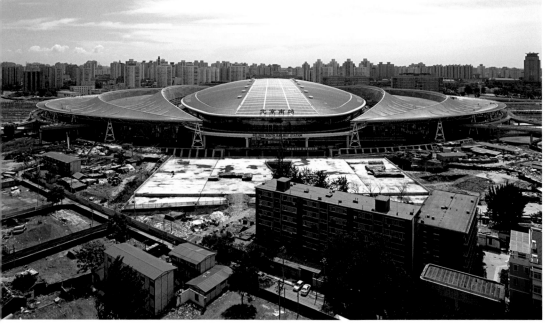

# MAOSI ECOLOGICAL DEMONSTRATION PRIMARY SCHOOL
## MAOSI VILLAGE, GANSU PROVINCE
## SCHOOL OF ARCHITECTURE, THE CHINESE UNIVERSITY OF HONG KONG

CLIENT **KADOORIE FARM & BOTANIC GARDEN**
STRUCTURAL/SERVICES ENGINEER **BUILDING DESIGN INSTITUTE OF QINGYANG CITY**
QUANTITY SURVEYOR **XIFENG AUDIT CENTRE OF FINANCIAL BUDGETEERING**
CONTRACTOR **QINGYANG SI LITIAN CONSTRUCTION**
CONTRACT VALUE **RMB 714,700**
DATE OF COMPLETION **AUGUST 2007**
GROSS INTERNAL AREA **1006 SQ. M**
IMAGES **JUN MU**

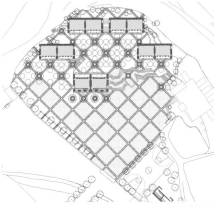

**SITE PLAN**

This elegant primary school is in a poor region where the climate is extreme. Thick mud walls to the classrooms provide thermal mass, and the clay-tiled roof is insulated with exposed timber beams, which were bought from local villagers, one beam per family. Villagers built the school using simple tools. Traditional building techniques were employed, so there is little environmental impact and embodied energy is kept to a minimum.

The school's ethos is relevant to anyone designing schools, but is especially relevant in developing regions. It is environmentally and architecturally ambitious, and sets an admirably high standard for rural village schools anywhere in the world. The Chinese government is already promoting the prototype eco-school, and some 200,000 schools could be built using this exemplar.

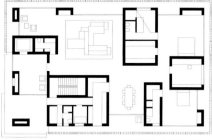

GROUND-FLOOR PLAN

# NINETREE VILLAGE
## HANGZHOU, ZHEJIANG PROVINCE
## DAVID CHIPPERFIELD ARCHITECTS

EXECUTIVE ARCHITECT/STRUCTURAL ENGINEER/ENVIRONMENTAL ENGINEER
ZHEJIANG SOUTH ARCHITECTURAL SERVICES DESIGN COMPANY
CLIENT ZHEJIANG JOYON REAL ESTATE COMPANY
LANDSCAPE ARCHITECT LEVIN MONSIGNY LANDSCHAFTSARCHITEKTEN
CONTRACTOR CHINA STATE CONSTRUCTION ENGINEERING
CORPORATION (CSCEC)
CONTRACT VALUE £30,000,000
DATE OF COMPLETION JANUARY 2008
GROSS INTERNAL AREA 23,500 SQ. M
IMAGES SHU HE (BOTTOM LEFT); CHRISTIAN RICHTERS – VIEW (TOP LEFT
AND RIGHT; CENTRE; BOTTOM RIGHT)

Ninetree Village is further evidence of the mastery that
David Chipperfield Architects has attained in harnessing
the benefits of contemporary design to local tradition. The
loggia zone that wraps round the apartment on each floor
provides a transitional space between the interior living
space and surrounding nature. Each loggia is fitted with
sliding wooden screens of oiled Kampala wood to give the
privacy and shading desired by the residents. The plan is
remarkable for its freedom, with the only supporting walls
being those of the cellular elements of bathrooms,
cupboards and closets.

This is luxury achieved through space, light and texture,
without any hint of ostentation, creating a delightful place
in which to live.

# SAXO BANK
## PHILIP HEYMANNS ALLÉ, HELLERUP, COPENHAGEN
## 3XN

CLIENT **CARLSBERG EJENDOMME**
LANDSCAPE ARCHITECT **LAND+**
STRUCTURAL ENGINEER **RAMBØLL DANMARK**
CONTRACTOR **KPC BYG**
CONTRACT VALUE **€28,400,000**
DATE OF COMPLETION **AUGUST 2008**
GROSS INTERNAL AREA **22,700 SQ. M**
IMAGES **ADAM MORK**

Saxo Bank is a story of two geometries: straight lines and sharp angles, counterpointed by sweeping curves. It is reminiscent of a yacht in full sail. Old warehouses form the building's context and provide the language. Internally, a sculptural staircase snakes its way up inside the atrium before emerging on the bank's main trading floor.

The aim of the project was to realize the virtual. Saxo is primarily an internet bank, so in order to lend it substance and therefore added credibility, the architects were asked to come up with a building that would be memorable and significant; an icon that would be a landmark both in space and in cyberspace.

# ALTO VETRO RESIDENTIAL TOWER
## GRAND CANAL QUAY, DUBLIN
## SHAY CLEARY ARCHITECTS

**GROUND-FLOOR PLAN**

CLIENT **TREASURY HOLDINGS IRELAND**
LANDSCAPE ARCHITECT **HYLAND EDGAR DRIVER**
STRUCTURAL ENGINEER **DBFL CONSULTING ENGINEERS**
SERVICES ENGINEER **HOMAN O'BRIEN ASSOCIATES**
QUANTITY SURVEYOR **BRUCE SHAW PARTNERSHIP**
FACADE ENGINEER **BILLINGS DESIGN ASSOCIATES**
CONTRACTOR **CMP**
CONTRACT VALUE **€10,000,000**
DATE OF COMPLETION **JUNE 2008**
GROSS INTERNAL AREA **2620 SQ. M**
IMAGES **ROS KAVANAGH**

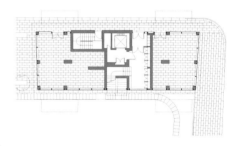

This is the tower every city wants. Elegant and slim, it rises sixteen storeys off a plan that measures just 21 metres by 8 metres and contains only two flats per floor so that they enjoy views in three directions. Maintaining the simple rectangular form, the tower avoids any sculptural gymnastics and instead relies for its architectural effect on the qualities of its glass skin. A simple rhythm of vertical mullions holds a variety of transparent and insulated panels articulated by strong horizontal stone bands at each floor level and interrupted by an informal pattern of projecting balconies.

As an urban marker, the tower works perfectly with the scale of the city, and helps to define the character of its quayside setting.

# EUROPEAN INVESTMENT BANK
## BOULEVARD KONRAD ADENAUER, LUXEMBOURG CITY
## INGENHOVEN ARCHITECTS

CLIENT **EUROPEAN INVESTMENT BANK**
LANDSCAPE ARCHITECTS **INGENHOVEN ARCHITECTS WITH WKM LANDSCHAFTSARCHITEKTEN WEBER KLEIN MAAS**
STRUCTURAL ENGINEER **WERNER SOBEK**
SERVICES ENGINEERS **HL-TECHNIK ENGINEERING PARTNER; INGENIEUR CONSULT; PBE-BELJULI PLANUNGSGESELLSCHAFT; S&E CONSULT ALS ARGE TGA**
CONTRACTORS **VINCI CONSTRUCTION GRANDS PROJETS AND COMPAGNIE D'ENTERPRISES CFE (JOINT VENTURE)**
CONTRACT VALUE **CONFIDENTIAL**
DATE OF COMPLETION **AUGUST 2008**
GROSS INTERNAL AREA **71,500 SQ. M**
IMAGES **H.G. ESCH (CENTRE; BOTTOM LEFT); INGENHOVEN ARCHITECTS (TOP; BOTTOM RIGHT)**

The European Investment Bank is linked by its cafeteria to the existing bank building by Sir Denys Lasdun, completed in 1980. Although it picks up on the curves of the original (also suggested by the site), the new building is by no means a deferential homage to the old; rather, it borrows an idea developed for Ingenhoven's 2008 RIBA European Award-winning Lufthansa headquarters in Frankfurt, and takes the form of an over-arching 13,000 square metres of lightweight steel-and-glass roof. The roof encompasses office space, dividing it into fingers of accommodation with full-height winter gardens. These naturally ventilated atria act as climate buffers, and help the building – the first in Europe outside the United Kingdom to be assessed under BREEAM – to achieve a 'Very Good' rating.

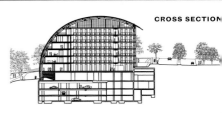

CROSS SECTION

# COCOON – EXCLUSIVE OFFICE HEADQUARTERS
## SEEFELDSTRASSE, ZURICH
## CAMENZIND EVOLUTION

CLIENT **SWISS LIFE**
STRUCTURAL ENGINEER **GRUNER**
SERVICES ENGINEER **HAUSTEC ENGINEERING**
ELECTRICAL ENGINEER **HEFTI HESS MARTIGNONI ZUG**
CONTRACTOR **ZÜBLIN-MURER**
CONTRACT VALUE **£4,500,000**
DATE OF COMPLETION **SEPTEMBER 2007**
GROSS INTERNAL AREA **1940 SQ. M**
IMAGES **NICK BRÄNDLI (TOP LEFT); CAMENZIND EVOLUTION (TOP RIGHT; BOTTOM RIGHT); FERIT KUYAS (BOTTOM LEFT)**

It is a brave move to take an idea by Frank Lloyd Wright – the spiralling ramp of the Guggenheim Museum in New York – transpose it to the shores of Lake Zurich and apply it to an office building. Cocoon is set amid a group of mature trees, and borrows its geometry directly from its surroundings. The shell-like structure produces an excellent working environment on twenty-five segmented levels with 40-centimetre 'treds' between them.

A fine stainless-steel mesh wraps the building, making it more a piece of sculpture than a piece of real estate. By day it appears almost secretive, certainly intriguing; at night it puts on its shimmering glad rags and becomes the talk of the town.

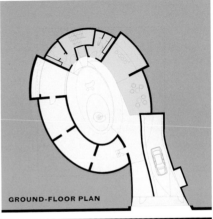

GROUND-FLOOR PLAN

# CHING FU SHIPBUILDING
## KAOHSIUNG, TAIWAN
## ROGERS STIRK HARBOUR + PARTNERS

CO-ARCHITECT **HOYA ARCHITECTS & ASSOCIATES**
CLIENTS **CHING FU SHIPBUILDING COMPANY; WEELEE INTERNATIONAL**
STRUCTURAL ENGINEER **SUPERTECH CONSULTANTS INTERNATIONAL**
SERVICES ENGINEER **CO-YOUNG ENGINEERING CONSULTANTS**
LIGHTING ENGINEER **CWI LIGHTING DESIGN**
FAÇADE ENGINEER **BRIGHT CURTAIN METAL**
CONTRACTOR **FU TSU CONSTRUCTION COMPANY**
CONTRACT VALUE **CONFIDENTIAL**
DATE OF COMPLETION **DECEMBER 2007**
GROSS INTERNAL AREA **25,178 SQ. M**
IMAGES **KATSUHISA KIDA**

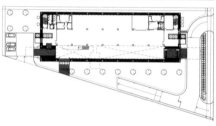

**GROUND-FLOOR PLAN**

Rogers Stirk Harbour + Partners has taken the language of the Centre Pompidou, Lloyd's of London and Lloyd's Register of Shipping – extractor funnels, ducts and pipework colour-coded according to function, but also, happily, the corporate colours – and has translated it into Mandarin. This, however, is not mainland People's Republic of China, but the offshore Republic of China – Taiwan to the rest of the world. As ever, the architects have adapted their own vernacular to suit local conditions: thus, the apparently free-floating boxes, hung from the building's steel structure, not only provide meeting rooms and cellular offices with decks on top, but also are part of a sophisticated environmental strategy.

The client is delighted to have a landmark Rogers building that sells its company to the world.

106

# ADVANCED RESEARCH AND DEVELOPMENT FACILITY, NORTHERN ARIZONA UNIVERSITY
## FLAGSTAFF, ARIZONA
## HOPKINS ARCHITECTS

EXECUTIVE ARCHITECT **BURNS WALD-HOPKINS ARCHITECTS**
CLIENT **NORTHERN ARIZONA UNIVERSITY**
LANDSCAPE ARCHITECT **T. BARNABAS KANE & ASSOCIATES**
STRUCTURAL ENGINEERS **ARUP; SCHNEIDER & ASSOCIATES**
SERVICES ENGINEER **ARUP**
CONTRACTOR **KITCHELL**
CONTRACT VALUE **$21,000,000**
DATE OF COMPLETION **OCTOBER 2008**
GROSS INTERNAL AREA **6503 SQ. M**
IMAGES **TIMOTHY HURSLEY**

Hopkins Architects has used its first major commission in the United States to deliver a tour de force of understated ecological design for Northern Arizona University. This research facility is a cool and gently curved linear block in which the south-facing double-skin glazed wall, and triple-height atrium behind, passively capture the winter sun and let in plentiful rays to reduce the internal heating and lighting load. The building uses 90 per cent less energy than its equivalent counterparts on other US university campuses. In fact, it might be claimed to be the most environmentally efficient building to date in the United States.

Typical of the work of Hopkins Architects, this exemplar of sustainable design shows that remarkable environmental savings can be made without hysterical formal manipulation or self-congratulatory eco-posturing.

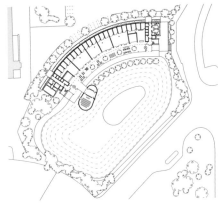

GROUND-FLOOR PLAN

# THE RIBA AWARDS

The RIBA Awards were established in 1966. RIBA members are invited to enter projects for all the RIBA building awards in the first two months of the year. Entries are first visited by a local architect to see if they merit a visit from a full regional jury of three, consisting of an architect chair from outside the region, one from that region and a 'lay' juror, such as an engineer, client, artist or journalist. The chairs of the regional juries report to the Awards Group (the scheme's advisory panel), which has the right to query if a scheme not given an award was, in its view, worthy of one. In this case, the jury chair may, in consultation with the other members of his or her jury, agree to an award. The Awards Group has no right to overturn an award. These awards are presented in the RIBA regions.

## JUDGES

The regional judges are listed in the following order: chair, regional representative and lay assessor.

**SCOTLAND**
PIERS GOUGH
ALLAN MURRAY
ROB GREGORY

**NORTHERN IRELAND**
SALLY MACKERETH
AIDAN MCGRATH
MARY WRENN

**NORTH-EAST**
ALASTAIR LANSLEY
DOLAN CONWAY
MARTINE HAMILTON KNIGHT

**NORTH-WEST**
PHILIP GUMUCHDJIAN
ROD HUGHES
SIR DUNCAN MICHAEL

**YORKSHIRE**
ALASTAIR LANSLEY
PETER CARTWRIGHT
MARTINE HAMILTON KNIGHT

**WALES**
SHAHRIAR NASSER
JONATHAN JONES
NICK TUNE

**WEST MIDLANDS**
GARETH HOSKINS
KEVIN SINGH AND COLIN WAY
POORAN DESAI

**EAST MIDLANDS**
KATHRYN FINDLAY
JULIAN MARSH
PATRICK MADDAMS

**EAST**
KEN SHUTTLEWORTH
STEVEN KEARNEY
JILL GODDARD

**SOUTH-WEST**
INGRID BILLE
TANYA GRIFFITHS
LOREN BUTT

**WESSEX**
INGRID BILLE
GEORGE TASKER
LOREN BUTT

**SOUTH**
MIKE TONKIN
ROBIN HADDOW
MIKE GAZZARD

**SOUTH-EAST**
RICHARD COTTRELL
GRAHAM WHITEHOUSE
HUGH MERRELL

**LONDON (NORTH)**
NEVEN SIDOR
SELINA MASON
CHARLIE BUNCE

**LONDON (SOUTH)**
GRAHAM STIRK
SOPHIE TWOHIG
MARK IRVING

**LONDON (EAST)**
KEITH WILLIAMS
ROBERT SAKULA
ELEANOR YOUNG

**LONDON (WEST)**
ALISON BROOKS
CHRIS HAMPSON
MADELON VRIESENDORP

**EUROPEAN UNION**
BOB ALLIES
GIANNI BOTSFORD
TONY CHAPMAN
PETER CLEGG
TOM DYCKHOFF
MURRAY FRASER
RICHARD GRIFFITHS
RACHEL HAUGH
PAUL MONAGHAN
SHEILA O'DONNELL
DEBORAH SAUNT
BILL TAYLOR
CINDY WALTERS

# THE BEATSON INSTITUTE FOR CANCER RESEARCH, UNIVERSITY OF GLASGOW
## GARSCUBE ESTATE, GLASGOW
## REIACH AND HALL ARCHITECTS

CLIENT **UNIVERSITY OF GLASGOW**
STRUCTURAL ENGINEER **URS CORPORATION**
SERVICES ENGINEER **HULLEY & KIRKWOOD**
QUANTITY SURVEYOR **TURNER & TOWNSEND**
ACCESS CONSULTANT **REIACH AND HALL ARCHITECTS**
CONTRACTOR **BALFOUR BEATTY CONSTRUCTION**
CONTRACT VALUE **£12,900,000**
DATE OF COMPLETION **DECEMBER 2007**
GROSS INTERNAL AREA **6475 SQ. M**
IMAGES **PAUL ZANRE**

The spare elegance and apparent simplicity of this glass pavilion, set within a walled garden, are a worthy and understated foil to the technical precision of the state-of-the-art research facilities it houses. Although the budget was relatively modest for a facility of this scale and complexity, the architects have created a world-class research environment in a crystalline cube.

By combining all its cancer-research facilities on one site and creating such a welcoming new building, the University of Glasgow has greatly enhanced its chances of attracting the best cancer researchers. One of the judges suggested that the Institute was the most 'lickable' of all this year's Scottish submissions.

# DRUMMOND HOUSE – THE SHED
## DUNDEE
## LEADINGHAM JAMESON ROGERS + HYND CHARTERED ARCHITECTS

CLIENTS **MR AND MRS P. DRUMMOND**
STRUCTURAL ENGINEER **SINCLAIR ASSOCIATES**
SERVICES ENGINEER/CONTRACTOR **PETER M. DRUMMOND**
CONTRACT VALUE **£600,000**
DATE OF COMPLETION **DECEMBER 2008**
GROSS INTERNAL AREA **475 SQ. M**
IMAGES **GRAEME HUTTON**

This purpose-built home in the Perthshire agricultural landscape is essentially a contemporary and playful reinterpretation of a rural barn, configured as a very sophisticated contemporary dwelling.

The materials palette, like the form, is a careful response to the setting. Rising from earthen brick perimeter walls, the zinc roofing reflects the colour temperature of the prevailing daylight. The steel-framed structure allows the flourish of a bold cantilever at the south-west corner, extending the roofscape over the countryside and emphasizing the building's joy in its setting between earth and sky.

The death of one of the architects, David Jameson, before the completion of the building imbues this award with particular poignancy.

# MOORE STREET HOUSING
## GALLOWGATE, GLASGOW
## RICHARD MURPHY ARCHITECTS; ELDER & CANNON ARCHITECTS; JM ARCHITECTS; PAGE\PARK

CLIENT **MOLENDINAR PARK HOUSING ASSOCIATION**
STRUCTURAL ENGINEER **SKM ANTHONY HUNT**
SERVICES ENGINEER **FULCRUM CONSULTING**
CONTRACTOR **CCG (SCOTLAND)**
CONTRACT VALUE **£10,010,000**
DATE OF COMPLETION **NOVEMBER 2008**
GROSS INTERNAL AREA **7550 SQ. M**
IMAGES **ANDREW LEE**

This development, the successor to the multi-award-winning Graham Square, amply demonstrates that the social-housing sector in Scotland remains a vital focus for innovation. Like its precursor, this new, larger development is a showcase not only for the skills of particular practices but also for joint working.

Each group of buildings declares a distinctive design identity. Scale, orientation, some shared materials and a robust landscape context, however, produce a unified, modest and attractive whole. The development is concerned less with bravura architectural performances than with the regeneration of the area and the creation of a new community.

The impressive entrance arch of the former meat market, retained as part of the development, is an elegant foil to the modernity and ingenuity of the new housing to which it is the prelude.

# NORTH GLASGOW COLLEGE
## SPRINGBURN, GLASGOW
### RMJM

CLIENT **NORTH GLASGOW COLLEGE**
STRUCTURAL ENGINEER/SERVICES ENGINEER/
ACCESS CONSULTANT **RMJM**
QUANTITY SURVEYOR **TURNER & TOWNSEND**
CONTRACTOR **BARR LIMITED**
CONTRACT VALUE **£27,500,000**
DATE OF COMPLETION **JANUARY 2009**
GROSS INTERNAL AREA **18,588 SQ. M**
IMAGES **KEITH HUNTER – ARCAID**

**Set in Springburn, once the focus of Glasgow's locomotive-manufacturing industry, this substantial new facility replaces North Glasgow College's historic premises. The building's scale, prominence, bold contemporary form and elegantly conceived landscape setting all signify major, positive change.**

**The impressive entrance atrium both welcomes and orientates visitors. The activity surrounding the atrium, particularly the cafe, large meeting spaces, winter garden and views into the games hall, ensures that the vivid life of the college and its central role within the Springburn community are well signalled.**

**The building provides a welcoming and inclusive teaching environment. The spare simplicity and honesty of its materials and the elegance of its form generate an effective architecture, free of gimmickry and unnecessary embellishment.**

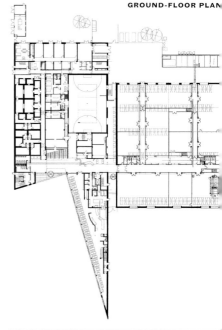

GROUND-FLOOR PLAN

# POLLOK CIVIC REALM
## COWGLEN ROAD, GLASGOW
## ARCHIAL ARCHITECTS

CLIENT **GLASGOW CITY COUNCIL**
STRUCTURAL ENGINEER **SCOTT WILSON**
SERVICES ENGINEER **THE HAWTHORNE BOYLE PARTNERSHIP**
QUANTITY SURVEYOR **DOIG HART**
CONTRACTOR **GRAHAM CONSTRUCTION**
CONTRACT VALUE **£6,500,000**
DATE OF COMPLETION **MAY 2008**
GROSS INTERNAL AREA **3211 SQ. M**
IMAGES **ANDREW LEE**

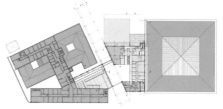

**SECOND-FLOOR PLAN**

As its name suggests, this project provides a range of public services for the Pollok area. The brief required the inclusion of a library, employment services, a local museum, a cafe, IT training, childcare and Citizens' Advice. The enclosure also allows access to the existing health and leisure centres, and works as an enclosed pedestrian thoroughfare, the main daytime route for visitors to the shops at the rear.

Internally, the different uses are highlighted through the employment of bold colours and strong, graphic signage. A brief that specified the linking of two existing mediocre structures could have produced a thoroughly compromised new building, but the architects have risen to the challenge.

# POTTERROW DEVELOPMENT, THE UNIVERSITY OF EDINBURGH
## CRICHTON STREET, EDINBURGH
## BENNETTS ASSOCIATES ARCHITECTS

CLIENT **THE UNIVERSITY OF EDINBURGH**
STRUCTURAL ENGINEER/SERVICES ENGINEER/ACCESS
CONSULTANT **BURO HAPPOLD**
QUANTITY SURVEYOR **TURNER & TOWNSEND**
CONTRACTOR **BALFOUR BEATTY CONSTRUCTION**
CONTRACT VALUE **£40,600,000**
DATE OF COMPLETION **JULY 2008**
GROSS INTERNAL AREA **16,528 SQ. M**
IMAGES **KEITH HUNTER – ARCAID**

These superbly detailed buildings form a new hub for the university. Faced in natural stone and polished quartz-aggregate concrete, they house the School of Informatics, the Informatics Forum (accommodating more than five hundred researchers) and the School of Philosophy, Psychology and Language Sciences. The façades of the buildings are aligned with the principal streets to reinstate the historic urban grain of the area. Two interlocking ribbons of accommodation, orientated to receive sunlight all year round, face each other across an open courtyard.

The internal communication routes and high-quality break-out spaces create a lively and friendly environment. Such amenities as comfortable seating areas and terraces create opportunities for interaction and quiet contemplation, a considerable remove from traditional educational provision. These buildings are powerfully contemporary in design and yet welcoming in their use of materials and creation of spaces.

# THE PRINTWORKS
## GLASGOW
## CAMERON WEBSTER ARCHITECTS

CLIENT **OTAGO DEVELOPMENTS**
STRUCTURAL ENGINEER **ALAN MCCULLOCH ASSOCIATES**
CONTRACTOR **CAMERON JOINERS & SHOPFITTERS**
CONTRACT VALUE **£200,000**
DATE OF COMPLETION **APRIL 2008**
GROSS INTERNAL AREA **225 SQ. M**
IMAGES **MARTIN PHILLIMORE (TOP LEFT AND RIGHT; BOTTOM LEFT);
CAMERON WEBSTER (BOTTOM RIGHT)**

This is quite literally a hidden gem, set behind a traditional
tenement block. The old building, once a glue factory
attached to an abattoir, was subsequently used as a
printworks. Since the existing brick structure was past
saving, it was demolished and a new steel-framed
structure built on its footprint. This increased both the
building's natural lighting and its usable space.

A central glazed courtyard brings natural light into
the centre of the space and provides lighting, ventilation
and a sense of connection with the outdoors, particularly
for the basement offices. The building now provides
225 square metres of office space, which is occupied by
three separate, complementary businesses, including
Cameron Webster Architects, its designer.

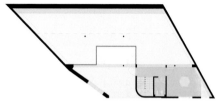

**GROUND-FLOOR PLAN**

# FALLAHOGEY HOUSE
## KILREA, COLERAINE
## MCGARRY-MOON ARCHITECTS

CLIENTS **JESSICA MCGARRY AND STEVEN MOON**
STRUCTURAL ENGINEER **STUCTURES 2000**
CONTRACTOR **ALAN MOON JOINERY & BUILDING**
CONTRACT VALUE **£325,000**
DATE OF COMPLETION **NOVEMBER 2008**
GROSS INTERNAL AREA **163 SQ. M**
IMAGES **JESSICA MCGARRY**

The design of this house demonstrates a pleasing duality
on a number of levels: it is both boldly uncompromising
and modestly contextual. Its form – a simple barn – houses
a series of sophisticated fluid spaces. Double-height
glazing to the rear façade allows the landscape to flow
into the living spaces, while letterbox windows in the
studio and bedrooms frame CinemaScope views to the
distant hills. Although the scale of the house is quite
grand, it remains humble in deference to the dramatic
landscape. The rawness of some of the materials used –
the rolled-zinc roof supported on galvanized-steel
columns, and the external sun-bleached timber louvres
and panels – gives the house a rural honesty.

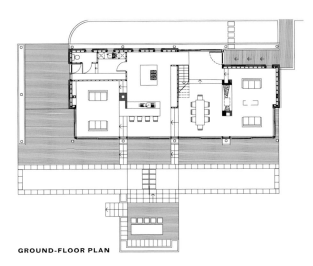

GROUND-FLOOR PLAN

# THE KNOCKBREDA CENTRE
## SAINTFIELD ROAD, BELFAST
## PENOYRE & PRASAD; TODD ARCHITECTS

CLIENT **BELFAST HEALTH AND SOCIAL CARE TRUST**
STRUCTURAL ENGINEER **PRICE & MYERS**
SERVICES ENGINEER **MAX FORDHAM**
CONTRACTOR **FARRANS HEALTHCARE**
CONTRACT VALUE **£7,350,000**
DATE OF COMPLETION **OCTOBER 2008**
GROSS INTERNAL AREA **4917 SQ. M**
IMAGES **TODD WATSON**

This building is an impressive example of a new breed of 'polyclinics'. Natural daylight filters through the soft organic curves of the atrium roof to bathe the space below, creating a calm, serene atmosphere. Combined with the long views from balcony to balcony, it makes the main waiting areas uplifting spaces. The design does not patronize, nor does it alienate with an uncompromising corporate vision, and the clarity of the plan makes it instantly user-friendly.

Although it is early days for this building type, the centre feels as though it is the culmination of a good deal of refining, careful consultation and planning, where a diverse and conflicting brief resolves into a welcoming place in the community.

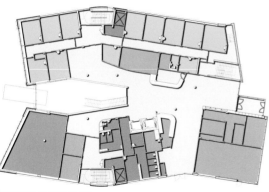

GROUND-FLOOR PLAN

# BERWICK WORKSPACE
## BERWICK-UPON-TWEED
## MALCOLM FRASER ARCHITECTS

CLIENT **BERWICK-UPON-TWEED BOROUGH COUNCIL**
STRUCTURAL ENGINEER **DAVID NARRO ASSOCIATES**
SERVICES ENGINEER **K.J. TAIT ENGINEERS**
QUANTITY SURVEYOR **MDA CONSULTING**
ACCESS CONSULTANT **BLUEKEEP**
CONTRACTOR **GB BUILDING SOLUTIONS**
CONTRACT VALUE **£3,100,000**
DATE OF COMPLETION **MAY 2008**
GROSS INTERNAL AREA **1503 SQ. M**
IMAGES **KEITH HUNTER – ARCAID**

The brief required this business incubation centre to
generate a creative bustle within the traditional grain of
Berwick's closes and courtyards, forming new links with
the surrounding streets, courts and buildings. The building
consists of a mixture of two- and three-storey structures
with four parallel pitched roofs, following the rich local
vernacular of eaves and gables. The development is an
essay in restraint, with a simple lime-based render on
a storey-height podium of local Doddington stone, and
vertically fixed untreated home-grown larch cladding,
which delineates the storeys.

    This simple and calm development sits comfortably
within its surroundings and gives Berwick a new courtyard
and delightful working space.

# CARDINAL HUME CATHOLIC SCHOOL
## OLD DURHAM ROAD, GATESHEAD
## GWK CHARTERED ARCHITECTS

CLIENT **DIOCESE OF HEXHAM AND NEWCASTLE**
STRUCTURAL/SERVICES ENGINEER **CUNDALL**
QUANTITY SURVEYOR **E.C. HARRIS**
ACCESS CONSULTANT **SOUTHERN GREEN**
CONTRACTOR **MILLER CONSTRUCTION**
CONTRACT VALUE **£21,000,000**
DATE OF COMPLETION **SEPTEMBER 2007**
GROSS INTERNAL AREA **1180 SQ. M**
IMAGES **ANDREW HEPTINSTALL**

The brief for this new school, to replace the old St Edmund Campion School in Gateshead, asked for a modern, state-of-the-art building to which teachers and pupils alike would be attracted, and which would not feel like a standard school. Briefing consisted of intensive sessions with staff and pupils over some weeks, to establish their vision.

The restricted site area and adverse ground conditions led the architects to design a medium-height tower in a departure from the conventional two-storey school arrangement; innovatively, it houses the noisier departments. This tower is now a landmark in the community, and its relatively small footprint has enabled more of the external area to be dedicated to sports.

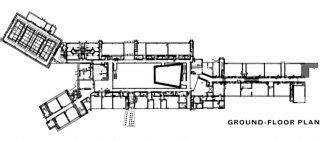

GROUND-FLOOR PLAN

# GATESHEAD HERITAGE @ ST MARY'S

## ST MARY'S CHURCH, OAKWELLGATE, GATESHEAD
## DESIGN SERVICES, GATESHEAD COUNCIL

CLIENT **GATESHEAD COUNCIL**
STRUCTURAL ENGINEER/SERVICES ENGINEER/QUANTITY
SURVEYOR **DESIGN SERVICES, GATESHEAD COUNCIL**
ACCESS CONSULTANT **GATESHEAD ACCESS PANEL**
CONTRACTOR **SURGO CONSTRUCTION**
CONTRACT VALUE **£1,150,000**
DATE OF COMPLETION **OCTOBER 2008**
GROSS INTERNAL AREA **595 SQ. M**
IMAGES **DESIGN SERVICES, GATESHEAD COUNCIL**

The redundant Grade I-listed church of St Mary has been transformed into Gateshead's first heritage centre by the removal of the late twentieth-century internal alterations to restore the building's original volume. The new service facilities are located in a contemporary timber-clad extension linked to the original building by a glazed enclosure, allowing educational and exhibition areas to be created in the church itself. New structural glass screens define office and storage areas.

Gateshead Council is to be applauded for its imaginative brief. It could have sought short-term financial gain by giving the building over to retail use; but instead the centre stands sentinel in its context of old and new architecture, reminding us of an era that has passed.

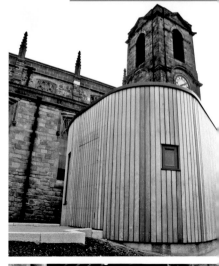

**GROUND-FLOOR PLAN**

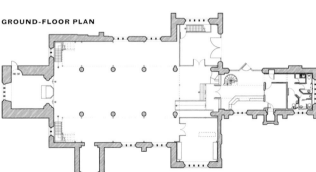

# KIELDER OBSERVATORY
## BLACKFELL, BEWSHAUGH, NORTHUMBERLAND
## CHARLES BARCLAY ARCHITECTS

CLIENT **KIELDER PARTNERSHIP**
STRUCTURAL/SERVICES ENGINEER **MICHAEL HADI ASSOCIATES**
QUANTITY SURVEYOR **BURKE HUNTER ADAMS**
CONTRACTOR **STEPHEN MERSH**
CONTRACT VALUE **£415,000**
DATE OF COMPLETION **MAY 2008**
GROSS INTERNAL AREA **100 SQ. M**
IMAGES **CHARLES BARCLAY ARCHITECTS**
KIELDER PARTNERSHIP WAS JOINT WINNER OF THE RIBA CLIENT
OF THE YEAR

In 2005 the Kielder Partnership, in association with
the RIBA, launched an open competition for a new
astronomical observatory located in Kielder Water & Forest
Park in Northumberland. Kielder has low levels of light
pollution and provides excellent observing conditions.

The observatory consists of a 42-metre-long 'land pier'
with two rotating telescope turrets, separated from each
other by the observation deck so that they do not interfere
with each other's sight lines. It was conceived as an all-
timber structure to reflect its forest location, and because
of timber's relatively low cost, eco-credentials and low
thermal mass, which means it does not release heat at
night in a way that can spoil conditions for observation.

**FIRST-FLOOR PLAN**

# THE PLACE
## ATHENAEUM STREET, SUNNISIDE, SUNDERLAND
## REID JUBB BROWN ARCHITECTURE

CLIENT **SUNNISIDE PARTNERSHIP**
STRUCTURAL/SERVICES ENGINEER **ARUP**
QUANTITY SURVEYOR **ELLIOTT DENT**
CONTRACTOR **GALLIFORD TRY PARTNERSHIPS NORTH**
CONTRACT VALUE **£3,500,000**
DATE OF COMPLETION **MAY 2008**
GROSS INTERNAL AREA **2930 SQ. M**
IMAGES **COLIN DAVISON**

The Place is an important part of the regeneration of the historic Sunniside area in the centre of Sunderland. A dramatic new building provides a hub through which six refurbished Grade II-listed Georgian buildings are accessed. The design of the new building, which houses offices, a cafe, conference rooms, a performance area and a much-needed gallery for local residencies, is key to the success of the project and to the regeneration of the Sunniside area as a whole.

The new building easily fulfils the criteria required to achieve a BREEAM 'Excellent' rating. Innovative elements include integrated artwork louvre panels on the façade, rainwater harvesting and natural ventilation.

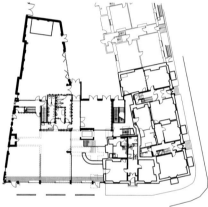

**GROUND-FLOOR PLAN**

## SALTHOLME WILDLIFE RESERVE AND DISCOVERY PARK VISITOR CENTRE
### SEATON CAREW ROAD, PORT CLARENCE, MIDDLESBROUGH
### JANE DARBYSHIRE AND DAVID KENDALL LIMITED

CLIENTS **RSPB; TEESSIDE ENVIRONMENTAL TRUST**
STRUCTURAL ENGINEER **BUILDING DESIGN (NORTHERN)**
SERVICES ENGINEER **ARUP**
QUANTITY SURVEYOR **TURNER & TOWNSEND**
ACCESS CONSULTANT **GATESHEAD ACCESS PANEL**
LANDSCAPE CONSULTANT **GLEN KEMP**
CONTRACTOR **LUMSDEN & CARROLL CONSTRUCTION**
CONTRACT VALUE **£4,300,000**
DATE OF COMPLETION **DECEMBER 2008**
GROSS INTERNAL AREA **944 SQ. M**
IMAGES **SALLY-ANN NORMAN – VIEW**

The architects were appointed by the RSPB and Teesside Environmental Trust following a limited design competition for the site at Port Clarence in Teesside, which consists of 405 hectares of former industrial land and is the largest wetland-creation project in the north of England.

The steel-and-timber-framed building stands next to one of the freshwater pools. The landscape design wraps the water around the building, and a swing bridge on the main access footpath acts as a security device, giving the appearance of a building set on an island. The spine of the building is a naturally lit double-height atrium extending up into the naturally ventilating monodraught feature, a focal point from outside.

# TYNESIDE CINEMA
## PILGRIM STREET, NEWCASTLE UPON TYNE
## FLETCHER PRIEST ARCHITECTS

CONSERVATION ARCHITECT **CYRIL WINSKELL**
CLIENT **TYNESIDE CINEMA**
STRUCTURAL ENGINEER **ADAMS KARA TAYLOR**
SERVICES ENGINEER **CUNDALL**
QUANTITY SURVEYOR **GLEEDS**
ACCESS CONSULTANT **BURDUS ACCESS MANAGEMENT**
CONTRACTOR **WATES CONSTRUCTION**
CONTRACT VALUE **£5,200,000**
DATE OF COMPLETION **MAY 2008**
GROSS INTERNAL AREA **2643 SQ. M**
IMAGES **SALLY-ANN NORMAN – VIEW**
**SHORTLISTED FOR THE CROWN ESTATE CONSERVATION AWARD**

Newcastle's Tyneside Cinema, designed in 1937, has a
unique place in the history of film in the north. A rare, fine
example of Art Deco work in Newcastle, it is significant
architecturally and historically as a prominent, high-quality
piece of architecture in the central conservation area.
    The original paintwork was analysed to reveal a palette
of subdued period colours that has been replicated
faithfully, and the original fittings and furnishings were
researched from period photographs and drawings.
As well as restoring the auditorium, the architects have
created a rooftop extension housing two new screens
linked by a foyer bar. Enclosed in translucent lightweight
polycarbonate sheeting, the bar at night becomes a
glowing opaque box.

# 13B PARADISE STREET
## LIVERPOOL
## ALLIES AND MORRISON ARCHITECTS

CLIENT **LIVERPOOL PARADISE STREET DEVELOPMENT AREA**
DEVELOPER **GROSVENOR**
STRUCTURAL ENGINEER **WATERMAN STRUCTURES**
SERVICES ENGINEER **WSP (BIRMINGHAM)**
CONTRACTORS **GROSVENOR; LAING O'ROURKE**
CONTRACT VALUE **£45,000,000**
DATE OF COMPLETION **OCTOBER 2008**
GROSS INTERNAL AREA **30,705 SQ. M**
IMAGES **DENNIS GILBERT – VIEW**

Allies and Morrison has created a building that acts as the focus of the Liverpool One development. Its elegant façades are of an impressive scale that generates strong symbolic links to Liverpool's grand nineteenth-century architecture. The project – more an articulated urban block than a building – links Paradise Street with Chavasse Park, dealing with public flow on four sides and providing parking, shopping and leisure facilities. Its robust and elegant stone façade is consistently detailed to give strong horizontal banding, and textured with a robust, almost rusticated finish reminiscent of the dock warehouses that once occupied the site. This skin is broken on the west side by glazing, allowing views out across the park to Albert Dock and beyond.

**SITE PLAN**

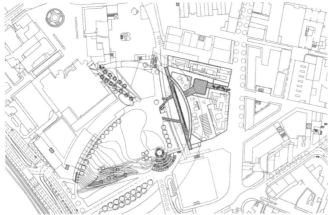

# BDP MANCHESTER STUDIO
## DUCIE STREET, MANCHESTER
### BDP

CLIENTS **BDP; TOWN CENTRE SECURITIES**
STRUCTURAL/SERVICES ENGINEER **BDP**
QUANTITY SURVEYOR **ARCADIS AYH**
CONTRACTOR **KIER NORTH WEST**
CONTRACT VALUE **£10,300,000**
DATE OF COMPLETION **SEPTEMBER 2008**
GROSS INTERNAL AREA **3840 SQ. M**
IMAGES **MARTINE HAMILTON KNIGHT – ARCAID**

BDP has pulled off a commercially viable, high-quality office building in functional, aesthetic and environmental terms, providing itself with an office that extracts full advantage from the limited site. Each floor creates a strongly characterized, flexible workplace. The scheme expresses its materials (wood, concrete, glass and steel) clearly, and is detailed to a very high standard.

This is Manchester's first office building with a **BREEAM** 'Excellent' rating. Maximum light is gained from the north façade, which faces the canal basin, while to the south (the street side) a protective stainless-steel-clad hull shades the building from solar gain. Natural ventilation decreases the low energy requirement even further. Such commitment to reducing its carbon footprint is the building's most remarkable feature.

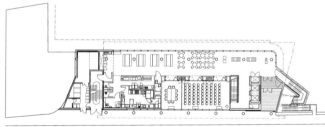

GROUND-FLOOR PLAN

# PARADISE STREET BRIDGE
## CANNING PLACE, LIVERPOOL
## WILKINSON EYRE ARCHITECTS

CLIENT **GROSVENOR**
STRUCTURAL/SERVICES ENGINEER **ARUP**
QUANTITY SURVEYOR **DAVIS LANGDON**
CONTRACTOR **TUCHSCHMID CONSTRUCTA**
CONTRACT VALUE **£2,400,000**
DATE OF COMPLETION **JUNE 2008**
GROSS INTERNAL AREA **57 SQ. M**
IMAGES **TIM SOAR**

Wilkinson Eyre has created a three-dimensional optical illusion that shamelessly transforms a simple link between car park and shop into a magnificently sculpted urban gateway. Internally, the tapering windows and illuminated wall panels create framed views of the city and the docks; at night the bridge becomes a remarkable piece of illuminated sculpture.

The Arup structure is quite simple, but the offsetting of the footway on top of a cranked structure and the wrapping of the bridge in triangular planes create an almost Escher-like illusion, with elements of the bridge apparently disappearing to a single line.

Symbolically and functionally this project creates wonder, then curiosity, and all in the simple act of walking from car to shop.

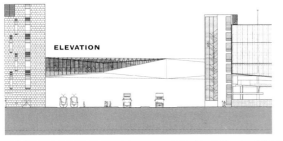

ELEVATION

# SCHAEFER HOUSE
## LADYBROOK ROAD, BRAMHALL, STOCKPORT
## MBLA ARCHITECTS + URBANISTS

CLIENTS **MR AND MRS PETER SCHAEFER**
STRUCTURAL ENGINEER **SCOTT HUGHES DESIGN**
CONTRACTOR **CONSTRUCTION NORTH WEST**
CONTRACT VALUE **£452,000**
DATE OF COMPLETION **FEBRUARY 2008**
GROSS INTERNAL AREA **286 SQ. M**
IMAGES **MBLA ARCHITECTS + URBANISTS (BOTTOM LEFT, CENTRE AND RIGHT); P. SCHAEFER (TOP)**

A remarkable partnership between architect MBLA and the Schaefer family in a street of suburban villas has created a contemporary home that responds in a refreshing and challenging way to the mores of suburbia. The single-storey L-shaped plan encloses the garden, which becomes an external room once the full-height glazed screens to the living space are opened. The house celebrates light, with rooflights in almost all rooms. A pleasing simplicity of materials and details renders the architectural form at once intimate and robust, while the building rejoices in its use of light, space and enclosure, generating a sense of calm delight.

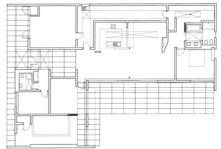

FLOOR PLAN

# THREE TOWERS
## DALTON STREET, COLLYHURST, MANCHESTER
## UNION NORTH

CLIENT/CONTRACTOR **URBAN SPLASH**
LANDSCAPE ARCHITECT **GROSS MAX**
STRUCTURAL ENGINEER **JOULE CONSULTING ENGINEERS**
SERVICES ENGINEER **LATHAM MILLER CONSULTING**
QUANTITY SURVEYOR **SIMON FENTON PARTNERSHIP**
CONTRACT VALUE **£13,800,000**
DATE OF COMPLETION **APRIL 2007**
GROSS INTERNAL AREA **13,182 SQ. M**
IMAGES **J. KEENAN (TOP LEFT; BOTTOM LEFT); PHOTOFLEX (TOP RIGHT; CENTRE; BOTTOM RIGHT)**

This project addresses the architectural and social problem of cost-effective refurbishment and re-emancipation of existing council tower blocks, a problem of national relevance. Union North has taken three thoroughly unpromising 1960s blocks and created a new sense of community with a strong visual identity and contemporary interior styling.

The external cladding creates a dramatic façade with wood-veneer panels and an irregular glazing module, giving the towers a dynamic skin while also upgrading them thermally. Extra floor space is created by simply including formerly external balconies in the floor plan. This has produced more pleasant interiors, where existing kitchens and living-rooms are combined as single spaces.

GROUND-FLOOR PLAN

# 1 NORTH BANK
## SHEFFIELD
## BDP

CLIENT **KENMORE PROPERTY GROUP**
STRUCTURAL/SERVICES ENGINEER **BDP**
QUANTITY SURVEYOR **RIDER LEVETT BUCKNALL**
CONTRACTOR **BOWMER & KIRKLAND**
CONTRACT VALUE **£9,500,000**
DATE OF COMPLETION **SEPTEMBER 2008**
GROSS INTERNAL AREA **7121 SQ. M**
IMAGES **DAVID BARBOUR**

BDP was commissioned to develop a masterplan for a site on the eastern fringes of Sheffield city centre. The client's brief called for more than 7000 square metres of speculative office space that would exploit the river frontage and meet the council's aspirations for the regeneration of the wider area.

This building is a new architectural landmark in Sheffield, worthy of its location at the gateway to the city. Notable civic gestures include careful scaling, which stitches the building into the existing context of the Wicker area, and the raising of the riverside frontage, to create new links with the Don riverside walks. The composition is further enhanced by meticulous detailing, and the arrays of bespoke solar shading provide character, depth and delight.

# CHARLES STREET CAR PARK
## ST PAUL'S PLACE, SHEFFIELD
## ALLIES AND MORRISON ARCHITECTS

CLIENT **CTP ST JAMES**
STRUCTURAL ENGINEER **CAPITA SYMONDS**
SERVICES ENGINEER **ERNEST GRIFFITHS & SONS**
QUANTITY SURVEYOR **TWEEDS CONSTRUCTION CONSULTANCY**
PROJECT MANAGER **GARDINER & THEOBALD**
CLADDING CONSULTANT **CLADTECH ASSOCIATES**
CONTRACTOR **J.F. FINNEGAN**
CONTRACT VALUE **£16,000,000**
DATE OF COMPLETION **OCTOBER 2008**
GROSS INTERNAL AREA **18,270 SQ. M**
IMAGES **DENNIS GILBERT – VIEW**

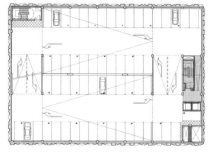

**TYPICAL FLOOR PLAN**

This multi-storey car park provides much-needed parking in Sheffield's city centre and forms part of the masterplan for the regeneration of the heart of the city. It provides 520 parking spaces over ten floors, with shops tucked under the spiral ramp. Columns, walls and floors are constructed from pre-cast concrete. The external envelope is finished in natural anodized aluminium panels painted green on the inside. Each panel is manufactured from a single sheet of folded aluminium cut to an angle on two sides, and is hung in one of four different orientations. This provides the required natural ventilation and hides the structure behind a homogenous surface. Locals refer to the car park as 'the cheese grater'.

# DE GREY COURT, YORK ST JOHN UNIVERSITY
## LORD MAYOR'S WALK, YORK
## RIVINGTON STREET STUDIO

CLIENT **YORK ST JOHN UNIVERSITY**
LANDSCAPE ARCHITECT **WHITELAW TURKINGTON**
STRUCTURAL ENGINEER **ROBINSON CONSULTING**
SERVICES ENGINEER **FABER MAUNSELL**
QUANTITY SURVEYOR **GLEEDS**
PROJECT MANAGER **GVA GRIMLEY**
ACOUSTIC CONSULTANT **SANDY BROWN ASSOCIATES**
CONTRACTOR **MORGAN ASHURST**
CONTRACT VALUE **£8,940,000**
DATE OF COMPLETION **JANUARY 2009**
GROSS INTERNAL AREA **4800 SQ. M**
IMAGES **SARAH B. LEE**

The university wanted an exciting, contemporary building
to complement a fine pair of Georgian terraced houses.
Rivington Street Studio won the design competition with
a solution that responds to the local context in terms of
scale, form and materials. The external walls are a mixture
of local hand-made bricks, dark-grey panels, fair-faced
concrete, render and timber – a combination that gives
the development a monastic feel.

The building enhances the area and the surrounding
listed buildings, and fits comfortably and significantly into
the historic core of this ancient city. The collegiate scale
of the streets is helped by the overhanging of the building
on to De Grey Street and by the bridge links that connect
the building to the rest of the campus.

SITE PLAN

# QUEEN'S CENTRE FOR ONCOLOGY AND HAEMATOLOGY, CASTLE HILL HOSPITAL
## COTTINGHAM, KINGSTON UPON HULL
## HLM ARCHITECTS

CLIENT **HULL AND EAST YORKSHIRE HOSPITALS NHS TRUST**
STRUCTURAL ENGINEER **WYG**
SERVICES ENGINEER **HULLEY & KIRKWOOD**
PROJECT MANAGER **GLEEDS**
ENVIRONMENTAL CONSULTANT **ENVIROS CONSULTING**
CONTRACTOR **SHEPHERD CONSTRUCTION**
CONTRACT VALUE **£42,000,000**
DATE OF COMPLETION **AUGUST 2008**
GROSS INTERNAL AREA **19,900 SQ. M**
IMAGES **IAN BRUCE**

Castle Hill hospital is a UK centre of excellence for the treatment of patients with cancer and blood disorders. The new centre was procured under the Private Finance Initiative and is based on the idea of an East Riding village that blends into its locale, where the entrance reads as the village hall, and wards and outpatient areas resemble residential cottages. Each wing of the unit is separated from its neighbour by a glazed link, providing natural sunlight as well as views across the countryside and into courtyards. All nine courtyards were designed solely for the benefit of patients, as natural environments are proven to have a positive effect psychologically and physically. It is a place of tranquillity, conducive to recuperation.

SITE PLAN

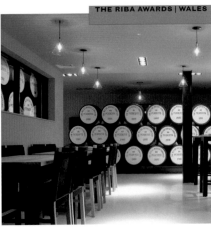

# PENDERYN DISTILLERY VISITOR CENTRE
## PENDERYN, RHONDDA CYNON TAF
## DAVID ARCHER ARCHITECTS

CLIENT **WELSH WHISKY COMPANY**
STRUCTURAL ENGINEER **CLARKE BOND**
SERVICES ENGINEER **SABA CONSULT**
QUANTITY SURVEYOR **FAITHFUL + GOULD**
ACCESS CONSULTANT **DAVID ARCHER ARCHITECTS**
CONTRACTOR **INTERSERVE**
CONTRACT VALUE **£500,000**
DATE OF COMPLETION **JUNE 2008**
GROSS INTERNAL AREA **288 SQ. M**
IMAGES **KEITH COLLIE**

Penderyn Distillery (the only distillery in Wales) is a small project in terms of both size and budget. The design is unfussy, consistent and effective, and manages to turn an industrial shed into a brand-enhancing building that is a pleasure to use.

The material used is simple. The façades are of overlapping waney-edged, black-stained oak boards sliced straight from the tree, a cladding that was used on a previous building (some of the old boards have been reused on the side elevations). The success of the scheme should encourage the owners of other abandoned industrial buildings in Wales to undertake work that could be both sustainable and sensitive.

# RUTHIN CRAFT CENTRE
## PARK ROAD, RUTHIN
## SERGISON BATES ARCHITECTS

CLIENT **DENBIGHSHIRE COUNTY COUNCIL**
STRUCTURAL ENGINEER **GREIG-LING**
SERVICES ENGINEER **BDP**
QUANTITY SURVEYOR **SMITH TURNER ASSOCIATES**
CONTRACTOR **POCHIN'S**
CONTRACT VALUE **£3,200,000**
DATE OF COMPLETION **JULY 2008**
GROSS INTERNAL AREA **1566 SQ. M**
IMAGES **DEWI LLOYD (TOP); IOANA MARINESCU (CENTRE; BOTTOM LEFT AND RIGHT)**

This inward-looking single-storey building has a courtyard at its heart, providing both circulation and a place for interaction between visitors and artists.

The simple plan contains artists' rooms, offices and educational facilities on the long arms of a U-shape. The gallery and cafe occupy the shorter span of the U, which rises to two storeys, culminating in a complex composition of sloping roofs. The roof is covered with zinc, which then turns to form part of the external enclosure with subtle but complex geometrical forms: beautiful.

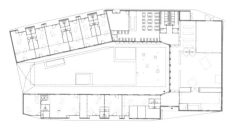

GROUND-FLOOR PLAN

# BOURNVILLE PLACE
## BOURNVILLE, BIRMINGHAM
## STANTON WILLIAMS; WEEDON
## PARTNERSHIP

CLIENT **CADBURY TREBOR BASSETT**
STRUCTURAL ENGINEER **FABER MAUNSELL**
SERVICES ENGINEER **CUNDALL**
QUANTITY SURVEYORS **EDMOND SHIPWAY (SHELL AND CORE);**
**RIDER LEVETT BUCKNALL (FIT-OUT)**
ACCESS CONSULTANT **APPROVED DESIGN CONSULTANCY**
INTERIOR DESIGN **MORLEY SMITH**
CONTRACTORS **BALFOUR BEATTY CONSTRUCTION (SHELL AND CORE);**
**ISG INTERIOR/EXTERIOR (FIT-OUT)**
CONTRACT VALUE **£33,040,000**
DATE OF COMPLETION **MAY 2008**
GROSS INTERNAL AREA **14,373 SQ. M**
IMAGES **PETER COOK – VIEW (TOP; CENTRE; BOTTOM RIGHT);**
**NATHAN WILLOCK (BOTTOM LEFT AND CENTRE)**

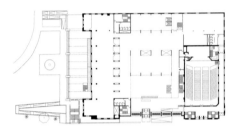

GROUND-FLOOR PLAN

This imaginative design-and-build project in the Bournville
Conservation Area carefully integrates new elements with
the re-use of the original factory dining building, to create
a new head office for Cadbury. Although (surprisingly)
unlisted, the old building occupies a prominent location
within the model factory complex.

Stanton Williams has removed the central bay of the
existing building and inserted a new section, forming a
simple 'H' configuration in place of the original square-
doughnut plan. This arrangement creates a full-height
atrium overlooked by the offices. The simple yet bold
architectural moves and the crisply detailed execution
have created a well-considered and enjoyable working
environment, and an elegant fusion of old and new.

# JOSEPH CHAMBERLAIN SIXTH FORM COLLEGE
## BELGRAVE ROAD, HIGHGATE, BIRMINGHAM
## NICHOLAS HARE ARCHITECTS

CLIENT **JOSEPH CHAMBERLAIN SIXTH FORM COLLEGE**
LANDSCAPE ARCHITECT **CAMLIN LONSDALE**
STRUCTURAL ENGINEER **BDP ENGINEERING**
SERVICES ENGINEER **CPW**
QUANTITY SURVEYOR **MADDISONS**
PLANNING SUPERVISOR **ROBINSON LOW FRANCIS**
CONTRACT VALUE **£28,000,000**
DATE OF COMPLETION **AUGUST 2008**
GROSS INTERNAL AREA **14,350 SQ. M**
IMAGES **ALAN WILLIAMS**

The Joseph Chamberlain Sixth Form College provides further-education facilities through the LSE Programme for a broadly Muslim community in the Highgate area of Birmingham. Set in a particularly harsh urban environment, the new college is a clearly organized series of buildings and spaces, both forming a protective environment and encouraging use by the community. While the architecture, with its simply and robustly detailed interiors, is relatively understated, it is the carefully considered urban and spatial moves of this scheme that make it a truly engaging and enjoyable place, in which students can learn and the wider community participate.

# THE PAVILIONS
## SANSAW BUSINESS PARK, HADNALL, SHREWSBURY
## ROSS SHARPE ARCHITECTS

CLIENT **JAMES THOMPSON**
LANDSCAPE ARCHITECT **FRAN TRUSCOTT JIM HODSON**
**LANDSCAPE ARCHITECTS**
STRUCTURAL ENGINEER **WILLIE HAIGH CONSULTING ENGINEER**
SERVICES ENGINEER **ENERGY BUILDING**
CONTRACTOR **RURAL SOLUTIONS CONSTRUCTION**
CONTRACT VALUE **£2,900,000**
DATE OF COMPLETION **NOVEMBER 2008**
GROSS INTERNAL AREA **1713 SQ. M**
IMAGES **EDWARD KINGSFORD**

Set against a backdrop of mature woodland on the
Hardwicke Estate, The Pavilions offers a high-quality
alternative to the ubiquitous out-of-town business unit.
Three distinct oak-clad buildings are placed symmetrically
in the estate's walled garden. The first impression on
arrival is relatively understated, but within the enclosure
one discovers a hidden garden of carefully planned lawns
and ponds, on to which the fully glazed 'internal' façades
of the pavilions look. Demonstrating that it is possible to
make this building type look beyond the typical tin
structure, The Pavilions makes a thoughtful architectural
statement that contributes positively to its environment.

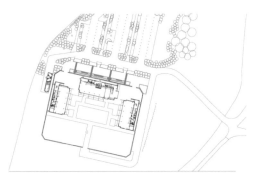

SITE/GROUND-FLOOR PLAN

# 82 DERNGATE
## NORTHAMPTON
## JOHN MCASLAN + PARTNERS

CLIENT **78 DERNGATE TRUST**
STRUCTURAL ENGINEER **JPP CONSULTING**
QUANTITY SURVEYOR **BOYDEN & COMPANY**
CONTRACTOR **MARRIOTT CONSTRUCTION (KIER)**
CONTRACT VALUE **£800,000**
DATE OF COMPLETION **JULY 2007**
GROSS INTERNAL AREA **1250 SQ. M**
IMAGES **JAMES BRITTAIN – VIEW**

This project is the final addition to the visitor centre for
Charles Rennie Mackintosh's exquisite last commission: a
house in Northampton. The centre was commissioned to
create level access across three adjacent properties: the
Mackintosh house at number 78; a narrow, Grade II-listed
Georgian building containing a small museum and the
circulation; and a Victorian house reworked for this project
to accommodate ticketing, a shop and a cafe. The interior
of the latter has been stripped out to give a contemporary
double-height volume between the house itself and its
neighbours. The architects' achievement is in the creation
of an uncluttered breathing space that is neutral but not
bland and takes its cue from the original in a fresh and
tactile manner.

# CURVE
## RUTLAND STREET, LEICESTER
## RAFAEL VIÑOLY ARCHITECTS

CLIENT **LEICESTER CITY COUNCIL**
STRUCTURAL ENGINEER **ADAMS KARA TAYLOR**
SERVICES ENGINEER **ARUP**
QUANTITY SURVEYOR **TURNER & TOWNSEND**
ACCESS CONSULTANT **BURO HAPPOLD**
CONTRACTOR **BOVIS LEND LEASE**
CONTRACT VALUE **£49,400,000**
DATE OF COMPLETION **AUGUST 2008**
GROSS INTERNAL AREA **13,364 SQ. M**
IMAGES **PETER COOK – VIEW (TOP LEFT AND RIGHT; CENTRE; BOTTOM RIGHT); WILL PRYCE – ARCAID (BOTTOM LEFT)**

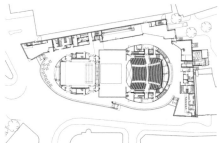

**GROUND-FLOOR PLAN**

Not a building for the faint-hearted, this enormous arts centre looms surreally large over the narrow streets. Curve is a state-of-the-art theatre: artists and performers love working in it, not least because of its ground-breaking idea of turning the typical configuration inside out. The auditoria are enclosed by a four-storey glazed curtain wall, a simple device that exposes production, construction, craft and technical components to the public and integrates the performance into the life of the city. The genuinely iconic Curve is strongly promoted by the council's leader, Ross Wilmott, as a driver for regeneration in a run-down area, and there are already signs of an upturn.

# DAVID WILSON LIBRARY, UNIVERSITY OF LEICESTER
## UNIVERSITY ROAD, LEICESTER
## ASSOCIATED ARCHITECTS

CLIENT **UNIVERSITY OF LEICESTER**
STRUCTURAL/SERVICES ENGINEER **AECOM**
QUANTITY SURVEYOR **FAITHFUL + GOULD**
CONTRACTOR **KIER MARRIOTT**
CONTRACT VALUE **£25,000,000**
DATE OF COMPLETION **APRIL 2008**
GROSS INTERNAL AREA **15,000 SQ. M**
IMAGES **MARTINE HAMILTON KNIGHT – ARCAID**

This is an exemplary and substantial reworking of an award-winning 1970s library by Castle Park Dean Hook, which had become outmoded in terms of both design and environmental performance. The architects overhauled the space, envelope and structure, replacing the dark-glass cladding with clear; cutting voids through the volume to allow more light into the depth of the building; re-cladding the front and side to improve solar performance; and bringing disabled access up to current standards. The building has received a BREEAM 'Excellent' rating.

The architecture is now legible and enjoyable, with a real buzz and a genuine sense of student study community. It has given the library complex a strong sense of being the centre of the campus.

# HIGHFIELDS AUTOMOTIVE AND ENGINEERING CENTRE, CASTLE COLLEGE
## UNIVERSITY BOULEVARD, NOTTINGHAM
## HAWKINS\BROWN

CLIENT **CASTLE COLLEGE, NOTTINGHAM**
LANDSCAPE ARCHITECT **GRANT ASSOCIATES**
STRUCTURAL ENGINEER **BWB CONSULTING**
SERVICES ENGINEER **BDSP PARTNERSHIP**
QUANTITY SURVEYOR **GLEEDS**
CONTRACTOR **MORGAN ASHURST**
CONTRACT VALUE **£9,200,000**
DATE OF COMPLETION **JANUARY 2009**
GROSS INTERNAL AREA **6600 SQ. M**
IMAGES **TIM CROCKER**

This facility, in the new development of Nottingham Science Park, is jointly occupied by Castle College and Toyota, and provides workshops and teaching space for trainees in automotive engineering and sales. It is not a refined or crafted building; its elements are many and conflicting, and its parts all do different things: float, dance, tilt and nestle. But there are some beautiful moments, and it is full of improvisation. Its success lies in its comfortable, unforced communication with its young occupants. It seems to work for them, creating joy and keeping them there, which is no small achievement for a building of this kind.

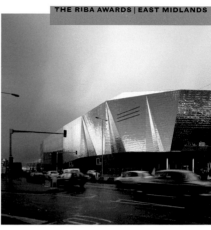

# JOHN LEWIS DEPARTMENT STORE AND CINEPLEX
## LEICESTER
## FOREIGN OFFICE ARCHITECTS

CLIENTS **SHIRES (GP); HAMMERSON; HERMES REAL ESTATE**
STRUCTURAL ENGINEER **ADAMS KARA TAYLOR**
SERVICES ENGINEER **WSP**
QUANTITY SURVEYOR **CYRIL SWEETT**
TRAFFIC CONSULTANT **WATERMAN BURROW CROCKER**
CONTRACTOR **SIR ROBERT MCALPINE**
CONTRACT VALUE **£44,000,000**
DATE OF COMPLETION **SEPTEMBER 2008**
GROSS INTERNAL AREA **32,000 SQ. M**
IMAGES **HÉLÈNE BINET (TOP RIGHT); FOA (BOTTOM RIGHT); PETER JEFFREE (BOTTOM LEFT); SATORU MISHIMA (TOP LEFT; CENTRE)**

This fresh and witty piece of architecture – a brave commission, for which the clients are to be congratulated – turns the department store inside out. It forms a unique exploration of the notion of the architectural skin, and adds a refreshing dimension to a world where there is usually tension between commercial requirement and signature design. The pattern, a 'net curtain' inspired by the city's historical textile and weaving industry, ethnic clothing and the store's own fabrics, was selected from archived local John Lewis pattern books, and, as such, celebrates regional identity. The cladding system allows levels of daylight unrivalled in most department stores. The adjacent cineplex, with its cladding of stainless-steel shingle-like scales, boasts another shimmering skin.

**GROUND-FLOOR PLAN**

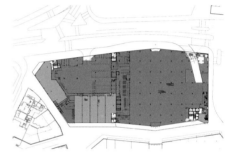

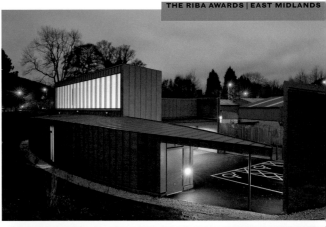

## LEVEL CENTRE
### ROWSLEY, MATLOCK
### CLASH ARCHITECTS

CLIENT **FIRST MOVEMENT TRUST**
STRUCTURAL ENGINEER **PRICE & MYERS**
SERVICES ENGINEER **HULLEY & KIRKWOOD**
QUANTITY SURVEYOR **NIGEL TATE ASSOCIATES**
ACCESS CONSULTANT **MICHELE TAYLOR**
CONTRACTOR **WILDGOOSE CONSTRUCTION**
CONTRACT VALUE **£841,590**
DATE OF COMPLETION **AUGUST 2008**
GROSS INTERNAL AREA **329 SQ. M**
IMAGES **MARTINE HAMILTON KNIGHT – ARCAID**

Situated on the edge of the Peak District National Park,
the centre is next to industrial units; its form and texture
connect it to both. The exterior wraps around different
interior volumes in a cladding of grey–green pre-weathered
zinc and handmade grey brindled brick. Such tough
materials and gloomy hues produce a strangely appealing,
poetic presence. As a building quite different from
anything to which local people are accustomed, it
promises to inspire more imaginative design in an area
that normally restricts itself to stone and slate.

First Movement develops arts projects for people
with learning difficulties. The facility provides a series
of multi-sensory environments, creating a stable, calm
yet inspiring space.

**GROUND-FLOOR PLAN**

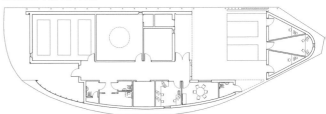

# NEW ART EXCHANGE
## NOTTINGHAM
## HAWKINS\BROWN

CLIENT **NEW ART EXCHANGE**
STRUCTURAL ENGINEER **PRICE & MYERS**
SERVICES ENGINEER **WATERMAN BUILDING SERVICES**
QUANTITY SURVEYOR **DAVIS LANGDON**
ACCESS CONSULTANT **NOTTINGHAM CITY COUNCIL**
CONTRACTOR **BODILL CONSTRUCTION**
CONTRACT VALUE **£3,100,000**
DATE OF COMPLETION **JUNE 2008**
GROSS INTERNAL AREA **1360 SQ. M**
IMAGES **HÉLÈNE BINET (TOP LEFT; BOTTOM LEFT AND RIGHT); TIM CROCKER
(TOP RIGHT)**

The challenge here was to bring together two rival arts
organizations, one Afro-Caribbean and the other Asian.
The architects' disciplined design approach has paid off
amply. The single-minded, driven design creates a building
of both consistency and surprise. Views out at all angles
connect the users to the streets outside. The simple cube-
like spaces are flexible, and the three galleries can be
either independent or continuous for exhibition use.

The building is unusual for a gallery in being totally
naturally ventilated, with wind-catchers on the roof and
natural stack ventilation incorporated into the walls. It is
making its mark as a catalyst for the regeneration of this
tough inner-city area.

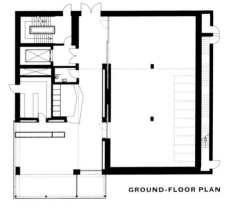

GROUND-FLOOR PLAN

## ANGLESEY ABBEY VISITOR CENTRE
### QUY ROAD, LODE, CAMBRIDGE
### COWPER GRIFFITH ARCHITECTS

CLIENT **THE NATIONAL TRUST**
STRUCTURAL ENGINEER **SCOTT WILSON**
SERVICES ENGINEER **MAX FORDHAM**
QUANTITY SURVEYOR **DAVIS LANGDON**
CONTRACTOR **HAYMILLS**
CONTRACT VALUE **£3,300,000**
DATE OF COMPLETION **JANUARY 2008**
GROSS INTERNAL AREA **1100 SQ. M**
IMAGES **PETER COOK – VIEW**

**The National Trust required facilities for visitors to Anglesey Abbey, a twelfth-century former monastery that was demolished by Henry VIII and rebuilt at the beginning of the seventeenth century (as a country house), in the nineteenth century and again in the 1920s.**

**The highly successful new building comprises two series of cedar-clad vaulted structures linked by a low, shallow, flat-roofed entrance lobby, and houses the visitor centre, a shop and a restaurant. A stepped plan and carefully detailed gables reduce the massing. Strong roof shapes contrast with the landscape yet are reminiscent of the agricultural heritage of the area, and the building is robust enough to receive the hordes of visitors to the park and house.**

# CLAY FIELD
## ELMSWELL, BURY ST EDMUNDS
## RICHES HAWLEY MIKHAIL ARCHITECTS

CLIENT **ORWELL HOUSING ASSOCIATION**
LANDSCAPE ARCHITECT **J. & L. GIBBONS**
STRUCTURAL ENGINEER **BTA STRUCTURAL DESIGN**
SERVICES ENGINEER **INVIRON**
QUANTITY SURVEYOR **HYAMS AND PARTNERS**
SUSTAINABILITY ENGINEER **BURO HAPPOLD**
CONTRACTOR **O. SEAMAN & SON**
CONTRACT VALUE **£3,900,000**
DATE OF COMPLETION **AUGUST 2008**
GROSS INTERNAL AREA **2072 SQ. M**
IMAGES **NICK KANE – ARCAID (TOP; SECOND FROM TOP; BOTTOM);**
**RICHES HAWLEY MIKHAIL ARCHITECTS (SECOND FROM BOTTOM)**

Clay Field is a group of twenty-two rural houses and four flats resulting from an RIBA competition. The site layout is very successful, and the form and positioning of the buildings ensure that the adjoining gardens and houses are not overshadowed. The project includes a wild-flower meadow, allotments, herb gardens and a playground in an orchard: the atmosphere is one of community. Inside, the well-designed homes are delightfully light and airy.

The scheme aspires – in the words of the architects – to 'a low-maintenance durability and a gentle minimalist ecology'. That means rainwater recycling, whole-house ventilation and a shared biomass boiler. The houses are constructed from sprayed hemp finished with cedar and lime render; they are south-facing and very well insulated.

**GROUND-FLOOR PLAN**

# GILLESPIE CENTRE, CLARE COLLEGE
## QUEEN'S ROAD, CAMBRIDGE
## VAN HEYNINGEN AND HAWARD ARCHITECTS

CLIENT **CLARE COLLEGE**
STRUCTURAL ENGINEER **SCOTT WILSON**
SERVICES ENGINEER **MAX FORDHAM**
QUANTITY SURVEYOR **GLEEDS**
LANDSCAPE CONSULTANT **ROBERT MYERS ASSOCIATES**
CONTRACTOR **HAYMILLS**
CONTRACT VALUE **£6,600,000**
DATE OF COMPLETION **DECEMBER 2008**
GROSS INTERNAL AREA **2000 SQ. M**
IMAGES **WILL PRYCE – ARCAID**

The centre provides a 150-seat lecture theatre, meeting-rooms, study bedrooms and offices for Fellows. The client also took the opportunity to explore the possibility of creating a whole new court. The architects have responded in their accustomed fitting way, quietly completing Giles Gilbert Scott's masterplan with an L–shaped building of brick and timber, and indulging in none of the visual clutter that could so easily have spoiled the modest composition.

The plan uses the site cleverly, clearly articulating the asymmetrical nature of the setting. The new court – a handsome addition to the history of Cambridge courts – is accessed via finely designed new tunnels through the existing buildings. The centre is beautifully detailed inside and out; the student bedrooms are spacious, light and airy.

148

SITE PLAN

# HOUSE AT PIPER'S END
## LETTY GREEN, HERTFORD
## NÍALL MCLAUGHLIN ARCHITECTS

CLIENTS **JIMMI AND LIZ BRADBURY**
STRUCTURAL ENGINEER **PRICE & MYERS**
SERVICES ENGINEER **XCO2**
QUANTITY SURVEYOR **JIMMI BRADBURY**
CONTRACTOR **CLAREMONT CONSTRUCTION**
CONTRACT VALUE **£644,235**
DATE OF COMPLETION **DECEMBER 2007**
GROSS INTERNAL AREA **220 SQ. M**
IMAGES **NICK KANE – ARCAID**
SHORTLISTED FOR THE MANSER MEDAL

A new house to replace a crumbling farmhouse in the Hertfordshire green belt was justified to planners on grounds of sustainability; they accepted that this approach was more sustainable in terms of embedded energy than the alternative plan of renovating the existing building. An impressive level of rigour and thinking has gone into the project, which clearly addresses both the front and back aspects of the site and its orientation, and a strong architectural feature is provided by exterior shading. The new house and landscaping form five complementary ribbons: a thicket of silver birch, a timber cabinet, a timber-framed vitrine, a loggia of white steel columns and a concrete-framed strip of pool for the house to admire itself in. And it is very beautiful: a fine house on a tight budget.

# SLIDING HOUSE
## HUNTINGFIELD, SUFFOLK
## DRMM

CLIENT **ROSS RUSSELL**
STRUCTURAL ENGINEER **MICHAEL HADI ASSOCIATES**
CONTRACTOR **SELF-BUILD**
CONTRACT VALUE **£340,000**
DATE OF COMPLETION **JANUARY 2009**
GROSS INTERNAL AREA **200 SQ. M**
IMAGES **ALEX DE RIJKE (CENTRE; BOTTOM LEFT AND RIGHT);
ROSS RUSSELL (TOP)**
SHORTLISTED FOR THE MANSER MEDAL

Architect and client shared a taste for the local vernacular. Alex de Rijke of dRMM has therefore turned the common timber-framed and -clad shed into something extraordinary, simply in the way the three elements are arranged. The garage is pulled off-axis to create a courtyard, while the house extends itself like a telescope: a 20-ton greenhouse-like structure slides out of the larch box of the main house on railway tracks by means of hidden wheels and electric motors. An ingenious and fun response to overwhelming conformity, this solution is exciting in its audacity, if not a little eccentric. It is also very responsive to its environment, and makes a great home.

# STUDIO SPACE
## MAULDEN, BEDFORD
## NICOLAS TYE ARCHITECTS

CLIENTS **NICOLAS AND ALISON TYE**
STRUCTURAL ENGINEER **AKERA ENGINEERS**
CONTRACTOR **SELF-MANAGED BY CLIENT/ARCHITECT**
CONTRACT VALUE **£220,000**
DATE OF COMPLETION **AUTUMN 2008**
GROSS INTERNAL AREA **220 SQ. M**
IMAGES **PHILIP BIER – VIEW (TOP LEFT; SECOND FROM TOP); NERIDA HOWARD (TOP RIGHT; SECOND FROM BOTTOM; BOTTOM)**
SHORTLISTED FOR THE STEPHEN LAWRENCE PRIZE

Projects designed and built by and for an architect can lack control, but this brief was precise and compelling: a creative and demonstrative studio space that would provide a comfortable, healthy and inspiring working environment. The result – a long, low glass box pinned down at both ends with larch walls – is beautifully executed and provides a modern building that sits comfortably next to an existing barn conversion, not least because of the attention paid to massing and materiality. It is an exercise in a single-minded approach, exercised with total control and fine detailing. It is well considered yet surprising in its use of Cor-Ten steel and timber in combination with planar glazing. It is, in short, a little gem.

# STUDY CENTRE AND MUSIC RECITAL ROOM, THE MØLLER CENTRE, CHURCHILL COLLEGE
## STOREY'S WAY, CAMBRIDGE
## DSDHA

CLIENT **THE MØLLER CENTRE**
STRUCTURAL ENGINEER **JANE WERNICK ASSOCIATES**
SERVICES ENGINEER **MAX FORDHAM**
QUANTITY SURVEYOR/PROJECT MANAGER **GARDINER & THEOBALD**
CONTRACTOR **HAYMILLS**
CONTRACT VALUE **£2,450,000**
DATE OF COMPLETION **JULY 2007**
GROSS INTERNAL AREA **708 SQ. M**
IMAGES **HÉLÈNE BINET (CENTRE); CRISTOBAL PALMA – VIEW (TOP; BOTTOM LEFT AND RIGHT)**

DSDHA won this project in a limited competition. The structure contrasts beautifully with, and is an effective foil for, its heavier neighbours. The black-glass cladding provides an enigmatic façade, enclosing a variety of spaces containing voids and solid walls as well as glazed areas. The building is well detailed and thoroughly considered, and provides a handsome addition to the richness of the Churchill College campus.

Internally, timber linings soften the sharp geometry and bring the materiality of the surrounding trees inside the building. The calm interior conceals a range of sophisticated technology and flexible facilities to transform the building for its many functions.

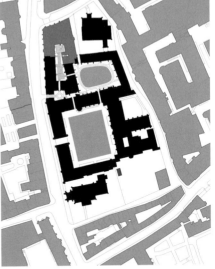

SITE PLAN

# TAYLOR LIBRARY, CORPUS CHRISTI COLLEGE
## TRUMPINGTON STREET, CAMBRIDGE
## WRIGHT & WRIGHT ARCHITECTS

CLIENT **CORPUS CHRISTI COLLEGE**
STRUCTURAL ENGINEER **ALAN BAXTER & ASSOCIATES**
SERVICES ENGINEER **MAX FORDHAM**
QUANTITY SURVEYOR **DAVIS LANGDON**
ACCESS CONSULTANT **THE MENZIES PARTNERSHIP**
CONTRACTOR **HAYMILLS**
CONTRACT VALUE **£6,500,000**
DATE OF COMPLETION **MARCH 2008**
GROSS INTERNAL AREA **1600 SQ. M**
IMAGES **PETER COOK – VIEW (LEFT); DENNIS GILBERT – VIEW (RIGHT)**

This building resulted from a competition to turn a workaday branch of NatWest into a sophisticated undergraduates' library. Wright & Wright won by proposing the removal of the main banking-hall structure and the lowering of the basement by half a metre, creating a large volume into which a three-storey oak building-within-a-building has been dropped.

Entered from the newly formed Library Court, it is a building of impeccable quality and with exemplary environmental credentials, using materials that are designed to last. The clever insertion of a library into an existing shell, without appearing to touch the walls, creates a dialogue between the two. It is exquisite and enjoyable to experience.

# DESIGN & TECHNOLOGY STUDIO, FALMOUTH SCHOOL

## TRESCOBEAS ROAD, FALMOUTH
## URBAN SALON

CLIENT **FALMOUTH SCHOOL**
STRUCTURAL ENGINEER **MOMENTUM CONSULTING ENGINEERS**
SERVICES ENGINEER **FULCRUM CONSULTING**
QUANTITY SURVEYOR **CYRIL SWEETT**
ACCESS CONSULTANT **URBAN SALON**
CONTRACTOR **COWLIN CONSTRUCTION**
CONTRACT VALUE **£550,000**
DATE OF COMPLETION **AUGUST 2008**
GROSS INTERNAL AREA **95 SQ. M (EXTENSION); 580 SQ. M (REFURBISHMENT)**
IMAGES **GARETH GARDNER**
SHORTLISTED FOR THE RIBA SORRELL FOUNDATION SCHOOLS AWARD

The new workshop space – creative and rather funky – is a welcoming contrast in shape and material to the rest of the school. A student group acted as the client, presenting the scheme to the Education Secretary in London, securing funding and collaborating with the architects until completion. The group was involved in all phases of the project and selected all materials based on their sustainability credentials. One student has been inspired by the project to take up structural engineering.

The walls and roof are of solid timber panels, in a staggered arrangement of shells that opens the room up to the north to provide abundant natural light.

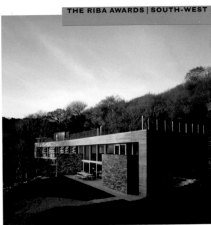

# PENCALENICK HOUSE
## PONTPILL, LANTEGLOS-BY-FOWEY, POLRUAN, CORNWALL
## SETH STEIN ARCHITECTS

CLIENT **JOHNNY SANDELSON**
STRUCTURAL ENGINEER **BARRY HONEYSETT CONSULTING STRUCTURAL & CIVIL ENGINEERS**
CONTRACTOR **CLIVE RALPHS PLUMBING AND HEATING**
CONTRACT VALUE **£1,000,000**
DATE OF COMPLETION **JANUARY 2007**
GROSS INTERNAL AREA **500 SQ. M**
IMAGES **RICHARD DAVIS**

The drive to this house is a wonderful adventure. The building, which at first seems to be dominated by the sheer beauty of its challenging location, is well integrated into the landscape by following the close contour lines of the site: its shape, in fact, springs from its surroundings.

The grass roof blends in well with the landscape, and the long glazed rooflight above the circulation route gives an idea of the building below. Because of the sensitive use of local materials – stone, glass and timber – the house has a wonderful Arts and Crafts feeling. The stone, beautifully laid in a traditional setting and rich in texture and colour, works well with the untreated cedar cladding.

# SCOTT BUILDING EXTENSION, UNIVERSITY OF PLYMOUTH
## GLANVILLE STREET, PLYMOUTH
## NICHOLAS BURWELL ARCHITECTS

CLIENT/ACCESS CONSULTANT **UNIVERSITY OF PLYMOUTH**
STRUCTURAL ENGINEER **SCOTT WILSON**
SERVICES ENGINEER **HOARE LEA**
QUANTITY SURVEYOR **GARDINER & THEOBALD**
CONTRACTOR **COWLIN CONSTRUCTION**
CONTRACT VALUE **£1,600,000**
DATE OF COMPLETION **SPRING 2007**
GROSS INTERNAL AREA **862 SQ. M**
IMAGES **NICK HUFTON**

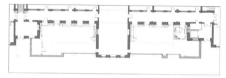

GROUND-FLOOR PLAN

This very successful extension is well integrated into the existing arts building. Although only a small volume, it has a big impact and provides an interesting spatial experience: industrial, and with all studios flooded with north light. In an inspirational use of colours and materials, the existing stonework is matched with a modern interpretation of natural Plymouth stone, rich in colour and texture. The building is carefully detailed, and the glass rainscreen façade is formed from a good choice of materials and colours, blending in with the surrounding buildings. Natural ventilation is both innovative and practical, delivered by a mix of manual and electrical systems.

# THE APPRENTICE STORE
## DE MONTALT MILL, SUMMER LANE, COMBE DOWN, BATH
## THREEFOLD ARCHITECTS

CLIENTS **MR AND MRS IAN COOPER**
STRUCTURAL ENGINEER **KING SHAW ASSOCIATES**
QUANTITY SURVEYOR **BARE, LEANING & BARE**
CONTRACTOR **TAYLOR ALLISON**
CONTRACT VALUE **£700,000**
DATE OF COMPLETION **OCTOBER 2008**
GROSS INTERNAL AREA **410 SQ. M**
IMAGES **CHARLES HOSEA (TOP RIGHT; BOTTOM LEFT); THREEFOLD ARCHITECTS (TOP LEFT; CENTRE; BOTTOM RIGHT)**

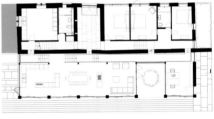

GROUND-FLOOR PLAN

The Apprentice Store is a wonderful restoration project with a very contemporary feel. Despite the complexity of the four existing buildings, which were quite dilapidated, the concept for linking them – with a modern steel gantry and stairs – is very clear. The project shows great respect for the existing structure, and additions are sensitively rendered with new materials. The mix of old and new, together with the careful choice of a few high-quality finishes, creates an industrial feel that refers to the historic use of the building as a paper mill.

The client has taken on a structure close to collapse and, with great enthusiasm, vision and attention to detail, has created a stunning contemporary home with beautiful views across the landscape.

# DEPARTMENT STORE, BRISTOL
## CABOT CIRCUS, BRISTOL
## STANTON WILLIAMS

CLIENTS **BRISTOL ALLIANCE; HAMMERSON; LAND SECURITIES**
STRUCTURAL ENGINEER **WATERMAN GROUP**
SERVICES ENGINEER **HOARE LEA**
QUANTITY SURVEYOR **CYRIL SWEETT**
ACCESS CONSULTANT **ACCESS DESIGN CONSULTANTS**
ARTIST **SUSANNA HERON**
CONTRACTOR **SIR ROBERT MCALPINE**
CONTRACT VALUE **£16,000,000**
DATE OF COMPLETION **SEPTEMBER 2008**
GROSS INTERNAL AREA **17,000 SQ. M**
IMAGES **HÉLÈNE BINET (TOP LEFT; RIGHT, ALL IMAGES); PAUL GRUNDY (BOTTOM LEFT)**

This building appears calming and dignified – terms not often applied to department stores. A wonderful cladding of local Portland stone has been executed with great attention to detail, while the lighting, carefully integrated into the façade, reverses the appearance of the volumes at night and creates a landmark for visitors arriving in Bristol. A full-height shop window and a double-height space filled with natural light create a very pleasant ambience and provide excellent visibility and orientation. The 7-metre-high ground floor, with views across and out, centred on a light-filled atrium, provides a great shopping experience, and the structural concept allows adaptation for future requirements. A fruitful collaboration with the artist Susanna Heron has created cladding and glass panels with integrated artwork.

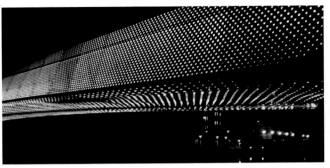

# MEADS REACH BRIDGE
## TEMPLE QUAY, BRISTOL
## NÍALL MCLAUGHLIN ARCHITECTS

CLIENT **CASTLEMORE SECURITIES**
STRUCTURAL ENGINEER **PRICE & MYERS**
QUANTITY SURVEYOR **GLEEDS**
PROJECT MANAGER **CYRIL SWEETT**
STAINLESS STEEL SUB-CONTRACTOR **M-TEC**
LIGHTING ENGINEER **BURO HAPPOLD**
LIGHTING ARTIST **MARTIN RICHMAN**
CONTRACTOR **DEAN & DYBALL CIVIL ENGINEERING**
CONTRACT VALUE **£2,200,000**
DATE OF COMPLETION **AUGUST 2008**
IMAGES **CASTLEMORE SECURITIES (TOP LEFT); NÍALL MCLAUGHLIN (RIGHT, ALL IMAGES); M-TEC PHOTOGENICS (BOTTOM LEFT)**

This is a wonderful addition to Bristol's long history of civil-engineering projects, and bridges in particular. With its reflecting stainless-steel structure, it is a perfect foil to its neighbours: an elegant brick railway bridge by Brunel and an over-designed suspension bridge.

Meads Reach Bridge is the result of intelligent architecture and engineering: restrained, functional, beautiful, poetic. The elegant form, the use of a single material and the shape of the perforations were driven by structural requirements; the pattern tells the story of the span's structural forces. The bridge is a perfect synthesis of the work of architect Níall McLaughlin, structural engineers Price & Myers and lighting artist Martin Richman: a true piece of art, flawlessly executed, delightful and magical. Eat your heart out, Isambard.

# MERCHANTS' ACADEMY
## WITHYWOOD, BRISTOL
## PENOYRE & PRASAD

CLIENT **MERCHANTS' ACADEMY TRUST**
STRUCTURAL/SERVICES ENGINEER **BURO HAPPOLD**
QUANTITY SURVEYOR **APPLEYARDS DWB**
CONTRACTOR **COWLIN CONSTRUCTION**
CONTRACT VALUE **£22,400,000**
DATE OF COMPLETION **JULY 2008**
GROSS INTERNAL AREA **10,230 SQ. M**
IMAGES **ROB PARRISH (BOTTOM LEFT); TIM SOAR (TOP; CENTRE; BOTTOM RIGHT)**
SHORTLISTED FOR THE RIBA SORRELL FOUNDATION SCHOOLS AWARD

The new Merchants' Academy convinces with a clear, straightforward concept: a central courtyard with all the departments placed around it. This works very well for the school and allows good orientation and supervision. The external envelope is reduced to brick and render, while the façades around the inner courtyard provide a boost in the form of different shades of blue. An inspiring colour scheme throughout distinguishes the different departments. Above all, the building delivers the education performance required by the client. This new academy has already made an impact on the local community by substantially raising standards of education.

# BIOCHEMISTRY DEPARTMENT, UNIVERSITY OF OXFORD
## SOUTH PARKS ROAD, OXFORD
## HAWKINS\BROWN

CLIENT **OXFORD UNIVERSITY ESTATES DIRECTORATE**
STRUCTURAL ENGINEER **PETER BRETT ASSOCIATES**
SERVICES ENGINEER **FOREMAN ROBERTS**
QUANTITY SURVEYOR **TURNER & TOWNSEND**
PROJECT MANAGER **PDCM**
LABORATORY CONSULTANT **HDR CUH2A**
CONTRACTOR **LAING O'ROURKE**
CONTRACT VALUE **£47,800,000**
DATE OF COMPLETION **SEPTEMBER 2008**
GROSS INTERNAL AREA **12,545 SQ. M**
IMAGES **KEITH COLLIE (RIGHT, ALL IMAGES; BOTTOM LEFT); TIM CROCKER (TOP LEFT; BOTTOM CENTRE)**

The biochemistry building embodies the notion that ideas are developed through dialogue. A vast, chasm-like central atrium, where everyone can see and be seen, is criss-crossed with staircases linking its four sides. The naturally ventilated space becomes the connection between all users of the building, both metaphorically and physically. A place that one might imagine to be hectic or frenetic is surprisingly calm; top light and careful attention to acoustics engender a sense of peace. Conventional wisdom would place people on the outside around central laboratories, but Hawkins\Brown reversed the formula. Write-up spaces overlook the atrium, so that students and fellows are continually communicating and moving science forwards.

GROUND-FLOOR PLAN

# BURNHAM COPSE PRIMARY SCHOOL
## NEW CHURCH ROAD, TADLEY, BASINGSTOKE
## HAMPSHIRE COUNTY COUNCIL
## ARCHITECTURE AND DESIGN SERVICES

CLIENT **HAMPSHIRE COUNTY COUNCIL CHILDREN'S SERVICES DEPARTMENT**
LANDSCAPE ARCHITECT **HAMPSHIRE COUNTY COUNCIL LANDSCAPE GROUP**
STRUCTURAL ENGINEER **R.J. WATKINSON**
QUANTITY SURVEYOR **HAMPSHIRE COUNTY COUNCIL QUANTITY**
**SURVEYING SERVICES**
MECHANICAL/ELECTRICAL ENGINEER **HAMPSHIRE COUNTY COUNCIL**
**ENGINEERING SERVICES UNIT**
CONTRACTOR **BRAZIER CONSTRUCTION**
CONTRACT VALUE **£2,800,000**
DATE OF COMPLETION **AUGUST 2008**
GROSS INTERNAL AREA **1795 SQ. M**
IMAGES **DANIEL KEELER (RIGHT, SECOND FROM TOP–BOTTOM);**
**PETER NOYCE (TOP RIGHT; BOTTOM LEFT)**

Burnham Copse Primary School sends out the very important message that sustainability involves making the best of what we already have. Rather than demolish and start again, the council's architecture division made a thorough critique of how the building was failing and how best to adapt it to meet the client's needs.

Like many post-war school buildings, the environmental performance was poor and there were not enough outdoor covered areas. The solution was to add a loggia to the building's southern aspect. The steel-framed flat-roof structure provides shade and external accommodation on two levels, as well as improving links between the three blocks without taking up valuable internal floor area.

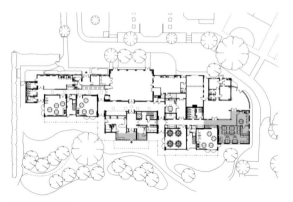

**GROUND-FLOOR PLAN**

# HIND HOUSE
## WARGRAVE, READING
## JOHN PARDEY ARCHITECTS

CLIENTS **STEVE AND DEE HIND**
STRUCTURAL ENGINEER **BARTON ENGINEERS**
CONTRACTOR **CLIVE HICKS, RIDGETREE PROJECTS**
CONTRACT VALUE **£620,000**
DATE OF COMPLETION **DECEMBER 2008**
GROSS INTERNAL AREA **294 SQ. M**
IMAGES **JOHN PARDEY ARCHITECTS**
SHORTLISTED FOR THE STEPHEN LAWRENCE PRIZE

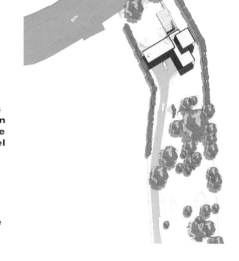

SITE PLAN

As one approaches Hind House one understands why it is elevated above the completely flat land: the River Loddon is at the bottom of the garden, and it floods regularly. The building is not overtly technical in any way (even the steel columns that support it are painted black so that they recede); rather, the building works for the quiet comfort of the clients. So, although the house's pedigree lies in the Californian Case Study Houses, its techniques and aesthetic are very much part of the new millennium. Hind House retains the formal clarity of its architectural forefathers while responding to the conditions of the site and the material aspirations of the client.

# MOUNTBATTEN BUILDING, UNIVERSITY OF SOUTHAMPTON
## HIGHFIELD CAMPUS, SOUTHAMPTON
## JESTICO + WHILES

CLIENT **UNIVERSITY OF SOUTHAMPTON**
LANDSCAPE ARCHITECT **PLINCKE LANDSCAPE**
STRUCTURAL ENGINEER **GIFFORD**
LEAD DESIGNER AND SERVICES ENGINEER **CH2M HILL IDC**
QUANTITY SURVEYOR **TURNER & TOWNSEND**
PROJECT MANAGER **WYG TRENCH FARROW**
CONTRACTOR **BOVIS LEND LEASE**
CONTRACT VALUE **£50,000,000**
DATE OF COMPLETION **JANUARY 2009**
GROSS INTERNAL AREA **14,200 SQ. M**
IMAGES **UNIVERSITY OF SOUTHAMPTON**

The old Mountbatten Building was lost in a fire in 2005. The brief for the new one was for a building that would bring the university the very latest in technology in the shortest possible time. The building, which houses two separate science departments, needs to perform as a world-class research facility as well as an attraction in its own right, drawing world-class students to the university.

The general arrangement grew out of the dialogue between scientist and architect, and is simple and very effective. The external graphics of fractal patterns speak of the energy that has gone into this complex project and the excitement with which the heads of department face the future.

**LOCATION PLAN**

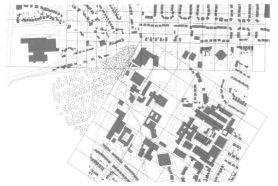

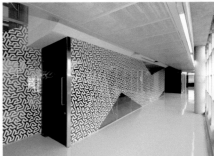

# QUEEN'S AND STANHOPE HOUSE, STOWE SCHOOL
## STOWE, BUCKINGHAM
## RICK MATHER ARCHITECTS

CLIENT **STOWE SCHOOL**
LANDSCAPE ARCHITECT **LAND USE CONSULTANTS**
STRUCTURAL ENGINEER **ECKERSLEY O'CALLAGHAN**
QUANTITY SURVEYOR **MICHAEL EDWARDS ASSOCIATES**
CONTRACTORS **WILLIAM SAPCOTE & SONS (PHASE 1); MARRIOTT CONSTRUCTION (PHASE 2)**
CONTRACT VALUE **£10,100,000**
DATE OF COMPLETION **JANUARY 2008 (PHASE 1); JANUARY 2009 (PHASE 2)**
GROSS INTERNAL AREA **1925 SQ. M (PHASE 1); 1310 SQ. M (PHASE 2)**
IMAGES **JAMES MORRIS – VIEW**

This new dormitory house has been configured as a sweeping linear block stepping gracefully back and down the slope, allowing the projecting windows to enjoy views over the landscape. The main façade has a Modernist clarity, but its hierarchical form shows respect for its Classical neighbour. The interior benefits from the same careful attention to detail: a host of functional elements in pale timber serve the communal and private spaces.

Stowe's ensemble of buildings by such great architects as Sir John Vanbrugh, Robert Adam, William Kent, James Gibbs and Sir John Soane has been graciously adorned by this masterful piece of work by Rick Mather. This is architecture that grows out of its historical context but finds its own identity by admirably fulfilling its purpose.

# WESTWELL MANOR FARM STABLE CONVERSION
## WESTWELL, BURFORD
## MUNKENBECK + MARSHALL
## WITH CAMERON WEBSTER

CLIENTS **MR AND MRS T. GIBSON**
STRUCTURAL ENGINEER **PETER ROCHE**
QUANTITY SURVEYOR **STOCKDALE**
CONTRACTOR **R. & T. STACEY**
CONTRACT VALUE **£750,000**
DATE OF COMPLETION **NOVEMBER 2008**
GROSS INTERNAL AREA **300 SQ. M**
IMAGES **RICHARD BRYANT – ARCAID**

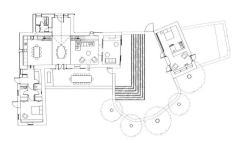

**GROUND-FLOOR PLAN**

A collection of rustic farm buildings in the Cotswold village of Westwell has been converted into a delightfully light and airy family home. The lofty character of the existing stable block has been retained with a double-height space in the centre between tall doors to front and back. Two oak staircases serve the bedrooms, which look at each other through oak-shuttered openings across the void of the central dining space below.

The architects' work shows a great understanding of the quality of the existing building, and a clear vision that enables the farm buildings to be appreciated, not with nostalgia, but for the simplicity of their materials and detailing.

# BOFORS TOWER
## DUNKIRK, CANTERBURY
## ROBERT MAXWELL, ALLIES AND MORRISON ARCHITECTS

CLIENT **FRANCES EUSTACE**
STRUCTURAL ENGINEER **PRICE & MYERS**
SERVICES ENGINEER **ATELIER TEN**
QUANTITY SURVEYOR **BOYDEN & COMPANY**
CONTRACTOR **W.W. MARTIN (THANET)**
CONTRACT VALUE **£350,731**
DATE OF COMPLETION **MAY 2007**
GROSS INTERNAL AREA **119 SQ. M**
IMAGES **CHARLOTTE WOOD – ARCAID**
**SHORTLISTED FOR THE CROWN ESTATE CONSERVATION AWARD**

The conversion of a decaying Second World War gun emplacement (listed as a scheduled monument) into a weekend retreat has all the ingredients of an impossible enterprise. However, by working closely with the relevant authorities and by treating the existing structure with creative respect, the building has been reinvented as an unusual home.

The emplacement has been restored and a new roof added to the first floor. The project celebrates the materials of brick and concrete, and uses the existing spaces to create bespoke interrelationships among the kitchen, the living-room and the bedrooms, which are intertwined. The house requires a degree of hardy living, however, as the first floor can be reached only via the existing external concrete staircase.

## CRADDOCK COTTAGES
### GOMSHALL, GUILDFORD
### STEPHEN TAYLOR ARCHITECTS

CLIENT **BAYLIGHT PROPERTIES (STEPHEN DODD)**
STRUCTURAL ENGINEER **THOMASONS**
CONTRACTOR **GOLDWAY PROPERTIES**
CONTRACT VALUE **£270,000**
DATE OF COMPLETION **FEBRUARY 2009**
GROSS INTERNAL AREA **191.6 SQ. M**
IMAGES **DAVID GRANDORGE**

These two small houses located on the main road through a rural village are a modern, sensitive and poetic addition to the area. Arranged around three courtyards on two levels, they are designed like a three-dimensional puzzle, interlocking in both plan and section to create a series of intriguing inside/outside domestic spaces that belies the small size of the plot.

The buildings are composed of traditional forms and materials, in which brick is predominant. They are detailed simply and consistently, and the overall feel is of a well-proportioned and subtle interplay of material and colour. A wonderfully understated but confident design, Craddock Cottages fit their context but provide appropriately modern accommodation.

**FIRST-FLOOR PLAN**

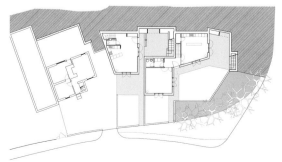

# DEAL PIER
## DEAL
## NÍALL MCLAUGHLIN ARCHITECTS

CLIENT **DOVER DISTRICT COUNCIL**
STRUCTURAL ENGINEER **PRICE & MYERS**
SERVICES ENGINEER **MAX FORDHAM**
QUANTITY SURVEYOR **SWORN KING & PARTNERS**
CONTRACTOR **BARWICK CONSTRUCTION**
CONTRACT VALUE **£738,640**
DATE OF COMPLETION **NOVEMBER 2008**
GROSS INTERNAL AREA **190 SQ. M**
IMAGES **NICK KANE – ARCAID (SECOND FROM BOTTOM); NÍALL MCLAUGHLIN
(TOP; SECOND AND THIRD FROM TOP; BOTTOM LEFT AND RIGHT)**
SHORTLISTED FOR THE STEPHEN LAWRENCE PRIZE

This timber-framed cafe–restaurant at the end of Deal
Pier makes a beautiful addition to the townscape and the
seascape. It does exactly what a pier building should: form
part of views of the sea, as well as framing them. It also
gives protection from the water, so that one can sit and
look back towards the seafront. The winged skeletal forms
lift to provide louvred shading according to the time of
year, as well as sheltering the seating outside. The building
was prefabricated and assembled on site, allowing the
fine detailing to be simple and bespoke. The materials will
weather naturally, and the colours are natural and subtle.

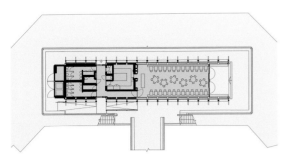

**GROUND-FLOOR PLAN**

# POND MEADOW SCHOOL
## LARCH AVENUE, GUILDFORD
## DSDHA

CLIENT **SURREY COUNTY COUNCIL**
STRUCTURAL ENGINEER **ADAMS KARA TAYLOR**
SERVICES ENGINEER **ATELIER TEN**
QUANTITY SURVEYOR **DAVIS LANGDON**
ACCESS CONSULTANT **RBC**
CONTRACTOR **WATES CONSTRUCTION**
CONTRACT VALUE **£8,800,000**
DATE OF COMPLETION **OCTOBER 2008**
GROSS INTERNAL AREA **3600 SQ. M**
IMAGES **HÉLÈNE BINET (SECOND FROM TOP; BOTTOM LEFT); DSDHA (TOP); TIM SOAR (LEFT, SECOND FROM BOTTOM; RIGHT, BOTTOM AND SECOND FROM BOTTOM)**

Pond Meadow School caters for children from the ages of three to nineteen with profound physical and learning difficulties. A canopy protects a deep-plan single-storey building, allowing in plenty of direct and diffuse light and creating a series of open internal courtyards. The palette is simple: dark, glazed brick, glass and painted plasterboard.

Staff at the school had expected some resistance to and fear of the new environment from the children with more profound difficulties, but through consultation and a brave design, the building has belonged to its users from the very beginning. The students could not wait to get inside.

# QUARTERHOUSE
## TONTINE STREET, FOLKESTONE
## ALISON BROOKS ARCHITECTS

CLIENT **CREATIVE FOUNDATION**
STRUCTURAL ENGINEER **AKERA ENGINEERS**
SERVICES ENGINEER **ATELIER TEN**
QUANTITY SURVEYOR **GPM PARTNERSHIP**
ACOUSTIC ENGINEER **SANDY BROWN ASSOCIATES**
THEATRE CONSULTANT **CHARCOALBLUE**
CONTRACTOR **D.J. ELLIS CONSTRUCTION**
CONTRACT VALUE **£4,000,000**
DATE OF COMPLETION **FEBRUARY 2009**
GROSS INTERNAL AREA **1550 SQ. M**
IMAGES **DENNIS GILBERT – VIEW**

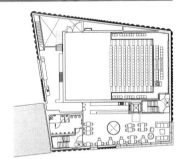

**FIRST-FLOOR PLAN**

This is the centrepiece of a brave and exciting regeneration scheme that seeks slowly to claim Folkestone town centre for artists and performers through a series of refurbishments. Quarterhouse is the first newly built project, and the focal point and symbol of the regeneration plans for the town. It provides an adaptable arts venue for local performers, a cafe–bar and flexible office accommodation for start-up businesses.

The building is a bold icon within the street scene, and a beacon at night. The façade is an undulating sheet of perforated metal, which softens the building form while providing opportunities for natural and artificial light to express its contours. The spaces inside are simple, practical and well organized.

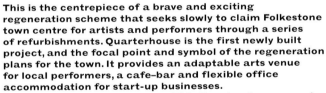

# RUNNYMEDE CIVIC CENTRE
## STATION ROAD, ADDLESTONE
## FEILDEN CLEGG BRADLEY STUDIOS

CLIENT **RUNNYMEDE BOROUGH COUNCIL**
STRUCTURAL ENGINEER **DEWHURST MACFARLANE AND PARTNERS**
SERVICES ENGINEER **MAX FORDHAM**
QUANTITY SURVEYOR **DAVIS LANGDON**
PROJECT MANAGER **BURO FOUR**
CONTRACTOR **WILLMOTT DIXON**
CONTRACT VALUE **£12,700,000**
DATE OF COMPLETION **MARCH 2008**
GROSS INTERNAL AREA **6196 SQ. M**
IMAGES **PETER COOK – VIEW**

This new civic centre – containing a library, town hall, council offices and police station – forms the first part of a masterplan to regenerate the place where Magna Carta was signed.

The major feature of the building is daylight. The public areas at the front are washed with natural light, and the deep-plan offices are naturally lit through large north lights and light-wells within the offices.

The palette of materials is simple. Brick, glass and colour clearly articulate the various functions of the building. The project successfully integrates itself into the townscape, managing to be at once a modest neighbour and a public building.

# 1 VINE STREET
## W1
## ALLIES AND MORRISON ARCHITECTS

CLIENT **THE CROWN ESTATE**
STRUCTURAL ENGINEER **CAMPBELL REITH HILL**
SERVICES ENGINEER **MECSERVE**
QUANTITY SURVEYOR **GARDINER & THEOBALD**
CONTRACTOR **SIR ROBERT MCALPINE**
CONTRACT VALUE **£33,900,000**
DATE OF COMPLETION **APRIL 2008**
GROSS INTERNAL AREA **10,570 SQ. M**
IMAGES **DENNIS GILBERT – VIEW (RIGHT, ALL IMAGES); PAUL RIDDLE – VIEW (TOP LEFT); SMALL BACK ROOM (BOTTOM LEFT)**

This is a fine example of the selective removal and replacement of buildings within a city block, integrating new façades and fenestration into the nineteenth- and twentieth-century structures without using pastiche or borrowing from adjacent buildings. On the primary, Regent Street elevation the stone façade has been restored and refurbished; to the rear, the external treatment is a study in detail and proportion. The side street has been pedestrianized, allowing restaurant tables to spill out on to the pavement. An atrium has been carved into the building, creating a calm, controlled space that both gives access to and is visible from each office floor. The building's clear sustainable agenda has attracted energy-conscious tenants to the offices.

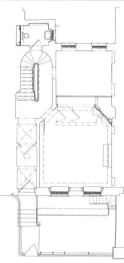

**GROUND-FLOOR PLAN**

# 14 LINCOLN'S INN FIELDS
## WC2
## JULIAN HARRAP ARCHITECTS

CLIENT **THE TRUSTEES OF SIR JOHN SOANE'S MUSEUM**
STRUCTURAL ENGINEER **HOCKLEY & DAWSON**
SERVICES ENGINEER **SPENCER CLARKE PARTNERSHIP**
QUANTITY SURVEYOR **D.R. NOLANS**
ACCESS CONSULTANT **DAVID BONNETT ASSOCIATES**
CONTRACTOR **FULLERS**
CONTRACT VALUE **£969,000**
DATE OF COMPLETION **JUNE 2007**
GROSS INTERNAL AREA **2057 SQ. M**
IMAGES **JUNE BUCK (TOP RIGHT); JULIAN HARRAP ARCHITECTS (TOP LEFT);
LYALL THOW (BOTTOM RIGHT)**
SHORTLISTED FOR THE CROWN ESTATE CONSERVATION AWARD

Conservation is a frequently neglected sector within the architectural profession, and its exponents are rarely credited fully for what they do. After years as a solicitor's office, 14 Lincoln's Inn Fields was bought by Sir John Soane's Museum with the intention that the museum should grow to occupy all three of the Soane-designed houses on the square. Julian Harrap's great achievement is to have left the property as if it had never been anything other than a Soane house. To achieve this required not only restraint but also ingenuity, as exemplified in the reconstruction of the rooflight over the main stairwell. Although it looks like a lantern designed by Soane, it incorporates discreet intruder-resistant features. Just imagine the galvanized roof-mounted cage that would have been designed by a less sensitive architect.

# 100 VE – UNILEVER LONDON HEADQUARTERS
## VICTORIA EMBANKMENT, EC4
## KOHN PEDERSEN FOX ASSOCIATES

CLIENT **UNILEVER**
LANDSCAPING **CHARLES FUNKE ASSOCIATES**
STRUCTURAL/SERVICES ENGINEER **ARUP**
QUANTITY SURVEYOR **DAVIS LANGDON**
ACCESS CONSULTANT **GELDER AND KITCHEN**
SPACE PLANNING **PRINGLE BRANDON; DEGW**
CONTRACTOR **BOVIS LEND LEASE**
CONTRACT VALUE **CONFIDENTIAL**
DATE OF COMPLETION **JULY 2007**
GROSS INTERNAL AREA **35,700 SQ. M**
IMAGES **H.G. ESCH (ALL EXCEPT SECOND FROM BOTTOM); MORLEY VON STERNBERG – ARCAID (SECOND FROM BOTTOM)**

Starting by restoring the iconic Grade II-listed 1930s Lever House – a highly complex piece of conservation in itself – and retaining part of a 1970s addition, the architects created a dramatic atrium that rises through nine storeys. Four open meeting decks rotate with dizzying geometry through the upper levels, and high-speed exposed lifts tear up and down, connecting all floors.

The architects have responded dynamically to the client's brief, which demanded an open, flexible and transparent working environment capable of attracting and retaining the best staff. Particular effort was taken to create pleasant break-out spaces, not least the large roof terrace. The building has achieved a BREEAM 'Excellent' rating.

## ARTS COUNCIL ENGLAND, NATIONAL OFFICES
### GREAT PETER STREET, SW1
### CARUSO ST JOHN ARCHITECTS

CLIENT **ARTS COUNCIL ENGLAND**
STRUCTURAL ENGINEER **PRICE & MYERS**
SERVICES ENGINEER **GDM**
QUANTITY SURVEYOR **JACKSON COLES**
CONTRACTOR **KNIGHT HARWOOD**
CONTRACT VALUE **£3,200,000**
DATE OF COMPLETION **APRIL 2008**
GROSS INTERNAL AREA **3500 SQ. M**
IMAGES **HÉLÈNE BINET**

The design philosophy is evident throughout the project: to work with the existing building with minimal intervention, using colour and well-designed furniture. At entrance level, a floor was removed to give a double-height space, and within this the entrance desk and built-in furniture have a simplicity that follows the design ethos. At the upper levels, the original gridded ceilings were removed and the services exposed and adapted, then spray-painted in a single colour, dramatically increasing the ceiling heights.

Remarkably, all the work on the building was undertaken while the Arts Council was in residence. The client is exceedingly pleased with this carefully and sensitively crafted piece of design.

# BLOCK 3, TARLING REGENERATION
## JAMES VOLLER WAY, E1
## S333 ARCHITECTURE + URBANISM;
## STOCK|WOOLSTENCROFT

CLIENT **ONE HOUSING GROUP**
STRUCTURAL ENGINEER **PAUL OWEN ASSOCIATES**
QUANTITY SURVEYOR **WALKER MANAGEMENT**
MECHANICAL ENGINEER **NORMAN GUTTERIDGE**
CONTRACTOR **GALLIFORD TRY**
CONTRACT VALUE **£6,200,000**
DATE OF COMPLETION **JUNE 2008**
GROSS INTERNAL AREA **4635 SQ. M**
IMAGES **JAN BITTER**
**SHORTLISTED FOR THE MANSER MEDAL**

This is a bold and successful attempt to import a
continental housing model into London's East End, and
to reinterpret it both in the context of a tough urban
environment and in response to the needs of a ward that
is more than one-third Bengali. The architects are to be
congratulated on producing an economic model for large
houses just a mile from the City of London.

The mixed-tenure project, which is part of a larger
masterplan, consists of a strip of primarily four-storey units,
with taller stacks of flats at either end of the terrace. The
flats are well planned, and the materials – dark-brown
sculpted concrete and strident yellow panels – add vibrancy
to the composition.

# CENTRAL LIBRARY, IMPERIAL COLLEGE LONDON
## SOUTH KENSINGTON CAMPUS, SW7
## A-EM STUDIO

CLIENT **IMPERIAL COLLEGE**
STRUCTURAL ENGINEER **CURTINS CONSULTING**
SERVICES ENGINEER **NORMAN DISNEY & YOUNG**
QUANTITY SURVEYOR **DAVIS LANGDON**
CONTRACTOR **PARKERAY**
CONTRACT VALUE **£6,800,000**
DATE OF COMPLETION **JULY 2008**
GROSS INTERNAL AREA **2425 SQ. M**
IMAGES **ALAN WILLIAMS**

This scheme reinvents the base of a distinctly brutalist 1970s academic building as a chic, multi-facility student hub, a kind of garden of digital delights for Imperial College's bright young things. The architects have accommodated with wit and invention the students' informal ways of working and socializing. A foyer leads to both library reception and student cafe. Immediately apparent is the coffered concrete underbelly of the 1970s building exposed in all its glory, along with ducting and shiny pipework worthy of a role in Terry Gilliam's *Brazil*: this is no drearily dry-lined library. In summer weather, the cafe opens on to the green, further reinforcing the new library's urbane relationship with the campus around it.

# CITY OF LONDON INFORMATION CENTRE
## ST PAUL'S CHURCHYARD, EC4
## MAKE

CLIENT **CITY OF LONDON CORPORATION**
STRUCTURAL/SERVICES ENGINEER **ARUP**
QUANTITY SURVEYOR **DAVIS LANGDON**
ACCESS CONSULTANT **REEF ASSOCIATES**
CONTRACTOR **SKANSKA**
CONTRACT VALUE **£1,300,000**
DATE OF COMPLETION **OCTOBER 2007**
GROSS INTERNAL AREA **146 SQ. M**
IMAGES **HUFTON & CROW – VIEW (TOP; SECOND FROM TOP; BOTTOM RIGHT); BENEDICT LUXMOORE – ARCAID (BOTTOM LEFT); ZANDER OLSEN (SECOND FROM BOTTOM)**

This small information centre, although a modest single storey, is hard to miss – which is exactly as it should be, given its function. Approximately triangular in plan, it has a complex form derived from two folded plates, which coalesce on its central axis. At its broadest, entrance façade the plates take the shape of a butterfly, or a paper aeroplane, as the architects describe it. The resulting carapace is elegantly made from crisply detailed mill-finished aluminium panels, clad inside in vibrant yellow panels that resemble the lining of an expensive suit.
The plan works well, with a series of information points arrayed along the fixed counter that runs the length of the building, meaning that large numbers of visitors can be attended to at any one time.

# THE CLOISTERS, ST BENEDICT'S SCHOOL
## EATON RISE, W5
## BUSCHOW HENLEY

CLIENT **ST BENEDICT'S SCHOOL**
STRUCTURAL ENGINEER **TECHNIKER**
SERVICES ENGINEER **FURNESS GREEN PARTNERSHIP**
QUANTITY SURVEYOR **GLEEDS**
CONTRACTOR **JERRAM FALKUS**
CONTRACT VALUE **£4,460,000**
DATE OF COMPLETION **NOVEMBER 2008**
GROSS INTERNAL AREA **2197 SQ. M**
IMAGES **DAVID GRANDORGE**

The architects were asked to integrate a range of new facilities – an entrance, a central hall, classrooms and a chapel – into the centre of an existing school campus made up of separate buildings. The materials used have an innate simplicity; they are aesthetically appropriate but also have the robustness needed in a school. Internally, timber, glass and concrete are used with rich paint colours. Externally, a misty-grey cementitious panel is integrated with a composite aluminium-and-timber window system. The palette of materials and the quietly stacked forms at the eye of the campus act as an effective foil for the older buildings. This deeply considered architecture combines the modesty and monumentality that befit an institution with monastic origins.

## FRAME HOUSE
### ROWE LANE, E9
### FLACQ ARCHITECTS

CLIENTS **MARCUS LEE AND RACHEL HART**
STRUCTURAL/SERVICES ENGINEER **ARUP**
CONTRACTORS **COWLEY TIMBERWORK; M&G JOINERY; COWAN ENGINEERING; ERIC WILSON AND CO.; MARTIN HAYWARD**
CONTRACT VALUE **£300,000**
DATE OF COMPLETION **SEPTEMBER 2008**
GROSS INTERNAL AREA **250 SQ. M**
IMAGES **KEVIN LAKE**

This house represents the development of ideas on timber-framed construction first used in the late 1980s by the same architect; of note is the use of a newer, more sustainable system of glue-laminated Siberian larch. The building's principal elevation is triangular, a form determined by the simple extruded section. The cladding is primarily a cedar rainscreen, which forms the envelope to part of the roof and walls, while a large glazed section brings light into the kitchen and dining area. Frame House is an exemplar for low-energy inner-city living, with wood-pellet heating, rainwater recycling and very high levels of insulation. The spaces are ingeniously planned and flexible, and the design was able to respond to changing family circumstances during construction.

# GARDEN PAVILION
## SW4
## ANDREW PILKINGTON ARCHITECTS
## AND DESIGNERS

CLIENT **MARTIN PILKINGTON**
STRUCTURAL ENGINEER **ELLIOTT WOOD**
CONTRACTOR **EDDIE KELLY**
CONTRACT VALUE **£65,000**
DATE OF COMPLETION **OCTOBER 2008**
GROSS INTERNAL AREA **24 SQ. M**
IMAGES **ANDREW PILKINGTON ARCHITECTS AND DESIGNERS (TOP LEFT AND RIGHT); RICHARD COLLINS – LIGNUM (CENTRE; BOTTOM)**

There is much to admire in this small, carefully composed garden pavilion. First is the decision not to fuse it to the rear of the main house, but to place it in the garden and in the sun. Secondly, the pavilion is literally without walls. A simple coffered timber roof structure floats independently from the garden wall, connected only by glazing. This is not simply a summer house: its walls can close to make a thermally insulated, energy-efficient living space that is usable all year round. There is poetry in its compositional intent, function and language of construction. It is a joy to experience.

# HOTHOUSE
## RICHMOND ROAD, E8
## ASH SAKULA ARCHITECTS

CLIENT **FREE FORM ARTS TRUST**
STRUCTURAL ENGINEER **DEWHURST MACFARLANE AND PARTNERS**
SERVICES ENGINEER **MICHAEL POPPER ASSOCIATES**
QUANTITY SURVEYOR **FAITHFUL + GOULD**
ACCESS CONSULTANT **DESIGN ACCESS**
CONTRACTOR **MANSELL**
CONTRACT VALUE **£2,200,000**
DATE OF COMPLETION **OCTOBER 2007**
GROSS INTERNAL AREA **1550 SQ. M**
IMAGES **ASH SAKULA ARCHITECTS (BOTTOM LEFT); NICK GUTTRIDGE – VIEW (TOP LEFT AND RIGHT; BOTTOM RIGHT); IOANA MARINESCU (SECOND AND THIRD FROM TOP)**

This is a textbook example of the difference creativity can make to an oddly shaped piece of unwanted land and a modest budget. Although the brief was for a flexible workspace, the result – a million miles from the product served up by the average developer – brims with playfulness.

First, there is the London Fields elevation, where the architects played a game with the brick boundary wall, peppering it with random organic openings. Next is the boomerang-shaped double-height workspace with its false perspectives. Then a generous, informal primary stair corkscrews around an open platform lift. And finally, the roof: a complete park environment of its own, with open areas of timber decking and semi-open glass houses shaded by photovoltaics. It is a complete delight.

# HOUSE IN BELSIZE PARK
## NW3
## ELDRIDGE SMERIN

CLIENTS **CHARLES AND SEEMA PEREZ**
STRUCTURAL ENGINEER **ELLIOTT WOOD**
SERVICES ENGINEER **MENDICK WARING**
QUANTITY SURVEYOR **AB ASSOCIATES**
CONTRACTOR **HARRIS CALNAN CONSTRUCTION**
CONTRACT VALUE **£985,000**
DATE OF COMPLETION **NOVEMBER 2007**
GROSS INTERNAL AREA **2460 SQ. M**
IMAGES **LYNDON DOUGLAS**

This scheme exploits its triangular site to reinvent the Victorian house extension as a building type. Instead of leaning a new volume against the original structure, at the edge of the garden, a modern addition has been boldly placed in the middle. Whereas in most back extensions one sees the garden in a single view, here one appreciates it close at hand from various perspectives.

The original house now contains all the cellular rooms, while modern open-plan living is confined to the new, single-storey, glass-clad pavilion. This distinction is softened, however, by the complete remodelling of vertical circulation in the house: a generous atrium open to the roof contains a beautifully crafted spiral stair of glue-laminated timber.

**GROUND-FLOOR PLAN**

# HOUSE IN HIGHGATE CEMETERY
## N6
## ELDRIDGE SMERIN

CLIENT **RICHARD ELLIOTT**
STRUCTURAL ENGINEER **ELLIOTT WOOD**
SERVICES ENGINEER **MENDICK WARING**
QUANTITY SURVEYOR **AB ASSOCIATES**
CONTRACTOR **HARRIS CALNAN CONSTRUCTION**
CONTRACT VALUE **£1,700,000**
DATE OF COMPLETION **JULY 2008**
GROSS INTERNAL AREA **4000 SQ. M**
IMAGES **LYNDON DOUGLAS**
SHORTLISTED FOR THE MANSER MEDAL AND THE STEPHEN
LAWRENCE PRIZE

This project is a drop of the hard stuff: uncompromising
and single-minded. The house completely fills its site, right
up to a party wall, with Swain's Lane on two boundaries
and Highgate Cemetery on the other two. Upper-floor
balconies are its only usable areas of external space,
but with views like these, who needs a garden?

The house is a completely flush rectangle, an abstract
composition of three opaque materials: etched glass,
painted steel and black granite. No fixings are visible. On
entering, one can see the underside of the roof through
two areas of clear-glass floor. The knock-out moment,
however, comes in the kitchen, on the third floor, when the
rooflight above slides away to transform the room into an
external courtyard.

# KING'S CROSS CONSTRUCTION SKILLS CENTRE
## RANDELL'S ROAD, N1
## DAVID MORLEY ARCHITECTS

CLIENT **ARGENT**
STRUCTURAL ENGINEER **TPS**
SERVICES ENGINEER **SCOTT WILSON**
QUANTITY SURVEYOR/CONTRACTOR **CARILLION**
CONTRACT VALUE **£2,700,000**
DATE OF COMPLETION **DECEMBER 2008**
GROSS INTERNAL AREA **1765 SQ. M**
IMAGES **DAVID MORLEY ARCHITECTS (TOP RIGHT); MORLEY VON STERNBERG – ARCAID (TOP LEFT; CENTRE; BOTTOM)**

This modest temporary scheme exploits the slope and narrow triangular shape of its site to create a building with much more personality and presence than might reasonably have been expected from such a brief. It is a planning-gain project required by Camden Council as part of the consent for Argent's wider plans for the area, and its aim is to foster construction skills in the neighbourhood. As such, the project could easily have been a metal-clad portal-frame shed. Instead, it is a highly visible building, intelligently planned to minimize energy use. A series of north lights and photovoltaic cells forms the main roofline, and timber louvres shield the offices from the western sun.

# KINGS PLACE
## YORK WAY, N1
## DIXON JONES

CLIENT **PARABOLA LAND**
STRUCTURAL/SERVICES ENGINEER **ARUP NEWCASTLE**
QUANTITY SURVEYOR **GARDINER & THEOBALD**
ACCESS CONSULTANT **TUFFIN FERRABY TAYLOR**
CONTRACTOR **SIR ROBERT MCALPINE**
CONTRACT VALUE **£96,000,000**
DATE OF COMPLETION **APRIL 2008**
GROSS INTERNAL AREA **2007 SQ. M**
IMAGES **RICHARD BRYANT – ARCAID (TOP LEFT AND RIGHT; BOTTOM RIGHT);
GUY MONTAGU-POLLOCK – ARCAID (BOTTOM LEFT)**
**PARABOLA LAND WAS JOINT WINNER OF THE RIBA CLIENT OF THE YEAR**

Kings Place is both an arts centre and an office building. It fulfils the dream of Peter Millican, ophthalmologist- turned-client and now arts administrator. A genuinely mixed-use building with a vibrant public environment at its heart, it has a restaurant, a bar, shops, a gallery and two concert halls good enough to offer residencies to two national orchestras.

Received wisdom says that atria must be glass-roofed. All this building's natural light comes through vertical gaps in the office floor-plates – an arrangement that suits the tenants: two national newspapers, which have colonized the space to create an attractive working environment. The architects have created an externally well-mannered building, which, through its exploitation of the possibilities offered by the brief, is completely absorbing internally.

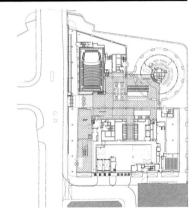

GROUND-FLOOR PLAN

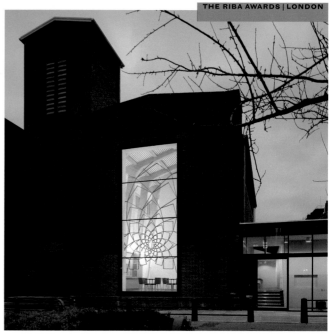

# LUMEN UNITED REFORMED CHURCH AND COMMUNITY CENTRE
## TAVISTOCK PLACE, WC1
## THEIS + KHAN ARCHITECTS

CLIENT **UNITED REFORMED CHURCH THAMES NORTH TRUST**
STRUCTURAL ENGINEER **F.J. SAMUELY**
SERVICES ENGINEER **ENG DESIGN**
QUANTITY SURVEYOR **BOYDEN GROUP**
ACCESS CONSULTANT **ANDREW WALKER**
CONTRACTOR **DOLLMAN RALSTON**
CONTRACT VALUE **£1,800,000**
DATE OF COMPLETION **SEPTEMBER 2008**
GROSS INTERNAL AREA **2022 SQ. M**
IMAGES **NICK KANE – ARCAID**

It is difficult to fault the interventions that have consolidated worship and community facilities in and around this neglected United Reformed church; each displays great architectural assurance and judgement. The existing nave was divided – to accommodate a cafe and a church big enough for the reduced congregation – by an elongated light cone designed for meditation and constructed from rendered, laser-cut polystyrene blocks. Crucially, the east window cill was lowered to connect street and cafe. A platform-lift was inserted behind a screen in the reception area, and a sequence of community facilities is set around the edge of the site, including a cloistered courtyard designed to work with the adjoining two largest community rooms. The scheme is brilliant.

# NEW STREET SQUARE
## EC4
## BENNETTS ASSOCIATES ARCHITECTS

CLIENT **LAND SECURITIES**
STRUCTURAL ENGINEER **PELL FRISCHMANN**
SERVICES ENGINEER **CUNDALL**
QUANTITY SURVEYOR **DAVIS LANGDON**
CONTRACTOR **SIR ROBERT MCALPINE**
CONTRACT VALUE **£200,000,000**
DATE OF COMPLETION **JUNE 2008**
GROSS INTERNAL AREA **102,193 SQ. M**
IMAGES **PETER COOK – VIEW**
SHORTLISTED FOR THE RIBA CABE PUBLIC SPACE AWARD

The architects were charged with the creation of a whole new business district containing more than 100,000 square metres of office space for 6000 people. The result is five buildings of differing sizes and expressions arrayed around a new city square. Retail occupies most of the ground-floor fronts, and the scheme has achieved a BREEAM 'Excellent' rating. Facing materials include natural and reconstituted stone, aluminium, and glass cladding with timber louvres, ensuring that the objective of architectural diversity is achieved despite the fact that all the buildings are by the same hand (which was not the original intention). The architects' familiarity with London's traditional cityscape – its density and surprises – was pivotal in giving the development a sense of place and focus.

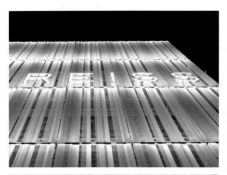

## REISS HEADQUARTERS
### BARRETT ST, W1
### SQUIRE AND PARTNERS

CLIENT **REISS**
STRUCTURAL ENGINEER **FLUID STRUCTURES**
SERVICES ENGINEER **HILSON MORAN**
QUANTITY SURVEYOR **DAVIS LANGDON**
CONTRACTOR **COMO**
CONTRACT VALUE **£16,000,000**
DATE OF COMPLETION **APRIL 2008**
GROSS INTERNAL AREA **4632 SQ. M**
IMAGES **WILL PRYCE – ARCAID**

This building manages to communicate a fashion brand simply yet powerfully, while responding sensitively to a dense and eclectic urban streetscape. Commissioned by the founder of Reiss, it speaks of a client's faith in the power of architectural imagery and the value of high-quality materials, impeccable construction and attention to detail. The glowing acrylic curtain developed by the architects is both enigmatic and seductive, and is very carefully detailed to produce a stunning effect when lit from behind. However, the veil is equally compelling during the day. It captures light within the thickness of each strip to become a vertical sunshower, while shading the south-facing office and showroom façades.

# RHIZOTRON AND XSTRATA TREETOP WALKWAY
## ROYAL BOTANIC GARDENS, KEW, RICHMOND
## MARKS BARFIELD ARCHITECTS

CLIENT **ROYAL BOTANIC GARDENS**
LANDSCAPE ARCHITECT **DAN PEARSON STUDIO**
STRUCTURAL ENGINEERS **ROYAL HASKONING (RHIZOTRON); JANE WERNICK ASSOCIATES (WALKWAY)**
SERVICES ENGINEER **ATELIER TEN**
QUANTITY SURVEYOR **FANSHAWE**
LIGHTING CONSULTANT **SPEIRS AND MAJOR ASSOCIATES**
ACCESS CONSULTANT **EARNSCLIFFE ACCESS FOR PEOPLE**
EXHIBITION DESIGNER **ENGINEERED ARTS**
CONTRACTOR **W.S. BRITLAND**
CONTRACT VALUE **£3,500,000**
DATE OF COMPLETION **MAY 2008**
GROSS INTERNAL AREA **450 SQ. M**
IMAGES **PETER DURANT – ARCAID**

**The Xstrata is a device for realizing childhood fantasies. A series of weathered-steel pylons supports an expanded-metal gangway that weaves through the treetops, providing a promenade 18 metres above ground. The introduction to this experience takes place in the Rhizotron, the concrete walls of which funnel visitors down to root level. One is then confronted by a pylon with a stair wound round it for a gradual but athletic ascent, along with a lift for disabled and older visitors. The walkway journey is short, but Kew will perhaps see the need for an extension, thus fulfilling this remarkable structure's potential for organic growth.**

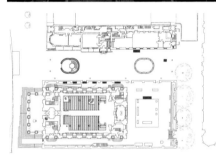

# ST MARTIN-IN-THE-FIELDS
## TRAFALGAR SQUARE, WC2
## ERIC PARRY ARCHITECTS

CONSERVATION ARCHITECT **CAROE & PARTNERS ARCHITECTS**
CLIENT **ST MARTIN-IN-THE-FIELDS**
STRUCTURAL ENGINEER **ALAN BAXTER & ASSOCIATES**
SERVICES ENGINEER **MAX FORDHAM**
QUANTITY SURVEYOR **GARDINER & THEOBALD**
CONTRACTOR **COSTAIN**
CONTRACT VALUE **£25,000,000**
DATE OF COMPLETION **OCTOBER 2008**
GROSS INTERNAL AREA **7180 SQ. M**
IMAGES **BENEDICT LUXMOORE – ARCAID (BOTTOM LEFT); TIM SOAR
(TOP LEFT; RIGHT, ALL IMAGES)**
SHORTLISTED FOR THE CROWN ESTATE CONSERVATION AWARD
ST MARTIN-IN-THE-FIELDS WAS JOINT WINNER OF THE RIBA CLIENT
OF THE YEAR

Eric Parry Architects' masterplan and design for St Martin's
has breathed new life into this landmark church. The
scheme includes the restoration of the church itself, but it
is below ground that the enormity and complexity of the
plan can be seen. Here, a grand public space has been
created where once there was a burial ground. Access
from the street is by a new jewel-like glass box.

The project has been painstakingly delivered with great
consideration and sensitivity at all levels of design, from
masterplan to detail. It was endorsed and supported by
an enlightened client, who is clearly delighted with the
architecture that has been created.

**GROUND-FLOOR PLAN**

## ST MARY MAGDALENE ACADEMY
### LIVERPOOL ROAD, N7
### FEILDEN CLEGG BRADLEY STUDIOS

CLIENT **LONDON DIOCESAN BOARD FOR SCHOOLS**
STRUCTURAL/SERVICES ENGINEER **BURO HAPPOLD**
QUANTITY SURVEYOR **DAVIS LANGDON**
CONTRACTOR **MACE PLUS**
CONTRACT VALUE **£27,760,000**
DATE OF COMPLETION **SEPTEMBER 2008**
GROSS INTERNAL AREA **2500 SQ. M**
IMAGES **NICK HUFTON**
**SHORTLISTED FOR THE RIBA SORRELL FOUNDATION SCHOOLS AWARD**

The architects' challenge was to squeeze an early-years centre, a primary school and a secondary school on to a relatively small Islington site. Liverpool Road reveals the project at its most public, with an 'educational shop window' and views into the lower-ground-floor assembly hall and playground beyond. The sports hall is above, elegantly clad both internally and externally in timber, and above it is a caged five-a-side football pitch. The early-years centre is organized around an external play area, with the primary school sitting above it.

The great achievement is to have integrated all these elements, which sit easily within their setting. The school is packed with measures to minimize carbon emissions, including natural ventilation, a biomass boiler and ground-coupling using earth tubes.

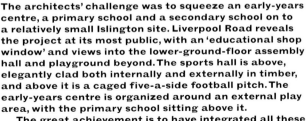

# UCL CANCER INSTITUTE: PAUL O'GORMAN BUILDING, UNIVERSITY COLLEGE LONDON
## HUNTLEY STREET, WC1
## GRIMSHAW

CLIENT **UNIVERSITY COLLEGE LONDON**
STRUCTURAL ENGINEER **BURO HAPPOLD**
SERVICES ENGINEER **FABER MAUNSELL**
QUANTITY SURVEYOR **GLEEDS**
CONTRACTOR **SHEPHERD CONSTRUCTION**
CONTRACT VALUE **£22,000,000**
DATE OF COMPLETION **SEPTEMBER 2007**
GROSS INTERNAL AREA **10,500 SQ. M**
IMAGES **MARK HUMPHREYS**

The Paul O'Gorman Building's complex, undulating, vertical terracotta louvres – a key determinant of its street aesthetic – make clear its contextual link with a nearby Waterhouse building. At a functional level, the louvres moderate the climate and reduce solar gain in the scientists' write-up spaces, which are in a strip immediately behind the façade.

The soffits of these internal spaces consist of beautifully made pre-cast concrete ceiling modules at the size of the structural bays, forming a sensuous, modulated surface overhead. They sit in welcome contrast to the necessarily hyper-functional rectilinear research laboratories, which are accessed directly from the write-up spaces. At the sixth and highest level the building becomes more open, showing a strong visual connection with London's roofscape.

# URBAN HOUSING, FINSBURY PARK
## SEVEN SISTERS ROAD, N4
## SERGISON BATES ARCHITECTS

CLIENT **CIRCLE ANGLIA**
STRUCTURAL ENGINEER **POWELL TOLNER & ASSOCIATES**
SERVICES ENGINEER **NC DESIGN**
QUANTITY SURVEYOR **ROBINSON LOW FRANCIS**
CONTRACTOR **HILL PARTNERSHIPS**
CONTRACT VALUE **£4,800,000**
DATE OF COMPLETION **JULY 2008**
GROSS INTERNAL AREA **1772 SQ. M**
IMAGES **DAVID GRANDORGE (BOTTOM RIGHT); STEFAN MUELLER (TOP LEFT AND RIGHT; CENTRE; BOTTOM LEFT AND CENTRE)**

With only a standard housing-association budget and tight space standards, the architects have managed to find an architectural language of great simplicity and presence that suggests robustness and permanence – both unusual qualities in this sector. The proportions and varying height of the three blocks recall the familiar forms of neighbouring nineteenth-century villas, and this reference is carried through to the choice of brick and to the vertical proportion of the fenestration. External walls are arranged as monolithic vertical piers between full-height openings and supported on thermally isolated in-situ concrete rails, which also create balconies and cantilevered roofs. The balconies are set within the building footprint, creating deep recesses and enclosed, usable outdoor spaces that are generous enough to allow seating.

# THE YELLOW BUILDING
## NICHOLAS ROAD, W11
## ALLFORD HALL MONAGHAN MORRIS

CLIENTS **NOTTINGDALE; MONSOON ACCESSORIZE**
LANDSCAPE ARCHITECT **MUF**
STRUCTURAL ENGINEER **ADAMS KARA TAYLOR**
SERVICES ENGINEER **NORMAN DISNEY & YOUNG**
QUANTITY SURVEYOR **JACKSON COLES**
CONTRACTOR **LAING O'ROURKE**
CONTRACT VALUE **£32,000,000**
DATE OF COMPLETION **JUNE 2008**
GROSS INTERNAL AREA **1393 SQ. M**
IMAGES **TIM SOAR**

Exuberance is a word not normally associated with office buildings, but this one expresses it in abundance. Its lemon-yellow striped façade and displaced sawtooth roof signal the building's role as flagship of a new, productive urban neighbourhood.

However, the real spectacle lies within: a muscular concrete lattice structure that frames a soaring eight-storey atrium. Part art gallery for the occupier's significant collection, part social space, part stage for catwalk shows and events, the atrium is both inspiring and generous on a scale rarely seen in commercial buildings in the United Kingdom.

The top floor is a huge open-plan samples workshop for Monsoon; symbolically, the creative production of the company takes place under the long-span sawtooth roof.

# BURREN HOUSE
## ANGLESEA ROAD, DUBLIN, IRELAND
## NÍALL MCLAUGHLIN ARCHITECTS

CLIENT **REG TUTHIL**
STRUCTURAL ENGINEER **CASEY O'ROURKE ASSOCIATES**
SERVICES ENGINEER **BURO HAPPOLD**
QUANTITY SURVEYOR **AUSTIN REDDY & CO.**
CONTRACTOR **MCINERNEY CONTRACTING**
CONTRACT VALUE **£2,100,000**
DATE OF COMPLETION **DECEMBER 2008**
GROSS INTERNAL AREA **490 SQ. M**
IMAGES **NICK KANE – ARCAID (BOTTOM LEFT AND RIGHT); NÍALL MCLAUGHLIN (TOP LEFT AND RIGHT; CENTRE)**

**GROUND-FLOOR PLAN**

A tantalizing view down a narrow lane between substantial red-brick Victorian houses shows a pristine glass box resting lightly on a granite wall. This initial view contains the two principal elements of the concept for Burren House: heavy, load-bearing stone garden walls enclosing the living and guest accommodation on the ground floor, and a delicate glass pavilion above. This first-floor bedroom element is made from a steel Vierendeel truss, and has multiple layers of glass, linen and blinds to all four elevations. The external skin is frameless glazing with natural linen laminated into the glass; this provides the privacy of net curtains during the day, and offers a unique sense of intimacy without diminishing the views over the lush surrounding gardens.

# HOOGVLIET HEERLIJKHEID
## ROTTERDAM, THE NETHERLANDS
## FAT

EXECUTIVE ARCHITECT **KORTEKNIE STUHLMACHER ARCHITECTEN**
CLIENT **WIMBY!**
EXECUTIVE LANDSCAPE ARCHITECT **DS+V**
STRUCTURAL ENGINEER **PIETERS BOUWTECHNIEK**
SERVICES ENGINEER **BOERSEMA INSTALLATIE ADVISEURS**
QUANTITY SURVEYOR **PRC VERSCHOOR**
CONTRACTOR **BAM**
CONTRACT VALUE **€2,400,000**
DATE OF COMPLETION **JUNE 2007**
GROSS INTERNAL AREA **500 SQ. M**
IMAGES **MAARTEN LAUPMAN (BOTTOM); ROB PARRISH (TOP; CENTRE)**

This project grew out of a collaborative approach with
WiMBY! ('Welcome into My Back Yard!'), the client, and
architect-led community consultation that included
festivals, exhibitions and events.

The architects were responsible for both the landscape
design and the buildings. They have transformed a dismal
piece of wasteland butting up to an enormous ICI oil-
refining plant by creating a bund to provide pasture
for cows, and acoustic and blast protection from the
neighbouring plant.

The Villa is the centrepiece of the new landscape, and
houses a large hall for parties and events, a cafe and what
will eventually be a small two-screen cinema. This is loose-
fit architecture, which concentrates on a supergraphic
façade that reflects the features that surround it.

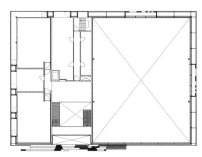

**GROUND-FLOOR PLAN**

# WEXFORD OPERA HOUSE
## HIGH STREET, WEXFORD, IRELAND
## KEITH WILLIAMS ARCHITECTS

ASSOCIATE ARCHITECT **THE OFFICE OF PUBLIC WORKS**
CLIENT **WEXFORD FESTIVAL OPERA**
STRUCTURAL ENGINEER **ARUP**
SERVICES ENGINEER **OPW M&E ENGINEERING SERVICES**
QUANTITY SURVEYOR **NOLAN RYAN TWEEDS**
THEATRE CONSULTANT **CARR & ANGIER**
LIGHTING CONSULTANT **SUTTON VANE ASSOCIATES**
CONTRACTOR **CLEARY DOYLE**
CONTRACT VALUE **€27,000,000**
DATE OF COMPLETION **SEPTEMBER 2008**
GROSS INTERNAL AREA **7235 SQ. M**
IMAGES **ROS KAVANAGH**

The incongruity of a major international opera house in a small Irish town is reflected in the boldness of the design. The unassuming entrance is a replica of what previously existed: a modest entrance foyer in a small domestic-scale street. From there, however, the building unfolds into an atrium space that links all three levels of the auditorium.

Inside, the rectilinear geometry of the outer layers gives way to sinuous curves generated by sight lines and acoustics – a poetic allusion to the soundbox of a cello. The richness of walnut, combined with the still new-smelling leather seats, provides an appropriate sense of luxury akin to the sensuousness of the interior of a classic car. It is a memorable experience for audience and performers alike.

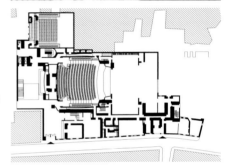

**GROUND-FLOOR PLAN**

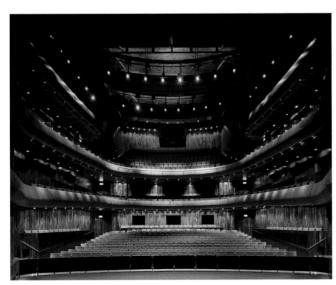

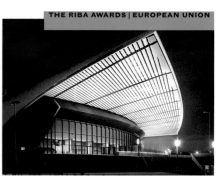

# ZÉNITH
## SAINT-ETIENNE, FRANCE
## FOSTER + PARTNERS

EXECUTIVE ARCHITECT **CABINET BERGER**
CLIENT **COMMUNAUTÉ D'AGGLOMÉRATION SAINT-ETIENNE MÉTROPOLE**
LANDSCAPE ARCHITECT **MICHEL DESVIGNE PAYSAGISTE**
STRUCTURAL/SERVICES ENGINEER **COTEBA**
QUANTITY SURVEYOR **CYPRIUM**
ACOUSTICS CONSULTANT **PEUTZ**
SUSTAINABILITY CONSULTANT **BATTLE MCCARTHY**
CONTRACTOR **LEON GROSSE**
CONTRACT VALUE **€40,000,000**
DATE OF COMPLETION **OCTOBER 2008**
GROSS INTERNAL AREA **12,599 SQ. M**
IMAGES **NIGEL YOUNG – FOSTER + PARTNERS**

Zénith is a purpose-built flexible music venue for
audiences ranging from 1000 to 7000 people. It was
conceived to raise the profile of Saint-Etienne as a
regional centre for the arts and to help drive the
regeneration of this post-industrial city.

With the exception of the dramatic canopy that shelters
and defines the entrance, the building is lean and mean,
the external form hugging the spaces within. Entrance
is at mid-level via a glazed foyer that not only ensures
the efficient distribution of crowds, but also allows the
ring road that bisects the site to be bridged by a large,
sloping public forecourt, lending the building an almost
'acropoline' quality. This clever integration of levels,
landscape and building mass is well executed.

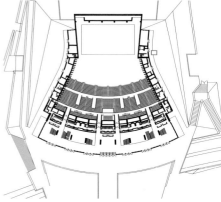

**FIRST-FLOOR PLAN**

# BIG PRIZE, SMALL PLANET: THE ENVIRONMENTAL CHALLENGE AND THE RIBA STIRLING PRIZE

**CHRIS TWINN, DIRECTOR, OVE ARUP & PARTNERS**

Chris Twinn co-founded Arup's sustainability group in building engineering. He is a former member of CABE's Design Review Panel, and a member of the RIBA Sustainable Futures Group, the BRE Global Sustainability Board, and numerous other professional committees. He also regularly acts as an adviser to UK central and local government.

Twinn's views do not necessarily reflect those of CABE or the RIBA.

As sustainability has climbed up the wider agenda, it would appear that the RIBA reacted well with its dedicated Sustainability Award. When it was initiated in 2000, the award was felt to be an appropriate response. But what has it achieved, and – ten years later – is that response still adequate?

There has been dramatic change during this period. In 2000 sustainability was a minority interest, the province of dedicated individuals struggling for some sort of market recognition, almost always in narrow sectors of the industry. For the wider audience it was an optional extra: desirable but by no means essential.

We now have a very different idea of what the future will bring and of the world in which our buildings will need to perform. It is one thing to say we will respond by replacing all our cars over the next fifteen years, but a very different proposition to replace all our buildings. We need to be resilient to a changing world.

These changes include increasing scarcity of materials, accelerating climate change, vastly curtailed carbon emissions, constrained finance, increasing taxation, and mounting individual and community expectations. We can no longer afford to produce buildings that are hungry for natural and financial resources, and that too often have obsolescence built in. We need more socially aware buildings – requiring less material and fewer systems, and ultimately costing less – if we are to support growing prosperity. As ever, less is more. Buildings that outlive their usefulness because they focus on short-life single-use and fashion are a luxury with a social and economic cost that is no longer acceptable. To all this must be added the future requirement for social responsibility by helping the developing world avoid the excesses we have shown in our pursuit of prosperity.

Are our buildings, and in particular those we put on pedestals, fit for such changes? Are these fundamental problems reflected in our priorities when we reward the great and the good in architecture? Anyone reading the Stirling Prize citations from the last ten years could be forgiven for believing that the word 'sustainability' has been purged from them. Such an impression reinforces the message that sustainability is not a worthwhile part of the buildings we regard as the very best.

It can be accepted that the absence of a particular label, and in particular the 'S' word, does not preclude its relevance to the work of the award-winners. Indeed, there is a logic in not using that tag, but instead acknowledging its constituent parts: social, environmental and economic responsibility. But do the words of the citations reflect that logic and describe how the buildings satisfy this new agenda?

Not surprisingly, social aspects tend to be covered very adequately within the winner's citation: it is clear that architecture struggles to warrant sufficient funding. But when it comes to the environment, there is silence. Nor is there any discussion of how buildings might retain their social and architectural merit in a changed future. The realization does not seem to have dawned that some of this good architecture will need to be fitted with ghastly insulated overcladding. Architecture must not appear to be above such problems when they concern the very future habitability of our planet.

Much of this kind of segregated response goes back to the first attempts, in the 1990s, to define sustainability. The 'triple bottom line' definition was typical, explaining that the three components each come with their own metrics, despite being under one larger heading. At least the recognition of differing metrics and assessments precluded the typical reductionist approach that might have attempted to drive such an aspect down to a single key performance indicator. However, this way of thinking of sustainability had the effect of placing it in pigeonholes too often occupied by separate groups speaking completely different languages and with little or no collaboration.

Such an approach polarizes design, focusing on the provision of 'either–or' solutions to the problem of what to spend the (limited) money on. It is only recently that those involved in these debates have started to acknowledge that it is not a matter of choice between social and environmental concerns, but rather that both have to be considered; and that good design demonstrates how the two can be integrated.

So, to go beyond the award citations, are the winners themselves devoid of environmental responsibility? It has to be acknowledged that many of the projects have very good environmental credentials. Accordia stands out, as does the Scottish Parliament, while 30 St Mary Axe makes valid claims. Some, however, are single-issue responses, such as Magna, which makes great play of bringing redundant buildings back into use, but seems to stop there.

The Stirling Prize assessment, however, appears not to judge environmental depth, and considers little how such factors might contribute to a building's status as exemplar. But must this be the case? Must one conclude that environmental subjects are irrelevant in the judging of exemplary building design? Others have decided that that is not the case: the experience of the Commission for Architecture and the Built Environment (CABE) in its Design Review role is but one example. Until about five years ago, environmental sustainability did not figure in CABE Design Review. It was felt that other, more technically competent bodies were better able to judge such matters, and thus that CABE should remain focused on design. However, considerable discussion of what constituted good design increasingly questioned the omission. Eventually the inevitable was acknowledged, and the particular role CABE took on was to champion the integration of sustainable measures at the earliest design stage, to avoid late – and compromising – add-ons. The significance of CABE's role was not so much in judging which particular solutions should be considered, but rather in bringing the environment into the top level of the design process, ensuring that it would be considered fully. CABE believes that good design should ensure that consideration of the environment and future resilience are properly integrated into the overall process.

So if CABE sees the problem of the environment as something to which all schemes must respond, why has the Stirling Prize seen it as a separate topic, divorced from what constitutes the supreme design exemplar? Perhaps it is the fear of not being able to judge to its usual very high standards what actually constitutes exemplary environmental design. Rapidly advancing knowledge in the field certainly makes judging it a challenge.

Here, too, there are lessons to be learned from others. CABE's experience of formally requesting a briefing on the environmental sustainability of a project has been interesting. At first, those preparing the submissions simply paid lip service, typically waxing lyrical about how environmentally friendly they were while doing little to hide the lack of integrated thought. Such phrases as 'low energy' were frequently and glibly used, without regard to what the energy use would be compared to. There were numerous examples of architectural aspirations that did not match the words: desire for façade transparency, for example, was inevitably followed in such a way that it was compromised when it was subsequently reconciled with energy targets. Submissions have been improving over the years, showing that the industry has slowly begun to climb the learning curve. The fundamental message is that good design must have environmental sustainability integrated within it.

Injecting environmental criteria into the Stirling Prize might seem a step too far and too fast. After all, it could be argued, it will come naturally, as sustainability becomes part of everything we do; and the industry needs time to embed this relatively new idea into the design of exemplars. But that argument implies that current candidates would have difficulty achieving architectural excellence with these new criteria. Such recent winners as the Scottish Parliament have shown the opposite, their architects delivering excellent architecture while achieving the highest BREEAM ratings. The designers of Accordia likewise accepted and succeeded with this challenge. Yet recognition is sadly lacking from their Stirling Prize winner citations.

It has also been suggested that environmental sustainability simply be codified into a list of criteria as represented by a BREEAM assessment. This can act as a reality check, since, as sustainability moves into the mainstream, there is a tendency for everything to offer its benefits. Even the slightest nod towards a single aspect is enough for much of the industry to claim to be sustainable. This 'greenwash' is set to increase as everyone feels the need to present what they do as following the sustainability agenda. Unfortunately, much of the public is likely to be taken in by such focus on presentation. The reality of the change needed is very different, however. It is absolutely essential for public understanding and for the development of a knowledgeable and critical public response that what makes a good building should be defined properly. Thus, it is important that the buildings chosen by the industry and presented as exemplars should not represent a greenwash. Assessment systems, such as BREEAM, can help to avoid that shallowness.

However, codifying environmental sustainability – whether as a BREEAM rating or in some other way – does not result in exemplary design, just as setting standards for fire escapes does not automatically bring about good design. Besides, with both knowledge and scope evolving so rapidly, no standard list can be expected to keep up to date; it can offer only a simplified representation.

In fact, it is innovative and creative design that is key in developing ever-higher levels of sustainability, presenting alternative approaches based on thorough understanding of the fundamental problems. This rapid rate of change and the development of knowledge must be driven by innovation and exemplars, rather than by standard compliance with tick-boxes. The Stirling Prize rewards the best design, where breaking the rules is part of forging better ways of doing things.

At which point, then, should an exemplar be judged? Good environmental performance is really established only once the building is in use. That is the dilemma for any architectural award: when does a building earn its success? There is a natural desire to assess it when it is pristine, but before there has been sufficient time to see how it works. For environmental aspects, this is a particular challenge, because all too frequently there are marked differences between predictions and in-use performance, especially highlighted by energy/carbon consumption and climate adaptation. The growing weight of evidence from building energy-efficiency labelling emphasizes this fundamental issue. If one reviews 30 St Mary Axe, one finds it makes some brave claims about the 50 per cent reduction in energy use. Has this been delivered in practice? It seems the façade vents are rarely, if ever, open, as required for natural-ventilation design. So, was this claim over-enthusiastic, or were there fitting-out and operating limitations? Is this an exemplary design of an enclosure that begged for that same exemplary standard to be carried through to the fit-out? Or perhaps could one be optimistic and say this is future-proofing waiting for the more frequent fit-out process to catch up? Similarly probing questions might also be asked about the long-term resilience of the Laban's plastic cladding. The exemplar test should consider whether a building really is environmentally resilient in operation.

While five years' good feedback would greatly help the judges, it is, of course, not practical. To a limited degree, the application of particular skills and healthy scepticism are useful. But it is only with the clear threat of subsequent detailed in-use review that designers will make more realistic claims and building owners be aware of their involvement in the building's overall performance.

In conclusion, it is excellent that the RIBA has finally recognized the importance of integrating sustainability into the Stirling Prize instead of packaging it in a separate box. But beware of the greenwash. It is essential that design claims are properly verified and then presented only as predictions, not as fact. Actual statistics should then be published. It is the performance of a building in practice that is the lasting legacy of an exemplar, not the claims of its designer.

The challenge for the RIBA now is to get this message across to the wider public, in spite of the media's tendency to focus on the sexy big 'A' of architecture. The message must be that sustainability is an essential part of all good building design.

# THE ROYAL GOLD MEDAL

ELIZABETH WALDER, MA, FRSA

The Royal Gold Medal was established by the RIBA in 1848 and is still awarded and celebrated today. It was conceived as a result of a conversation between the then President of the RIBA, Earl de Grey, and Prince Albert.

The idea for a Gold Medal had come about in 1846, twelve years after the foundation of the RIBA. Originally it was to be awarded to the winner of a competition to encourage young architects to design 'a building suitable and practical to house the Institute and its daily operations' – an idea that received royal approval from Buckingham Palace. Eleven designs were submitted, but – according to the RIBA's centenary history – 'they missed the mark so entirely: they were, most of them, so grandiose and expensive – in short, they so widely disregarded the conditions imposed, that the medal was not awarded. This fiasco sealed the fate of the junior members of the profession in regard to the medal and it was decided to award it in future not to the immature work of the young but in recognition of the actual achievements of the older men [*sic*].' (In fact, to date, shockingly, no woman has won the medal in her own right.)

Earl de Grey's fresh approach was communicated to Queen Victoria via Prince Albert. It was agreed that the medal should be 'conferred on some distinguished architect for work of high merit, or on some distinguished person whose work has promoted either directly or indirectly the advancement of architecture'. This has remained the basis of the criteria to this day.

The RIBA commissioned William Wyon, Chief Engraver of the Royal Mint, to execute the medal. The Vice-President of the RIBA, Ambrose Poynter, designed the reverse, showing a laurel wreath encircling text and the RIBA's coat of arms. The name of the winner is inscribed around the edge of the medal. Today the Royal Gold Medal is still made by the Royal Mint. As the gift of the monarch, it shares a coveted status with twenty-four other Royal Prize Medals awarded on an annual basis by Her Majesty The Queen. As originally conceived, previous winners include architects, engineers, historians, writers and theorists (see p. 263).

Nominations for Royal Gold Medallists are made by members of the RIBA in the first half of the year prior to the year of the award. Names are considered by a distinguished panel chaired by the President of the RIBA and including architects and non-architects from the United Kingdom and overseas. One name is presented to Her Majesty for approval, and the winner is announced in October. The formal presentation is held the following February.

This year's Honours Committee, which chooses the Medallist and the Fellows, comprised RIBA President Sunand Prasad; Peter Davey, OBE, writer; Sir Jeremy Dixon, Dixon Jones; Kenneth Frampton, Ware Professor at the Graduate School of Architecture and Planning, Columbia University; Despina Katsikakis, DEGW; Pankaj Patel, Patel Taylor; and Jane Wernick, Hon FRIBA, engineer.

# THE ROYAL GOLD MEDAL CITATION
## SUNAND PRASAD, RIBA PRESIDENT, 2007–09

Álvaro Siza is simply a profoundly complete architect who defies categorization.

As you arrive at Siza's Museu de Serralves (1997) in Porto, the shape of the entrance canopy immediately tells you that some special intelligence is at play. It is at once enticing and a little unsettling. A high white roof-edge over a white wall simply folds down to make a low white roof over the path to the front door. While the higher part – through which you glimpse some white cubic building shapes – lends majesty to these framed objects, the lower canopy is clearly there to guide your journey and provide shelter from the sun and the rain. In this sequence Siza has reinterpreted the ancient typology of the gatehouse in an entirely fresh, seemingly nonchalant way. The forms, though abstract, require no great interpretive effort, their impact being directly meaningful as experience. And as you move through the building, the same thing happens again and again. No other architect lays out buildings quite like this.

The forging of a masterful and seemingly inevitable architecture out of the possibilities of the site is one of the supreme characteristics of Siza's architecture. He manipulates his readings of place into sculptural forms that are never predictable or ordinary, yet are also never allowed to dominate over use or typological intelligibility.

Siza freely acknowledges his debt to Aalto, but the uncannily similarly named Alvar might have been a little jealous had he not been such a big-hearted man. In Siza's buildings, perhaps like no others, it is the relationships between the elements of the architecture that are given primacy rather than the shape or texture of the elements themselves.

This is an architecture in which an economy of expressive means is combined with an abundance of spatial revelation. In Santa Maria Church at Marco de Canavezes (1996) the congregation assembles in a very tall space, organized in plan specially to accommodate the familial style of modern liturgy, lit from above by indirect daylight. Out of quite ordinary elements Siza has here created an entirely new and deeply affecting spiritual space for our times.

Museu de Serralves, Porto, Portugal, 1997

'My architecture ... is a response to a concrete problem, a situation in transformation in which I participate.' In this famous statement, Siza sought to explain his approach of understanding and responding to the dynamics of programme and place, eschewing the facility of deploying already established theories to synthesize form. In that sense he has moved on from Modernism in the most explicit way. But rather than throwing away the compass, his architecture urges us to watch the needle more closely. He recognizes that the conditions in which architecture is created are contingent and unpredictable in ways that defeat the certainties of Modernism, but that does not lead him to relativism and a rejection of the great discoveries of Modernist pioneers. Rather, he applies them with a fluid mastery to the particularities of place and time in ways for which no method could be prescribed: 'We have gone beyond the stage whereby unity of language was believed to be the universal solution for architectural problems. Recognizing that complexity is the nature of the city, transformational movements take on very different forms.'

Siza's architecture matured in a Portugal under dictatorship, allowing little interchange with international architectural culture. After qualifying in 1955, he worked for three years with Fernando Tavora, with whom he is seen as the leading light of the 'Porto school'. Siza's approach is already evident in his first independent project, the charming Boa Nova Tea House and Restaurant (1958–63), albeit that the design there is overlaid with a measure of decorative detail, which displays his deep interest in construction more obviously than in later projects. Siza is emphatic about the importance of the unity of conception and execution in architecture, and has lamented the 'artificial separation between the phases of project and construction, which is characteristic of the contemporary production process'; furthermore, he has argued that 'the average low quality of contemporary architecture is, to a great extent, due to this division of work'.

After 1977 and the end of dictatorship, Siza was asked to design large numbers of low-cost houses for the local government of Evora, and later for the national housing association. Not only do these houses make adaptive and liveable dwellings, but also, collectively, they bring a gentle order to the city periphery, establishing Siza's command of the larger urban scale. At the same time, Portugal opened up to the outside world, and soon Siza was invited to enter competitions and take commissions abroad.

Ribera Serrallo Sports Complex, Barcelona, Spain, 2003

Siza has applied his unique architectural insights to buildings in Germany, Spain, Italy, France, The Netherlands and South Korea, and recently in London we saw the 2005 Serpentine Pavilion, a collaboration between Siza and Eduardo Souto de Moura. Siza has meanwhile continued to build inspiring buildings in Portugal, such as the College of Education, Setubal (1986–93); the University of Oporto Faculty of Architecture (1987–93); and the Adeaga Mayor Winery (2003–06).

Siza is, and always has been, a committed teacher and educator. He has enabled many younger architects to gain commissions through the work he was initially offered, and this selflessness is one of many examples of his commitment to the greater architectural project, rather than to personal success. Unusually for an architect of such international standing, Siza has deliberately kept his studio small to ensure his attention to every project. He is generous with his appreciation of other architects.

For the inspiring and instructive body of work he has produced during the past forty years, and for his immense contribution to architecture through dialogue and teaching, the RIBA, on behalf of Her Majesty The Queen, is honoured to present the 2009 Royal Gold Medal for Architecture to Álvaro Joaquim de Melo Siza Vieira. We wish him many more years of fulfilment of his unique vision of the possibilities of building.

**Santa Maria Church, Marco de Canavezes, Portugal, 1996**

# ÁLVARO SIZA
# IN CONVERSATION
# WITH TONY CHAPMAN

TC    I have spent two days filming some of your projects, in particular two early works – the swimming pool at Leça da Palmeira and the tea house. These were projects that engage with nature; they almost set out to tame nature. Is that a theme that has always interested you?

AS    Yes. I do not like to put up a building that does not seem as if it has been there since I don't know when. So whether I work in the town, in the urban scene or in open landscape, my preoccupation is that it fits the site, it fits the architecture. That does not mean mimesis, it means that when we approach a project there is a kind of predisposition in each site for what must follow. But as well as the appetite for transformation, there is also built-in inertia, things that we cannot see, and they leave marks, and I think the architect in a way is a kind of detective always looking for the facts.

TC    I went to see Buça [social housing] yesterday, and in a way that seems to symbolize some of the changes that have gone on in society.

AS    There were very bad conditions in Porto [in the 1960s and 1970s]. So when revolution came and there was a kind of void of power, all this exploded. And the government began a programme of support for people in bad conditions with social housing that involved participation. So we formed groups of architects and students to discuss with these communities, which had a real identity, what to do. We had about three hundred people discussing projects; it might be how to do the kitchen within the living-room, and so on. But gradually it became more structural, and suddenly what was under discussion was the town and problems with the town. And for architects, those that worked there, it was a period of both reflection and action, a time of enthusiasm. Nobody could be indifferent to the atmosphere then in Portugal.

TC    Materials are very important to you. How do you go about choosing your materials?

AS    Yes, it's a big problem. I was educated from the beginning in how to deal with difficult materials – stone, stucco, wood and things that sometimes are impossible to use. I remember sometimes in the old days, we young architects, our fight was to be able to use concrete, because to build a house in concrete was more expensive than using stone, and so our dream was to use concrete. And today sometimes our dream is to use stone, now it has become expensive. And our other dream was to make flat roofs; nobody wanted pitched roofs. Many things change – new materials, metal, treatment of wood – and so there are many masks appearing. That for me is difficult; I cannot think of architecture as masks. And so it's becoming more and more difficult for me.

TC    Another factor is the project manager, who is taking on another of the architect's roles.

AS    It's a fact that we are gradually losing control of what we do. The contractor's team has more power than the project team, and sometimes I think the wish of the client in a public building – but not only public buildings – is that the architects do a drawing,

214

they have to know the regulations, and how to get approval, and then bye-bye, we don't want you. It's happening more and more.

**TC** Let's turn to another building type of which you have a lot of experience: museums. I've been to Serralves, and I've been to Galicia before. It's been said that great architects earn the right to build on great sites. So how do you make sure you make the best of those sites?

**AS** I try to make the best of those sites. I don't know, there are different opinions among the critics. But what you can say is that good sites are those that are really asking to be transformed and that need a programme of transformation, and so the two things go together. And then you have to do a good work. If you do not do a good work you are not a good architect.

**TC** So it's not just the geography of a site, not just the physical position, the topography of a site?

**AS** It's also geography, but it's also history; it's everything.

**TC** Words are just as important to you as architecture; you write as succinctly as you draw. There is a brevity to your writing that is unusual in architects.

**AS** But I suffer in this. Because to write literature, it needs a concentration that I cannot always have, because I have so many other things to do. So when someone asks me to write a text about a project or an article, I really suffer, I really feel I should concentrate more: stop the architecture so now I can concentrate on writing. That is one reason. The other reason is I know I can never achieve the necessary quality. The thing I write most is poetry, and when you write poetry you see that each poem is so elaborated, and at the same time you do not feel all the effort involved – so it is like a jewel. But to arrive at that point – oh my God.

**TC** But your buildings have that simplicity, the simplicity but the concentration of a haiku perhaps.

**AS** I try to approach that, but I know them better than anyone, so I know where are the wrong things.

**TC** But your architecture is the opposite of instant architecture; you take your time. There's a term in cooking, 'slow cooking': it's slow architecture.

**AS** I don't like to work quickly. It can happen eventually in some state of euphoria – something allows the energy suddenly to go quickly – it can happen, but usually my work is slow, and also I want to take pleasure in the activity, because architecture without pleasure is a hell, it's terrible, so we must take as much pleasure as we can, because also it has its many constraints and bad moments, but the good moments compensate.

Iberê Camargo Foundation, Porto Alegre, Brazil, 1998

Ribera Serrallo Sports Complex, Barcelona, Spain, 2003

Boa Nova Tea House and Restaurant, Leça da Palmeira, Portugal, 1958

Portuguese Pavilion for Expo 98, Lisbon, Portugal, 1998

Viana do Castelo Municipal Library, Portugal, 2008

# THE RIBA
# INTERNATIONAL
# FELLOWSHIPS

Throughout its 175-year history, the RIBA has honoured men and women who have made a major contribution to the world of design and, in particular, architecture. Any architect outside the United Kingdom who is not a UK citizen, has a demonstrable interest in the objectives of the RIBA, and exhibits distinction and breadth of contribution to architecture may be elected an International Fellow of the RIBA. Prior to 2006, such people were elected Honorary Fellows; in 2006, with the creation of the new honour, all architect Honorary Fellows, including non-UK surviving Royal Gold Medallists, were made RIBA International Fellows.

Of the eleven architects made International Fellows in 2009, eight work in partnership. They come from Finland, France, Japan, The Netherlands, Portugal, Spain and Switzerland, and their work not only represents the spirit of their countries, but also transcends it to become truly international in its reference and influence.

This year's RIBA International Fellows were chosen by the Honours Committee, which also selects the Royal Gold Medallist and the RIBA Honorary Fellows (see pp. 226–33).

**ABALOS AND HERREROS
(SPAIN)**

Iñaki Abalos and Juan Herreros founded their practice more than twenty years ago, and as a consequence of their teaching and editorial, research and design activities have created their own identity as architects, demonstrating commitment to the contemporary world and concern for the urban context of new buildings. Their pragmatic approach to architecture is typified by their interest in the skyscraper, which dates back to the exhibition they designed in 1987, early in their careers, on the skyscrapers of Le Corbusier. They have gone on to build their own examples of the genre, including a Barcelona apartment block, the Woermann Tower in Las Palmas and – as part of Sociópolis – the Torre Solar in Valencia (all completed in 2005).

The work of Abalos and Herreros defies any easy stylistic categorization. It is based on a playful engagement with context. The architects take something from the place and usually add to it something unexpected from elsewhere: a material, a pattern or a way of making. They are committed to a clear tectonic articulation of constructional form, but they always infuse their designs with a marvellous quality of lightness: there is a sense that the building is only just there, and may disappear or fade at any moment. Additionally, although the buildings are often made of ordinary materials, they are nonetheless somehow transformed by the essential idea that underpins them.

Vitoria Towers, Bilbao, 2007

**GIGON AND GUYER
(SWITZERLAND)**

Annette Gigon and Mike Guyer have been working together for nearly two decades, and have become a fixed point of reference for younger Swiss architects. They achieved early success with their exemplary contributions to Swiss museums, and have since consolidated their architectural approach with international competition projects, housing and public buildings. Their buildings, despite their apparent simplicity, are highly considered, inventive solutions, sometimes appearing to dematerialize into their surroundings; this effect can be seen in such examples as the Kirchner Museum Davos (1992); the Erweiterung Kunstmuseum in Winterthur (1995); and the Sammlung Oskar Reinhart 'Am Römerholz', also in Winterthur (1998). Other work is more concerned with materiality: with the use of titanium, for example, in a family house in Graubünden (2007); the Cor-Ten-constructed Kalkriese Archaeological Museum and Park in Osnabrück (2002); or the use of iron-pigmented concrete on a signal-box in Zurich (1999).

The blind wall at the front of the Villa 'Am Römerholz' is made of concrete, and faces you as you come up the driveway. When the concrete was poured, copper grounds were mixed in with it. These have caused the surface to turn a cool grey-green. Above, a copper roof discharges its water directly on to the vertical surface of the wall. The copper carbonate flowing off the upper surface deposits fine layers of patina on to the face. On a wet day, this layering upon and within the surface causes the wall to glow with a lacquer-like lustre. Time and rain and weathering thus do not damage the architecture, but actually bring it into being.

In Davos, the Sports Centre is like a battered piece of hockey kit. The weathered-wood face covers blocks of acid-hued graphic colour. It is at once utilitarian and celebratory, as the architecture plays a knowing game between the materials that weather and those that stay bright and sharp. The thing seems unforced.

Gigon and Guyer manage to achieve striking, even theatrical effects, without appearing to have tried. Their work involves a fine balancing act between reserve and showiness; it also constantly provides the viewer with a sense of epiphany. It shows consistent control of the materials of architecture, and appears at once matter-of-fact and glorious.

Housing complex, Brunnenhof, Zurich, 2007

**KENGO KUMA
(JAPAN)**

Kengo Kuma was born in Japan and established his practice in 1990, with the aim of utilizing old and new materials in an experimentally expressive manner, in order to reinterpret the Japanese architectural tradition. He has become well known for his distinctive use of glass, wood and stone in works as diverse as private residences, Buddhist temples, and art museums. His buildings possess an extremely tactile character, which invariably harmonizes with the topography in which they are situated, irrespective of whether they are in the country or the city: for example, the Bamboo House that he constructed close to the Great Wall of China; the Hiroshige Museum in Nasu, Japan; the monumental louvred box of the Santory Museum, Tokyo; and the equally striking Fukusaki Hanging Garden offices in Osaka.

Kuma displays an acute sensitivity in relating a building to its context. In this regard he has created very varied works using quite different materials, for example – at the beginning of his career – the partition made entirely of glass, suspended on a sheet of water overlooking Atami Bay; an adobe cellar to house an ancient wooden Buddha; and a concrete observatory platform and steps cut into the top of a forested mountain. In each instance, whether the dominant material is plastic, stone, straw, paper or wood, the building is brought into a particularly sensitive rapport with its environment. In the timber-louvred Louis Vuitton headquarters in Tokyo, for instance, the façade is harmoniously linked to the tree-lined avenue of Omotesando; while at the Nagasaki Prefectoral Museum, the interplay of reflected light and transparency is mirrored in the water of the canal flowing through the museum. Similarly, at the small Masanari Murai Museum of Art, Tokyo, the old horizontal boarding of Masanari's house and studio has been stripped off the original shell and reused as a rustic screen of vertical timber louvres, which in effect serves to transform a private residence into a diminutive public building.

Water/Glass, Atami, 1995

**LACATON AND VASSAL
(FRANCE)**

**The Paris-based practice that Anne Lacaton and Jean-Philippe Vassal founded together aims to create buildings that are generous in space and spirit. The duo work at 'the edge of architecture' on social issues, and are keen to create a better living environment through social housing that incorporates 'freespace' that residents can use as they wish. The same principles apply to all Lacaton and Vassal's work, large and small, from single dwellings, such as the flexible living-space of Latapie House, Floriac (1993), which incorporates a large greenhouse-style living-area with moving wall panels and flexible floor plans, to the large scale of Nantes School of Architecture (2008), in which a significant proportion of the space is unassigned.**

**Lacaton and Vassal are interested in the intrinsic qualities of a place and the circumstances that surround the act of construction. They know that certain kinds of architecture can be detrimental to the unforced natural order of a situation. 'Why, more often than not, do things become fixed, freeze up, when architecture is installed?' they ask. Their work is undogmatic, but they have a strong commitment to the given and the imperfect. They tell us that they do not wish to address the whole issue of perfection. Their work has no virtuosity of a conscious kind; instead, it possesses a kind of indifference, a desire to avoid any self-conscious architectural form. They prefer buildings in a raw state, unadulterated, as though construction is somehow unfinishable.**

**Lacaton and Vassal's real passion is lightness. This could be the space beneath the broad sky, but really it means the skill, available to few designers, to do just enough or even to do nothing at all. It requires extraordinary judgement and tact to work in this way. This is architecture closely tuned to the music of what actually happens.**

Management Sciences University, Bordeaux, 2006

**JUHANI PALLASMAA (FINLAND)**

Juhani Pallasmaa is one of the most distinguished and influential architectural thinkers in the world. His voluminous production of articles and several books has increasingly identified him as a powerful advocate of the understanding of architecture as something that is appreciated by all the senses, meaning that architects need to design with more than just visual criteria in mind.

Pallasmaa's *The Eyes of the Skin: Architecture and the Senses*, first published in 1996, is a set book in many architectural schools throughout the world, and is the classic analysis of the phenomenological understanding of architecture. Other books have included discussions of the relationship of the cinema to architecture, and the unconscious work of animals and birds as architects.

Pallasmaa is not only a fine writer and a very approachable proponent of a most important theoretical and critical architectural position, but also a distinguished practising exponent of it, with project credits as diverse as the Helsinki Old Market Hall renovation; the Institut Finlandais in Paris (with Roland Schweitzer); the urban landscaping of the Ruoholahti housing scheme; the Bank of Finland Museum in Helsinki; and his contribution to the redevelopment of the Kamppi Centre, a new major part of the heart of the Finnish capital. He is an exquisite exhibition designer, whose thoughtful shows have illuminated many aspects of architecture.

Pallasmaa has shown himself to be an influential teacher in several countries apart from Finland, where he was until recently a professor at the Helsinki University of Technology. As a young man he also taught in Ethiopia, and he remains a visiting professor at Washington University in St Louis, Missouri. He is an Honorary Fellow of the American Institute of Architects, and a member of the International Committee of Architectural Critics.

House of Silence, Siikakoski, 2001

**EDUARDO SOUTO DE MOURA
(PORTUGAL)**

Eduardo Souto de Moura produces architecture that achieves harmony and balance between the natural and the man-made. Such buildings as the Braga Stadium and the interior of Álvaro Siza's Portuguese Pavilion at Expo 98, as well as his other work with Siza – for example, the Serpentine Pavilion in London in 2005 – have attracted attention both within and outside Portugal, not only because of Souto de Moura's capacity for reducing formal means, but also because of his sensitive treatment of situational factors and his ability to demonstrate a complex view of things.

Souto de Moura is a professor at the University of Oporto's Faculty of Architecture and has been a visiting professor at the architectural schools of Geneva, Paris-Belleville, Harvard, Dublin, ETH Zurich and Lausanne. He studied architecture at the School of Fine Arts in Oporto, and from 1974 to 1979 worked with Álvaro Siza at his practice. Souto de Moura began his professional career designing houses and achieving consistency and control of design by emphasizing adaptation to the site, reinforcing the idea that typology remains unchanged and universal, while materials and building systems are the elements of change.

Souto de Moura's focus has always been on the harmonious coexistence of the site and architecture through tension, an approach that has roots in contemporary American sculpture and the work of such artists as Robert Morris, Donald Judd and Sol Le Witt. Like them, Souto de Moura is concerned with making discreet, precise but convincing gestures so that his interventions generate a new balance that rearranges the components and imposes a new order upon them.

Souto de Moura's use of materials creates a fusion of monumentality, luxury, sustainability and contextual appropriateness that demonstrates the value he places on local traditions and appropriate solutions. His early work is more open and transparent, and the current work increasingly closed, while always being an elegant reinterpretation of mid-century Modernism.

Braga Stadium, Braga, 2004

**UNSTUDIO
(THE NETHERLANDS)**

Ben van Berkel and Caroline Bos co-founded their practice, UNStudio, in 1999. It is an international architectural practice that now boasts extensive experience in the fields of urbanism, infrastructure, and public, private and utility buildings. The practice strives to make a significant contribution to the discipline of architecture and continually to develop its quality of design and technology.

Underpinning UNStudio are several long-term goals, which are intended to define and guide the quality of its performance in the architectural field. The architects explain: 'We see the demands of the market and the wishes of the client as being equally important in enabling our work, and we aim for results in which our goals and our client's goals overlap.'

Van Berkel's early projects profoundly affected his understanding of the role of the architect today, and constituted the foundation of his collaborative approach to practising, leading to the foundation of UNStudio. Recent projects, which reflect his longstanding interest in the integration of construction and architecture, are the Mercedes-Benz Museum in Stuttgart and Arnhem Central (a bus terminal and station area). He is currently Professor of Conceptual Design and Head of Architecture at the Staedelschule in Frankfurt.

As an analyst, Bos has been involved in all UNStudio projects. Her observations about and synthesis of different programmatic issues have become integral to the work of the different project teams. With van Berkel, Bos was editor of *Forum* (1985–86) and the ANY publication 'Diagram Work' (1998). Her interest in the concept of the architect is reflected in the books she has co-written with van Berkel, including *Delinquent Visionaries* (1990), *Mobile Forces* (1994), *Move* (1999), *Unfold* (2003) and *Design Models* (2006).

La Défense offices, Almere, 2004

# THE RIBA HONORARY FELLOWSHIPS

In 2009 the RIBA awarded fourteen new Honorary Fellowships to men and women from a wide range of backgrounds, including journalism, art, engineering and property development.

RIBA Honorary Fellowships reward the particular contributions people have made to architecture in its broadest sense: its promotion, administration and outreach; its role in building more sustainable communities; and finally its role in the education of future generations. The lifetime honour, conferred annually, allows recipients to use the initials Hon FRIBA after their name.

All of these people, be they practitioners or commentators, have done much for architecture. In their very different ways, they have all helped to improve the quality of design and influence the delivery of the built environment in a sustainable and creative way.

This year's RIBA Honorary Fellows were chosen by the Honours Committee, which also selects the Royal Gold Medallist and the RIBA International Fellows (see pp. 218–25).

**PETER ACKROYD**

Peter Ackroyd was made an RIBA Honorary Fellow because of his deep understanding of the relationships between history and place, and between buildings and people. He has explored these in a series of acclaimed literary works, fictional and biographical, that has led readers (and viewers of his television explorations) to a greater understanding of the world. Overtly or not, Ackroyd's theme has generally been London, but his musings on the place of his birth always have universal application.

Ackroyd is the author of thirteen novels, many biographies and works of historical non-fiction, and has also presented television programmes. He is Honorary President of the London Festival of Architecture committee and chief book reviewer for *The Times*.

Ackroyd studied at Yale University and went on to act as Literary Editor (1973–77) and Joint Managing Editor (1978–81) of *The Spectator*. He is a Fellow of the Royal Society of Literature and was awarded a CBE in 2003. He blends past and present, fact and fiction in his writing, which often evokes the city of London as both a powerful physical presence and a sinister metaphor, haunted and animated by its past and its characters, both real and imaginary. He has been the recipient of the Somerset Maugham Award, *The Guardian* Fiction Prize and the Whitbread Biography Award.

Ackroyd's first novel, *The Great Fire of London* (1982), is a reworking of Dickens's *Little Dorrit*. The book set a formal pattern for many of Ackroyd's later novels, including *Hawksmoor* (1985) and *The House of Doctor Dee* (1993), by intertwining historical segments with present-day narratives. *London: The Biography* (2000) is a history of the city that has exerted such a powerful influence on his writing; the book was awarded the South Bank Show Annual Award for Literature. Ackroyd's latest book about London is *Thames: Sacred River* (2007).

**STEPHEN BAYLEY**

Stephen Bayley is a man for whom design, in all its manifestations, really matters. He has sought, almost obsessively and in a wide variety of ways, to interest the public in his subject, and has succeeded. Britain today looks very different from the way it looked in the 1980s, and that is due in no small measure to Bayley.

In 1981 Bayley was invited by Sir Terence Conran to run the Boilerhouse Project in a dilapidated basement at the Victoria and Albert Museum, where in five years he organized twenty exhibitions on subjects as diverse as the Ford Motor Company, Sony, Issey Miyake and Coca Cola. In 1987 the Boilerhouse transmuted into the Design Museum, with Bayley as its first, most controversial and innovative director. In 1989 he was made a Chevalier de l'Ordre des Arts et des Lettres, France's top artistic honour. Since 1990 he has worked as a freelance design consultant, advising numerous global brands, including Absolut Vodka, Marks & Spencer and Foster + Partners.

As architecture and design correspondent for *The Observer* newspaper since 2006, Bayley has shown a once largely design-illiterate public that design can improve their lives in many ways. Tom Wolfe said of him, 'I don't know anybody with more interesting observations about style, taste and contemporary design.'

Bayley is the author of eight books, including *Life's a Pitch* (2007) and *Work: The Building of the Channel Tunnel Rail Link* (2008); thirty exhibition catalogues; and countless articles, many of which treat his subjects with admirable and refreshing scepticism. Architecture and design need such forthright friends, and the RIBA is pleased to welcome Bayley as an honorary and perenially difficult fellow.

**LOREN BUTT**

Loren Butt is a mechanical engineer, and proud to be so called. He has developed a reputation for being an inventive and strategic thinker, committed to achieving architectural design intent. Not for him the fashionable 'environmental engineer' tag, although that is the job he has been doing supremely well for twenty years. Like many of the best engineers, Butt has worked relatively quietly in the background of any number of projects, making them succeed not only environmentally and economically, but also in terms of lifetime performance.

After working for various services engineering companies, both in the United Kingdom and in Canada, Butt joined Foster Associates as an engineering director. He contributed to the groundbreaking formative work of the practice, most notably the Willis Faber & Dumas Headquarters and the Sainsbury Centre for Visual Arts, but also, among others, the Hongkong and Shanghai Bank, Stansted Airport and the Sackler Galleries at the Royal Academy of Arts. Butt's involvement in these and other projects ensured that a strategy was developed in parallel with the architectural vision from the earliest stages of design. His memories of his former boss are mixed, however. Butt and his wife, Jenny, are keen gardeners, and well remember the occasion on which Norman Foster landed his helicopter on their lawn and blew away the runner beans.

Since 1987 Butt has worked as an independent consultant to a number of architectural practices, which consult him on conceptual services strategies at the early stages of design development. He has contributed to a great variety of projects, including the Tate Britain Pier; British Airways London Eye; London Underground Jubilee line Stratford Depot; White Cliffs Visitor Centre in Dover; HM British Embassy in Moscow; and the Brussels Opera House in La Monnaie.

**DAVID FISK, CB**

David Fisk is the thinking man's engineer and the thinking engineer's man. Fisk was one of the first to make the now obvious connection between engineering and the sustainable performance of buildings. As one of the key scientific advisers to government, he has had a beneficial influence on government policy in the areas of climate change, energy use, regional policy and transport. He has also done much to persuade everyone involved in the governance of our resources, as well as in the construction industry, that all future development has to be sustainable.

Fisk is the Royal Academy of Engineering Chair at Imperial College in Engineering for Sustainable Development. He is also Co-Director of the college's Urban Energy Systems project. He was previously Chief Scientist and Policy Director in the Department of Energy, the Department of the Environment, Transport and the Regions, and the Department of Transport, Local Government and the Regions. Until 2005 he was Chief Scientific Adviser to the Office of the Deputy Prime Minister. Among his responsibilities were UK climate change policy, including the Intergovernmental Panel on Climate Change; the Framework Convention and its Kyoto Protocol; the UK's first National Air Quality Strategy; and policy on the disposal of radioactive and other wastes.

Fisk has published in the fields of engineering, environment modelling and analysis, energy and resource economics, knowledge management, and risk. His research interests include approaches to understanding the onset of unsustainable development and how this might be best included in risk assessments, particularly for large complex systems, such as cities.

Fisk was made a Companion of the Bath in the 1999 New Year's Honours list.

**MICHAEL INGALL**

Michael Ingall has consistently shown himself to be a developer deeply concerned with architectural, urban, social and environmental issues. He has demonstrated that development is as much about the regeneration of our cities as about the making of money. An unsung role model for other developers, Ingall was a member of the team involved in the Manchester Civil Justice Centre – shortlisted for the 2008 Stirling Prize – a highly sustainable development that was also shortlisted for the RIBA English Partnerships Sustainability Award.

Ingall started his career at Drivers Jonas, managing several large estates, and went on to become a Director of Surveyors at Molyneux Rose, where he specialized in investment and development consultancy. He was then Property Director at Raglan Properties, where between 1990 and 1995 he was responsible for restructuring the company.

Throughout his career, but particularly as Chief Executive of Allied London Properties (ALP) since 2000, Ingall has encouraged the use of distinguished architects, including Foster + Partners, Sheppard Robson, Make, and John McAslan + Partners, and led the development of major mixed-use, inner-urban projects in Glasgow, London, Manchester and elsewhere.

ALP's Spinningfields regeneration scheme in Manchester demonstrates how ingenuity in development can be profitable while providing for an active, diverse community and incorporating major new civic buildings. Its restoration of the Brunswick Centre in London is an outstanding example of sensitive design-led regeneration of an innovative urban intervention of the late 1960s.

Current schemes in the ALP portfolio, such as the regeneration of Bracknell town centre, and the Granada Left Bank development in Manchester, show that Ingall and the company he heads have lost none of their imagination and determination to seek high quality in architecture and urban design.

**DOREEN LAWRENCE**

Doreen Lawrence's connection with architecture is both intimate and tragic, but out of the tragedy she has created an inspiring resource to make the study of architecture more accessible. Her son Stephen, who aspired to become an architect, was murdered in a racist attack in 1993, when he was eighteen years old. The perpetrators, while known, were never convicted. Not only did Doreen and Neville Lawrence display extraordinary strength and determination in their response to the loss of their son, but Doreen also went on to found the Stephen Lawrence Trust, which she directs.

Stephen dreamed of becoming an architect so that he could influence the design of inner cities from within. The Stephen Lawrence Trust seeks to make his dreams a reality for others by opening up the architectural and related professions to Britain's most disadvantaged young people. It awards bursaries to young people who want to train as architects or construction specialists; liaises between schools and construction companies; presents to educational institutions; and works with the government to find new ways to build communities with self-respect, and to regenerate urban areas. The Stephen Lawrence Centre opened in 2007 and provides much-needed mentoring and education, creative and business development facilities for disaffected young people.

The Trust is now a major force in education, with wide-ranging links to government and educational bodies, and to the businesses that benefit from the skills developed as a result. It has awarded many undergraduate and postgraduate bursaries to architectural students in the UK, the Caribbean and South Africa. With the support of the Marco Goldschmied Foundation, it has also established the Stephen Lawrence Prize, which is awarded annually at the Stirling Prize Dinner, for projects with a construction budget of less than £1,000,000.

**LAURA LEE**

Like Doreen Lawrence, Laura Lee's association with architecture arose through the misfortune of others. Lee is a cancer-care nurse, and one of her patients was Charles Jencks's wife, Maggie. Lee promised she would carry out Maggie's dying wish: to see cancer sufferers and their families offered humane facilities in which they could learn about the illness and receive support. Neither woman could have dreamt that within twelve years of Richard Murphy's first centre opening at the Western General Hospital in Edinburgh, six centres would be open, with a further three under construction and five more planned. All of the centres' services are free of charge.

Maggie's Centres are positioned close to major cancer-treatment units, so that they are easy to access. As CEO, Lee deals with fundraising, running the centres and persuading architect-led teams to produce great projects. Lee was made joint RIBA Client of the Year in 2009.

Opened in 2006, Maggie's Fife in Kirkcaldy was designed by Zaha Hadid, and was Hadid's first UK-based building. It has a sculptural, sparkling black exterior with sharp angles, contrasting with a light-filled interior of welcoming curves. Hadid said of her design: 'It's a great honour to create a building that will enhance the experience of people visiting the Maggie's Centre in Fife. I knew Maggie and we shared an understanding of how significantly environments can help enhance personal well-being.'

Further centres are planned for Nottingham (CZWG Architects), Newcastle (Foreign Office Architects), Cheltenham (MJP Architects), Monklands Hospital Lanarkshire (Reiach and Hall Architects), and South Wales (Kisho Kurokawa – his last work). The other existing centres are Dundee (Frank Gehry), Inverness (David Page, Page & Park), Edinburgh (Richard Murphy Architects) and London (Rogers Stirk Harbour + Partners, with landscaping by Dan Pearson Studio), which won the RIBA Stirling Prize in 2009.

**DUNCAN MICHAEL**

Duncan Michael was made an Honorary Fellow of the RIBA on account of his tireless efforts to help improve our built environment by means of a number of different avenues. Michael – an affably eccentric Highland Scot – was the third in a triumvirate of engineers in this year's list of RIBA Honorary Fellows. Through the Arup Foundation, he placed his vast experience as a teacher and practitioner with Arup at the disposal of a number of charitable construction-industry causes.

Michael studied engineering at Edinburgh University and later became a lecturer at Leeds University, where he also completed a PhD. He was Chairman of Arup from 1995 to 2000, expanding the organization into a global company, and became Chairman of the Trustees for Arup's Ownership from 1995 to 2004. He remains a trustee of the Ove Arup Charitable Foundation and continues to serve the company. Through his chairmanship Michael modernized Arup's constitution, governance and management, enabling it to prosper without abandoning its social values.

Again through the Arup Foundation, Michael has been very involved in establishing programmes run at the London School of Economics (Cities Programme) and the University of Cambridge (Interdisciplinary Design for the Built Environment). He also has a distinguished public-service career, advising many universities and professional institutions. Currently, his main focus, as Chairman of Investment at the Housing Corporation, is on the delivery of a massive social-housing programme in England, creating more than 40,000 new homes annually.

**JONATHON PORRITT**

Jonathon Porritt is a man of passion, conviction and eloquence. He also possesses a media-savviness that has enabled him to use those qualities successfully to argue the green case long before it became fashionable. For seven years the media associated him inextricably with his pressure group, Friends of the Earth. Since then he has had an equal impact on the Green Party and on Forum for the Future, the United Kingdom's leading sustainable-development charity, which has more than one hundred partner organizations, among them the world's most successful companies.

Porritt was formerly Chair of the UK Ecology Party (now the Green Party) from 1978 to 1984, during which time he gave the party credibility with the electorate, and helped membership grow from a few hundred to around three thousand. In 1984 he became Director of Friends of the Earth (FoE), a post he held until the turn of the decade. FoE was the first organization to campaign effectively on the issues of climate change and biodiversity.

Between 1993 and 1996 Porritt was Chairman of UNED-UK (United Nations Environment and Development, UK Committee). He has also been Chairman of Sustainability South West (1999–2001) and a trustee of WWF UK (1991–2005).

Porritt is a co-founder and currently Programme Director of Forum for the Future. He is an eminent writer, broadcaster and commentator on sustainable development, and in 2000 the Prime Minister appointed him as Chairman of the UK Sustainable Development Commission, the government's principal source of independent advice across the whole sustainable-development agenda. In addition, Porritt has been a member of the Board of the South West Regional Development Agency since 1999, and is Co-Director of the Prince of Wales's Business and Environment Programme, which runs seminars in Cambridge, Salzburg, South Africa and the United States.

**ALLAIN PROVOST**

Allain Provost is the *grand-papa* of French landscape architecture. His strongly geometrical work and benign influence can be seen on both sides of the Channel (not least where the Tunnel emerges near Calais). But it was with his designs for the Parc André Citroën in Paris that he began to rescue his profession and re-establish landscape architecture as much more than an adjunct to architecture and the rationalization of garden design.

Provost's other work includes designs for Courneuve Park in Paris, the Eurotunnel in Calais, the Technocentre Renault in Guyancourt, the reconstruction of the castle gardens of Villarceaux and the Thames Barrier Park in London. In 1990 he established Groupe Signe with Alain Cousseran, another landscape architect.

Working with architects Patel Taylor, Provost designed the Thames Barrier Park, an RIBA Award-winner in 1999 and a welcome addition to the capital's range of landscape-architecture projects. The park has a fresh, modern look, with adventurous planting and a dancing water fountain. In plan, the design bears a distinct resemblance to Provost's competition-winning scheme for Parc André Citroën. Both are dominated by a diagonal line slicing a rectangle, a geometrical idea found in many of Provost's landscape designs. In 2006 Patel Taylor with Allain Provost was announced as the winning design team, from a field of six international practices, to take forward the creation of Birmingham's first new City Park for more than a century. The winning design is composed of three interconnected gardens that form a centrepiece to Eastside and connect it to the core of the city.

Provost is an Honorary Member of the Fédération Française du Paysage (FFP; the French Federation of Landscape Architecture).

**ANDREW SCOONES**

Andrew Scoones has done more than anyone to drive cross-professional collaboration and to engender respect among the differing disciplines within the construction industry. In the past twenty years he has transformed the Building Centre Trust, of which he is now Director: while previously it was a place where architects would sneak in only to see the latest bricks, it is now a thriving industry community centre where architects are only too happy to breakfast with engineers and construction professionals, and discuss the latest thinking in environmental design.

The Building Centre Trust was established in 1963 as an independent charitable organization to provide support for educational, research and cultural activities connected with the built environment. Scoones ran the educational film unit there for ten years, producing more than fifty films for the construction industry. He has since developed the Trust's series of educational initiatives. These include 'The Art of the Structural Engineer', 'Renewable Energy in the Built Environment', 'Digital Fabricators', 'The Engineering Club', the 'Store Street' series with Peter Cook, and the 'Prefabulous Homes' series and publication.

Scoones has also co-curated and directed numerous exhibitions at the Building Centre, at Earls Court, London, and at the NEC, Birmingham. Most recently he collaborated with the London Mayor's Office to produce the travelling exhibition *No.1 Lower Carbon Drive*, which offers advice on how to transform a typical Victorian terrace into an environmentally friendly home. The exhibition debuted in 2007 in Trafalgar Square and has since travelled to the Ideal Home Show and Grand Designs Live.

Scoones's contribution to the discourse about our built environment has been tireless, enthusiastic and enormous. The Building Centre has become a forum for architects, engineers and many others with an interest in how we shape our environment.

**RICHARD SENNETT**

Chicago-born Richard Sennett was honoured by the RIBA for his profound thinking and teaching on the development of our cities. He is one of a long and honourable line of urban scholars, stretching back via Lewis Mumford to Ebenezer Howard. For four decades, Sennett's work has provided the sociological basis for the work of architects and urbanists.

Sennett is Professor of Sociology at the London School of Economics, where he teaches in the Cities Programme and trains doctoral students in the sociology of culture; he is also Bemis Professor of Social Sciences at the Massachusetts Institute of Technology.

Sennett's scholarly writing centres on the development of cities, the nature of work in modern society and the sociology of culture. His most recent books include *The Culture of the New Capitalism* (2006) and *The Craftsman* (2008). He is currently working on two projects, the first about cultural materialism, and the second a large-scale overview of urban design – a look at the evolution of cities, which Mumford traced in *The City in History* (1961).

Sennett founded, and directed for a decade, the New York Institute of the Humanities at New York University. He then chaired a United Nations commission on urban development and design. As President of the American Council on Work he led a forum for researchers trying to understand the changing patterns of American labour. He has been awarded the Amalfi and the Ebert prizes for sociology, and is a Fellow of the American Academy of Arts and Sciences, the Royal Society of Literature and the Royal Society of the Arts. He has written for numerous publications, among them *The Guardian*, *New Statesman*, *History Today*, *British Journal of Sociology*, *Contemporary Sociology*, *New York Review of Books*, *Times Literary Supplement*, *New Yorker* and *Harper's*.

**JAMES TURRELL**

It is rare for an artist to influence the progress of architecture directly. The work of James Turrell is an outstanding example of this unusual circumstance, and is the reason the RIBA wished to honour him.

As a sculptor, Turrell works directly with light and the impact it has on the perception of space. His installations can be seen throughout the world, and have moved even the harshest critics to wonder at the beauty and simplicity of Turrell's work. The result has been an increase in the critical sensibility of the observer, and in particular of architects, in relation to the mysterious beauty of light and how it is perceived through the eye. Architecture can fully exist only through the perception and illusions of light, and Turrell's work serves as a rousing challenge to architects to think afresh about the inventive possibilities of creating poetic space.

As a child Turrell was invited to 'go inside and greet the light' at Quaker meetings. Subsequently, at the age of sixteen, he learned to fly, and he has since explored the perception of vision through both the experience of flying and his studies on perceptual psychology and art. Inspiration then came from the work of Mark Rothko: Turrell preferred to see the paintings in the form of transparencies, where light is an active ingredient. An important exhibition in Berlin in 2001 was appropriately titled *On the Sublime: Mark Rothko, Yves Klein, James Turrell*.

Turrell has worked at many scales, from his extraordinary *Roden Crater* project (still in progress) to installations at the Yorkshire Sculpture Park, at Kielder Water & Forest Park in Northumberland, and for the Thames (unbuilt). His work has mystical overtones, but is firmly rooted in the reality of experience. It is preoccupied with how the eye responds to dramatic changes in light levels, and the actual nature of the moment of looking.

**MADELON VRIESENDORP**

The artist Madelon Vriesendorp has made a unique contribution to the visual culture of architecture, sometimes challenging architects, sometimes beautifying their work. Born in The Netherlands and now based in London, she studied at the Rietveld Academy, Amsterdam, in the 1960s. She later worked on the restoration of old frescoes and as a designer of jewellery, books and stage costumes. After graduating from Central Saint Martins in London, she moved to New York, where in 1975, with her husband, Rem Koolhaas, she co-founded the Office for Metropolitan Architecture.

Paintings Vriesendorp produced at the time were used for book and magazine covers, and were exhibited at the Guggenheim Museum and the Max Protetch Gallery in New York, the Centre Pompidou in Paris, the Stedelijk Museum in Amsterdam, the Aedes gallery in Berlin and Gallery Ma in Tokyo. Her paintings and drawings from this period were published in Koolhaas's *Delirious New York* (1978) and were widely acknowledged as beguiling and beautiful masterpieces. From the mid-1980s Vriesendorp taught art and design at a number of institutions, including the Architectural Association, London, and the Edinburgh College of Art.

During the last ten years Vriesendorp has worked in collaboration with Charles Jencks, producing drawings and models to accompany many of his publications, and with her own daughter on several books and art projects. Most recently she has produced illustrations for *Built*, *Domus* and *Abitare*, while working on costumes, built objects, paintings and short stories. In 2008 the Architectural Association hosted a show titled *The World of Madelon Vriesendorp*, and published an accompanying book of the same title, with contributions from Beatriz Colomina, Douglas Coupland, Charles Jencks, Shumon Basar and Stephan Trüby.

# THE RIBA PRESIDENT'S MEDALS STUDENT AWARDS

The RIBA has been awarding the President's Silver Medal since the 1850s. The President's Medals, in their current format, were established in 1984 and are regarded as an international benchmark for excellence in education. The aim of these prestigious awards is to promote excellence in the study of architecture, to reward talent and to encourage architectural debate worldwide. Each year students from schools of architecture in the United Kingdom and abroad aspire to be selected by their school to enter for the medals, and for the opportunity for their work to be recognized and publicly exhibited.

The President's Medals website (presidentsmedals.com) features all the nominations since 1998. On the site, which includes a database of projects and statements of intent from the students, schools define their educational policy and aims; tutors justify their nominations; and the judging panels explain their decision-making process.

Each year, the judging panels select up to twenty projects that receive awards. Medals are awarded in three categories: the Bronze Medal, for best design project at Part 1; the Silver Medal, for best design project at Part 2; and the Dissertation Medal. In addition, there is a maximum of three commendations in each category.

The winners of the 2008 awards received their medals and commendations in front of an audience of more than four hundred people at a prestigious ceremony held at the RIBA on 3 December. Previous guest speakers at the event have included Norman Foster, Alex James, Mark Lawson, Richard MacCormac, Richard Rogers, Martha Schwartz and Paul Smith.

The 2008 judging panels included Simon Allford (Chair), Hanif Kara, Benedetta Tagliabue and Ellen van Loon in the design project category, and Peter Blundell Jones (Chair), Gerry Adler, Catherine Slessor and Simon Unwin in the dissertation category.

Wynne Leung and Francesco Matteo Belfiore from the University of Greenwich won the Bronze Medal for their joint project 'Invisible University Library', and James Tait from the University of Strathclyde won the Silver Medal for his project 'Time and Tide for Seaweed'. Dominic Severs from the University of Westminster won the Dissertation Medal for his work 'Rookeries and No-go Estates: St Giles and Broadwater Farm'.

Atkins is the principal sponsor of the President's Medals. In 2008 the awards were also sponsored by iGuzzini, Paul Davis + Partners, the SOM Foundation and Komfort Workspace; *Architects' Journal* was the media partner.

Invisible University Library

Time and Tide for Seaweed

Rookeries and No-go Estates: St Giles and
Broadwater Farm

# INVISIBLE UNIVERSITY LIBRARY
## WYNNE LEUNG AND FRANCESCO MATTEO BELFIORE, UNIVERSITY OF GREENWICH

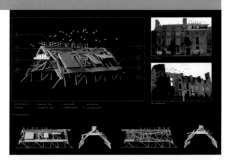

Hay-on-Wye, a small town in Wales, is famous for its second-hand bookshops, which receive internet orders from readers around the world. 'Invisible University Library' explores the position of the book, the writer, education and communication in today's society. The students identify a gradual shift from written language to technological media, particularly audio culture. Hay Castle offers an idealized pastoral landscape where books are read out, transferred to audio format, then broadcast to a live audience and on radio. Nature is inhabited by artifice as the castle becomes a mechanized, digitized rural artefact.

The students began by dismantling books. They dispersed the pages of a book entitled *The World Today* along the border between England and Wales, then collected the pages and interspersed them among the leaves of *An Outline of History*, their own portable border. Using a map of the town, they then identified the positions of scenes shown in old postcards. These were then introduced into the diagrams of a book called *The Process of Circuit Making*, thereby establishing a network of panoramas in the town. Their strategy was to reoccupy the historical 'postcard voids' by means of transposition: traffic islands become scenic views, postcard void becomes urban signal.

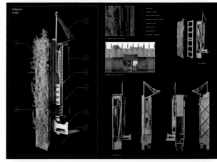

The students' 'hedgerow school' revives the urban tradition of storytelling. When Wales and Ireland were occupied by the English, Celtic languages were banned. Hedgerow schools emerged as a desperate attempt to pass the language on from one generation to the next. The students claim that the written word is less subject to alteration and reconstruction than the verbal language, and therefore the book is a museum. So books are shredded and used as a 'bird's nesting roof' or to make more paper, which is rolled out along the Welsh border for use by new writers.

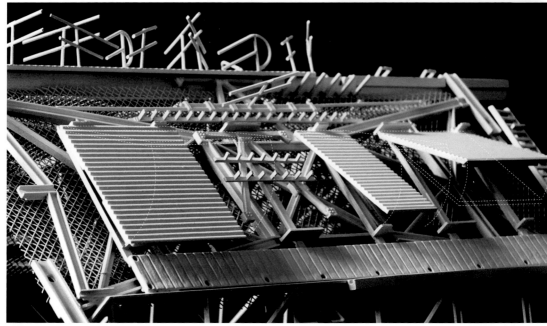

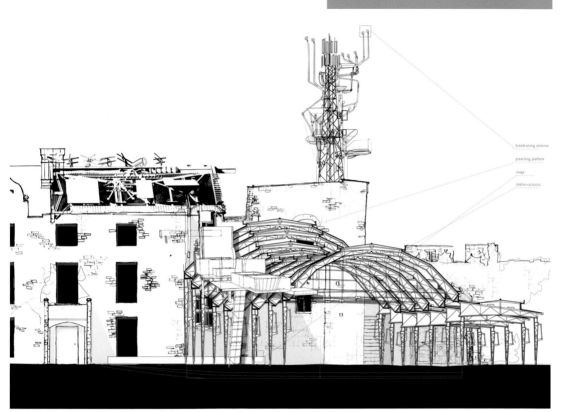

broadcasting antenna

preaching platform

stage

shelter+acoustic

# TIME AND TIDE FOR SEAWEED
## JAMES TAIT, UNIVERSITY OF STRATHCLYDE

James Tait's beautifully drawn and presented scheme proposes a productive landscape, based on the natural and abundant resource of seaweed, that would transform the coastal communities of the north-west Highlands. The student's expansive research allowed him to discover and substantiate the benefits of this unknown resource while ultimately forming the basis of his architectural proposal.

The seaweed-farm complex at Arisaig takes us through all aspects of the industry, from cultivation to consumption, and inventively explores existing and unprecedented building typologies. Comprising an offshore farm, a bothy, steam baths and a restaurant, the project's elegant structures are functionally arranged to facilitate optimum productivity while remaining proportionate and respectful to their environment.

The student draws on traditional coastal forms and textures yet remains thoroughly modern in his approach, creating an architecture that is sensitive and innovative, functional and beautiful. In an age of resource shortages and ecological awareness, the student's proposal provides a real alternative to fishing and migration, at the same time creating a landscape of purpose and poetry, all inspired by the humble seaweed.

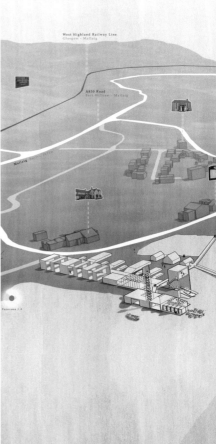

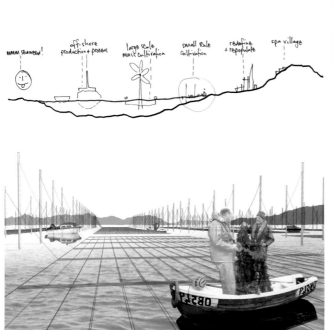

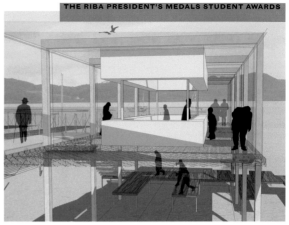

Loch Nan Uamh

Rhu Road

Loch Nan Ceall

Panorama 1.3

Panorama 1.2 & 1.3

# ROOKERIES AND NO-GO ESTATES:
# ST GILES AND BROADWATER FARM
## DOMINIC SEVERS, UNIVERSITY OF
## WESTMINSTER

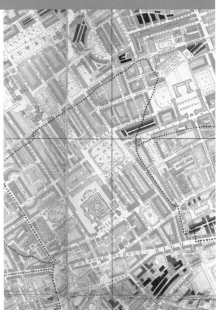

This outstanding dissertation investigates whether there
were parallels between the impulses and legislation that
lay behind the development of housing for the poor in late-
nineteenth-century so-called 'rookeries' and in the post-
war Modernist housing estates that feature so strongly in
contemporary London. Detailed documentary research on
the St Giles-in-the-Fields rookery and the Broadwater
Farm Estate, Tottenham, is supported by reference to the
literature of social conditions, behaviour and architecture,
particularly, for the nineteenth century, Blanchard
Jerrold's *London: A Pilgrimage* (1872) and Charles Booth's
*Life and Labour of the People in London*, first published
in the late 1880s, and, for the modern period, Oscar
Newman's seminal text *Defensible Space* (1972).

   The investigation of public and private space, and the
apparent and implied barriers between them, shows strong
similarities in the architectural strategies employed in
both forms, and leads the author of this dissertation into
a discussion of the ideologies that have coloured the
responses to both kinds of estate. The discussion is
enhanced and counterpointed through a consideration of
the rationale behind the development of the single-family
terraced house in late-nineteenth-century Tottenham.
There is full reference here to the enabling legislation
and literary representations that, in the case of both the
rookery and the estate, have taken shocked pleasure in
the depiction and gleeful description of the moral and
physical contagion, vice and violence inherent in these
'no-go' (for the middle classes) areas. Noting the hysteria
surrounding the description of the Broadwater Farm riot
of 1985, discussed in detail, with particular reference to
the subsequent official report, the author questions ideas
of community and safety, and raises the questions of
'whose community?' and 'safety from whom?' The possibility
of a new post-riot narrative for Broadwater Farm and
Modernist estates in general is proposed, and is entirely
original in its scope.

# THE HOUSING DESIGN AWARDS

The Housing Design Awards are now into their seventh decade. They represent a history of house-building in this country, chronicling changes in how homes are planned, designed and produced. The partnership promoting the awards also reflects shifts of emphasis in how new homes are funded. This year, the Homes and Communities Agency (HCA) joined the RIBA, the National House-Building Council and the Royal Town Planning Institute as a powerful new vehicle to deliver Communities and Local Government's drive for quality new homes. HCA's involvement helps to broaden the focus of the awards to address those bigger planning issues of infrastructure, employment, amenity and environment.

Shockwaves from the international banking crisis have affected developments everywhere. HCA is providing much-needed support to the industry by, for example, funding a programme that will reinvigorate and kick-start the best of the projects in England that have been stalled. Some of the unbuilt schemes shown in the Housing Design Awards' 'Exhibition of Excellence' (designforhomes.org/hda/2009/shortlist/project.html) could well be among those that deserve such help.

Small flats targeted at the rental investor have been hardest hit by economic conditions, but apartment-living can be very attractive when buildings are designed well, and this year there are great examples in both the Completed Scheme Award and Project categories. These schemes illustrate the emerging consensus on how to design apartments in which people would want to live over the longer term. The Completed Scheme Award-winner Angel Waterside maximizes the number of apartments with more than one aspect by using multiple cores. The design makes it difficult to distinguish between the social-rented flats and the market-sale ones.

It is notable that this year's Completed Scheme Award winners all include homes designed for families. While the winning schemes all go the extra mile, whether through their eco-credentials, their use of modern methods of construction, or a strong focus on design quality, it is the back-to-basics provision of good family homes, spaces and neighbourhoods that has given them the edge and has supplied what people want.

This is the first year in which entrants have been asked to score themselves against the 'Building for Life' criteria: government-endorsed design guidance that helps planners and developers deliver quality. A key part of this process requires an assessment of whether there is fair provision of both private and public amenities – something that has always been at the heart of the Housing Design Awards.

South Gate, Harrison Sutton Partnership

The importance of layout and the quality of private and public space are reflected in this year's Overall Winner, South Gate in Totnes. This scheme demonstrates the benefits of an ambitious local authority taking the lead: assembling a site; organizing a design competition, the brief for which was to maximize low-cost homes for local residents; and then managing a process whereby the intricate vision of the winning design made it to site intact. The judges noted how South Hams District Council recognized the limits of the private sector to fund everything, and worked supportively to achieve joint goals.

The success of this scheme reminds us what is possible. South Gate demonstrates how true partnership can still deliver our ambitions for quality homes and environments in which to live.

# SOUTH GATE
## TOTNES
## HARRISON SUTTON PARTNERSHIP

DEVELOPERS **SOUTH HAMS DISTRICT COUNCIL; MIDAS HOMES;
SOVEREIGN HOUSING ASSOCIATION**
CONTRACTOR **MIDAS HOMES**
PLANNING AUTHORITY **SOUTH HAMS DISTRICT COUNCIL**
IMAGES **TIM CROCKER/HOUSING DESIGN AWARDS**

South Gate comprises fifty-three new homes in Totnes across four sites so different in layout and form that the architects consider each a discrete development. Conversely, it is the total integration of planning authority, local people, architect and development team working together to deliver homes of every type that makes this scheme worthy of national attention.

The town did not like the original brief, and a community group called Design Our Space, in partnership with South Hams District Council and local architects Harrison Sutton, produced new proposals. South Hams then formed a partnership with Midas Homes and Sovereign Housing Association to deliver all four parcels.

The northernmost phase is a courtyard block of six town houses. The terrace is met at the top by a refurbishment of a historic building that retains a commercial unit at ground-floor level and puts two new two-bed apartments above it.

The second phase has an intricate arrangement of a three-storey house that sits back-to-back with a maisonette facing the street at first and second level. All the units use sun pipes to mitigate against the single-aspect nature. Both terraces are bookended at the bottom of the slope by prominent new-build blocks of seven apartments with spectacular views across the valley below.

The third phase is a development of ten town houses of four storeys in two runs of five. A landscaped area behind these houses will become a new public sculpture

**SITE PLAN**

garden and will feature running water as part of the sustainable drainage for dealing with flash flooding off the steep slope.

A final terrace of ten homes includes a small public park forming the corner to the road, so that the terrace can be pulled back to form a continuous line with the existing properties stepping down the valley.

South Gate achieves an EcoHomes 'Excellent' rating. The town houses have costed options of solar thermal or photovoltaic panels on the roofs. The approach of the partnership to boosting sustainability is refreshing, with the local authority agreeing to split the cost of upgrades to specification with its development partners.

# ANGEL WATERSIDE
## LONDON N1
## POLLARD THOMAS EDWARDS ARCHITECTS

DEVELOPER CITY WHARF DEVELOPMENT
CONTRACTOR CITY WHARF CONSTRUCTION
PLANNING AUTHORITY LONDON BOROUGH OF ISLINGTON
IMAGES TIM CROCKER/HOUSING DESIGN AWARDS

Angel Waterside is a single block of eighty-five apartments that has four cores when it might have had two. Multiple cores not only give more space and produce higher value dual-aspect apartments, but also facilitate the combination of social rent and highly priced market sale in a single block. The affordable core looks just like its market-sale neighbours.

The shallow block typically has a pair of smaller, single-aspect units on each side of the core, wrapped by dual-aspect apartments. The smallest, 40-square-metre studios have a hanging-bay balcony screened with metal louvres that can be independently twisted to control shading and manage privacy. The bays open due south for a view of City landmarks and plenty of light and air.

TYPICAL BLOCK PLAN

**FUTURE PROOF AWARD**

# CLAY FIELD
## ELMSWELL
## RICHES HAWLEY MIKHAIL ARCHITECTS

DEVELOPER **ORWELL HOUSING ASSOCIATION**
CONTRACTOR **O. SEAMAN & SON**
PLANNING AUTHORITY **MID SUFFOLK DISTRICT COUNCIL**
IMAGES **TIM CROCKER/HOUSING DESIGN AWARDS**

One tenet of sustainability is to use the local. This scheme of twenty-six homes in rural Suffolk has a communal boiler powered by biomass from the area's forestry. Homes are constructed in timber frame lined with hempcrete (lime mixed with locally produced hemp). The builder is from the next village.

The layout exploits the area's fabled flat landscape and low-angled winter sun. All houses face south, with the sun passing over the two-storey houses to reach the three-storey homes. Elevations and roofs are clad in a continuous cedar shingle, and the gable ends are finished in traditional local pastel renders.

A collaborative procurement process has not just led to local homes, but has also revitalized village life.

**FLOOR PLANS**

# HEREWARD HALL
## MARCH
## PROCTOR AND MATTHEWS ARCHITECTS

DEVELOPER **HOME GROUP DEVELOPMENTS**
CONTRACTOR **INSPACE**
PLANNING AUTHORITY **FENLAND DISTRICT COUNCIL**
IMAGES **TIM CROCKER/HOUSING DESIGN AWARDS**

Hereward Hall is one of three developments built in the Fenland towns of March and Chatteris as part of an Anglo-German-Swedish programme called SmartLIFE, which aims to share the skills needed for sustainable growth.

Hereward Hall is a rarity in being a low-rise residential development using Insitu Concrete Framework (ICF), so it is unusual that the ground floors are faced in brick. The upper storeys are clad in a hanging concrete tile, and roofs have traditional verges with the tile bedded in cement rather than being mechanically fixed. All the houses across the three schemes have modular bathroom layouts so that the same factory pods could be used.

Houses range from 76-square-metre two-bed homes to 86-square-metre four-beds.

**FLOOR PLAN**

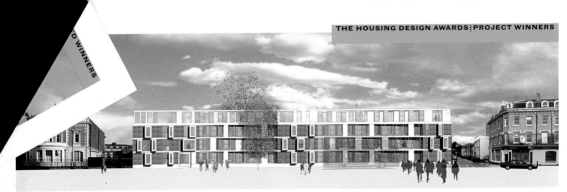

# ASHBURNHAM 3
## LONDON SE10
### FRASER BROWN MACKENNA ARCHITECTS

DEVELOPER **CATHEDRAL GROUP**
CONTRACTOR **NOT YET APPOINTED**
PLANNING AUTHORITY **LONDON BOROUGH OF GREENWICH**
IMAGES **HOUSING DESIGN AWARDS**

This development of two hundred student study bedrooms, to be built on Greenwich Road in south-east London, is in the heart of a conservation area. The building wraps a corner site with a continuous frontage; this gives the appearance of a single block, but in fact the project comprises three distinct 'villas' separated by stair cores that serve four storeys of 'apartments', with no more than three apartments on each floor. Each apartment contains between five and eight study bedrooms of typically 12 square metres, sharing a large kitchen-diner. Fifteen-square-metre studios are located mostly on the quieter southern corner of the layout.

The elevations use vertical bands of stonework and have panels of brickwork picking up on the Georgian buildings either side, complemented by white render. The top storey will be finished with a silvery untreated hardwood so that it has less presence and does not dominate its neighbours.

The scheme will be topped with a green flat roof – a response that tackles both climate issues and conservation anxieties.

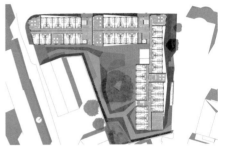

SITE PLAN

# BE
## SOUTH CHASE
## ALISON BROOKS ARCHITECTS

DEVELOPER/CONTRACTOR **GALLIFORD TRY PARTNERSHIPS**
PLANNING AUTHORITY **HARLOW COUNCIL**
IMAGES **HOUSING DESIGN AWARDS**

Be's houses co-opt the vernacular pitch-black weatherboarding found on mills and barns across Essex, as well as the commonplace slate roof. But then the plan, elevation and roof all have a little slice planed off, so that the orthogonal form becomes irregularly faceted, like a partly cut gem.

The scheme's most-used type is a 117-square-metre courtyard house, including a first-floor decked terrace. There are three other house types. The first two are 90- and 115-square-metre terraced houses built as part of the one-in-four provision of affordable housing, complete with photovoltaic roof tiles. The final house type is the scheme's largest: a 134-square-metre L-shaped-plan villa, where the short outrigger is two storeys high, and the rest three storeys.

**GROUND-FLOOR PLAN**

# CANNING TOWN
## LONDON E16
## MACCREANOR LAVINGTON

DEVELOPER/CONTRACTOR **COUNTRYSIDE PROPERTIES**
PLANNING AUTHORITY **LONDON BOROUGH OF NEWHAM**
IMAGES **HOUSING DESIGN AWARDS**

Working within a masterplan by Erick van Egeraat, Maccreanor Lavington re-use the surviving fragments of the Victorian neighbourhood, clustering a school and amenities around a square that will become the area's focal point.

New housing blocks reinforce the street pattern, with terrace houses bookended by apartment blocks. A short, single-storey wall screens small rear-parking courts, bicycle stores and storage provision for rubbish bins, while also acting as the parapet to a large first-floor terrace.

The terraced streets contain either three-storey houses (forty in total) or two-storey maisonettes with flats above. These are part of the strategy to give as many homes as possible direct access to the street, as well as private garden space or an outdoor terrace.

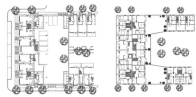

**FLOOR PLANS**

# DOWNTOWN
## LONDON SE16
## PROCTOR AND MATTHEWS ARCHITECTS

DEVELOPER/CONTRACTOR **BARRATT EAST LONDON**
PLANNING AUTHORITY **LONDON BOROUGH OF SOUTHWARK**
IMAGES **HOUSING DESIGN AWARDS**

This scheme of 212 homes is an early import of the Dutch *woonerf* (literally, a 'liveable street', used to describe a street in which pedestrians and cyclists have legal priority over drivers), and is partly the work of consultant Graham Smith, who has long called for streets to underpin a 'woonerful life'. Safety comes from bumper-bending obelisks and copses of trees in the road, directing vehicles first right then left as they track gingerly through.

The buildings are in seven discrete blocks. The elipse overlooking the site access is a new health centre, which will contain a community facility to replace existing provision on site. Other blocks contain homes ranging from 45-square-metre studios to 141-square-metre five-bed houses. A terrace of courtyard houses to the south-west of the site forms a lower density fringe to existing development.

**FLOOR PLAN**

# REAR 39–61 GWENDWR ROAD
## LONDON W14
## WESTON WILLIAMSON ARCHITECTS

DEVELOPER **STADIUM HOUSING ASSOCIATION**
CONTRACTOR **NOT YET APPOINTED**
PLANNING AUTHORITY **LONDON BOROUGH OF HAMMERSMITH AND FULHAM**
IMAGES **HOUSING DESIGN AWARDS**

The inspiration for this scheme is provided by a local landmark of 1890 on the Talgarth Road: Frank Wheeler's 'studio houses for the requirements of bachelor artists', with their triple-height picture windows.

Seven two-bed duplex units set on top of seven one-bed flats create fourteen homes in a building block of twelve and a final detached block of two. The gap between the blocks encloses the route into a deck access that serves the duplexes; the route is partly screened from the road by timber louvres.

All ground-floor apartments have private rear gardens. Residents in the duplexes have their own private outdoor space – a small secure garden at the west end of the site, which is reached directly from the deck access.

**FIRST-FLOOR PLAN**

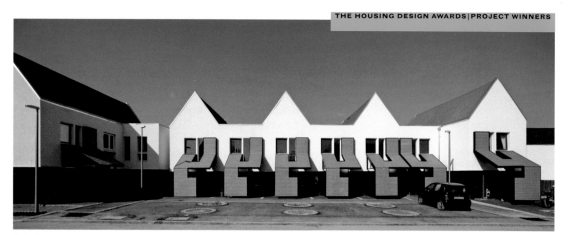

# SLO
## SOUTH CHASE
## PROCTOR AND MATTHEWS ARCHITECTS

DEVELOPER **SOUTH CHASE NEWHALL**
CONTRACTOR **SPACEOVER**
PLANNING AUTHORITY **HARLOW COUNCIL**
IMAGES **HOUSING DESIGN AWARDS**

FLOOR PLAN

This development, part of the much-feted Newhall, is a rare example of market-sale volumetric house-building on a greenfield site. It utilizes the FutureForm Building System, a monocoque steel construction. Modules arrive on site sealed and weather-tight, with a full internal fit-out. They are then stacked, roofed in clay tiles and faced in classic Essex white render before prefabricated porches, canopies and balconies complete the exterior elevations.

The aim is to allow customers to specify extensive internal variations in bathroom and kitchen fit-outs, but still have the homes ready in about sixteen weeks from reservation.

The scheme was launched as 'slo' (Simple Living Opportunities). The acronym soon reflected the market, and the judges chose to reclassify this half-finished scheme as a Project.

# TRIA
## LONDON E2
## FORMATION ARCHITECTS

DEVELOPER/CONTRACTOR **BARRATT EAST LONDON**
PLANNING AUTHORITY **LONDON BOROUGH OF TOWER HAMLETS**
IMAGES **HOUSING DESIGN AWARDS**

Someone walking past this scheme in east London would see six storeys stepping down to two storeys, all finished in a yellow stock flecked brick evoking that of houses in the adjacent conservation area. Behind and above the brickwork, however, is a series of inventions that gives this scheme a level of private amenity the Victorians would have envied.

The middle section of five floors has a sixth-floor set-back, allowing a communal roof terrace across most of the top floor. A similar set-back to four-, five- and six-bedroom three-storey town houses, with gardens on their roofs, makes them appear to be two-storey. Thirteen duplex apartments are faced with a medium-dark oak, which adds warmth and texture to the development.

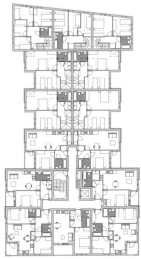

**FIRST-FLOOR PLAN**

258

# WOOLMER GATE
## LIPHOOK
## RE-FORMAT

DEVELOPER **TERRY BONNAR**
CONTRACTOR **NOT YET APPOINTED**
PLANNING AUTHORITY **EAST HAMPSHIRE DISTRICT COUNCIL**
IMAGES **HOUSING DESIGN AWARDS**

Small infill developments on the edge of villages create more resistance than anything sleek and soaring in the city. So, in spite of its environmental sensitivity and scale, this proposal, to replace two houses on the outskirts of Liphook, was bound to face opposition.

In the end, four rather than six units were approved. Each of the four detached two-storey villas has an inward-facing courtyard garden so that many principal windows are inverted.

Shallow-pitched roofs mean that the highest point of the villas is just 6.7 metres, less than the 9-metre ridge produced by the usual 40-degree pitch. The resulting scale will allow the houses to be wrapped with existing planting and screened from the plots beyond for much of the year.

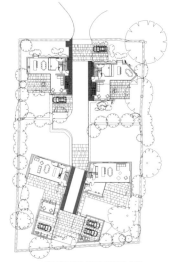

**GROUND-FLOOR PLAN**

# PREVIOUS WINNERS
# ROYAL GOLD MEDALLISTS
# SPONSORS
# INDEX

2004 Peabody Trust: RIBA Award-winning schemes

2005 Gateshead Council: art and architecture projects

2006 Royal Botanic Gardens: buildings at Kew and Wakehurst Place

2007 Derwent London: 28 Dorset Square, London

2008 Coin Street Community Builders: Coin Street Neighbourhood Centre, London


## THE ADAPT TRUST ACCESS AWARD

2001 Avery Associates Architects, Royal Academy of Dramatic Arts, London

2002 Malcolm Fraser Architects, Dance Base, Edinburgh

2003 Nicoll Russell Studios, The Space, Dundee College


## THE RIBA INCLUSIVE DESIGN AWARD

2004 Arup Associates, City of Manchester Stadium

2005 Foster + Partners, Sage, Gateshead

2006 Adjaye/Associates, Idea Store, Whitechapel, London

2007 Patel Taylor, Portland College New Learning Centre, Mansfield


## THE RIBA CABE PUBLIC SPACE AWARD

2008 Gustafson Porter, Old Market Square, Nottingham


## THE RIBA SUSTAINABILITY AWARD

2000 Chetwood Associates, Sainsbury's, Greenwich, London

2001 Michael Hopkins and Partners, Jubilee Campus, University of Nottingham

2002 Cottrell + Vermeulen Architecture, Cardboard Building, Westborough Primary School, Westcliff-on-Sea

2003 Bill Dunster Architects, BedZED, Wallington

2004 Sarah Wigglesworth Architects, Stock Orchard Street, London

2005 Associated Architects, Cobtun House, Worcester

2006 Feilden Clegg Bradley Architects, Heelis, Swindon

2007 Architype, Upper Twyford Barns, Hereford

2008 Denton Corker Marshall, Manchester Civil Justice Centre


## THE RIBA SORRELL FOUNDATION SCHOOLS AWARD

2007 Building Design Partnership, Marlowe Academy, Ramsgate

2008 Allford Hall Monaghan Morris, Westminster Academy at the Naim Dangoor Centre, London


## THE STEPHEN LAWRENCE PRIZE

1998 Ian Ritchie Architects, Terrasson Cultural Greenhouse, France

1999 Munkenbeck + Marshall, Sculpture Gallery, Roche Court, near Salisbury

2000 Softroom Architects, Kielder Belvedere, Northumberland

2001 Richard Rose-Casemore, Hatherley Studio, Winchester

2002 Cottrell + Vermeulen Architecture, Cardboard Building, Westborough Primary School, Westcliff-on-Sea

2003 Gumuchdjian Architects, Think Tank, Skibbereen

2004 Simon Conder Associates, Vista, Dungeness

2005 Niall McLaughlin Architects, House at Clonakilty, County Cork

2006 Alison Brooks Architects, Wrap House, London

2007 David Sheppard Architects, Wooda, Crackington Haven

2008 John Pawson, The Sackler Crossing, Royal Botanic Gardens, Kew, Richmond

## ROYAL GOLD MEDALLISTS

The Royal Gold Medal for the promotion of architecture, instituted by Queen Victoria in 1848, is conferred annually by the sovereign on some distinguished architect or group of architects for work of high merit, or on some distinguished person or group whose work has promoted either directly or indirectly the advancement of architecture.

1848   Charles Robert Cockerell, RA
1849   Luigi Canina, Italy
1850   Sir Charles Barry, RA
1851   Thomas L. Donaldson
1852   Leo von Klenze, Austria
1853   Sir Robert Smirke, RA
1854   Philip Hardwick, RA
1855   J.I. Hittorff, France
1856   Sir William Tite
1857   Owen Jones
1858   August Stuler, Germany
1859   Sir George Gilbert Scott, RA
1860   Sydney Smirke, RA
1861   J.B. Lesueur, France
1862   Revd Robert Willis
1863   Anthony Salvin
1864   E. Viollet-le-Duc, France
1865   Sir James Pennethorne
1866   Sir M. Digby Wyatt
1867   Charles Texier, France
1868   Sir Henry Layard
1869   C.R. Lepsius, Germany
1870   Benjamin Ferrey
1871   James Fergusson
1872   Baron von Schmidt, Austria
1873   Thomas Henry Wyatt
1874   George Edmund Street, RA
1875   Edmund Sharpe
1876   Joseph Louis Duc, France
1877   Charles Barry
1878   Alfred Waterhouse, RA
1879   Marquis de Vogue, France
1880   John L. Pearson, RA
1881   George Godwin
1882   Baron von Ferstel, Austria
1883   Francis Cranmer Penrose
1884   William Butterfield
1885   H. Schliemann, Germany
1886   Charles Garnier, France
1887   Ewan Christian
1888   Baron von Hansen, Austria
1889   Sir Charles T. Newton
1890   John Gibson
1891   Sir Arthur Blomfield, ARA
1892   César Daly, France
1893   Richard Morris Hunt, USA
1894   Lord Leighton, RA
1895   James Brooks
1896   Sir Ernest George, RA

1897   Dr P.J.H. Cuypers, The Netherlands
1898   George Aitchison, RA
1899   George Frederick Bodley, RA
1900   Professor Rodolfo Amadeo Lanciani, Italy
1901   Not awarded, owing to the death of Queen Victoria
1902   Thomas Edward Collcutt
1903   Charles F. McKim, USA
1904   Auguste Choisy, France
1905   Sir Aston Webb, PPRA
1906   Sir L. Alma-Tadema, RA
1907   John Belcher, RA
1908   Honoré Daumet, France
1909   Sir Arthur John Evans, FRS, FSA
1910   Sir Thomas Graham Jackson
1911   Wilhelm Dorpfeld, Germany
1912   Basil Champneys
1913   Sir Reginald Blomfield, RA, FSA
1914   Jean Louis Pascal, France
1915   Frank Darling, Canada
1916   Sir Robert Rowand Anderson, FRIAS
1917   Henri Paul Nenot, Membre de l'Institut, France
1918   Ernest Newton, RA
1919   Leonard Stokes
1920   Charles Louis Girault, Membre de l'Institut, France
1921   Sir Edwin Landseer Lutyens, OM, KCIE, RA, FSA
1922   Thomas Hastings, USA
1923   Sir John James Burnet, FRIAS, RA, RSA
1924   Not awarded
1925   Sir Giles Gilbert Scott, OM, DCL, RA
1926   Professor Ragnar Östberg, Sweden
1927   Sir Herbert Baker, KCIE, RA
1928   Sir Guy Dawber, RA, FSA
1929   Victor Alexandre Frederic Laloux, France
1930   Percy Scott Worthington, FSA
1931   Sir Edwin Cooper, RA
1932   Dr Hendrik Petrus Berlage, The Netherlands
1933   Sir Charles Reed Peers, CBE, PPSA
1934   Henry Vaughan Lanchester, PPTPI
1935   Willem Marinus Dudok, The Netherlands
1936   Charles Henry Holden, MTPI
1937   Sir Raymond Unwin
1938   Professor Ivar Tengbom, Sweden
1939   Sir Percy Thomas, OBE, JP, MTPI
1940   Charles Francis Annesley Voysey
1941   Frank Lloyd Wright, USA
1942   William Curtis Green, RA
1943   Professor Sir Charles Herbert Reilly, OBE
1944   Sir Edward Maufe, RA
1945   Victor Vessnin, USSR
1946   Professor Sir Patrick Abercrombie, FSA, PPTPI, FILA
1947   Professor Sir Albert Edward Richardson, RA, FSA
1948   Auguste Perret, France
1949   Sir Howard Robertson, MC, ARA, SADG
1950   Eliel Saarinen, USA
1951   Emanuel Vincent Harris, OBE, RA

| | |
|---|---|
| 1952 | George Grey Wornum |
| 1953 | Le Corbusier (C.E. Jeanneret), France |
| 1954 | Sir Arthur George Stephenson, CMG, AMTPI, Australia |
| 1955 | John Murray Easton |
| 1956 | Dr Walter Adolf Georg Gropius, USA |
| 1957 | Hugo Alvar Henrik Aalto, Finland |
| 1958 | Robert Schofield Morris, FRAIC, Canada |
| 1959 | Professor Ludwig Mies van der Rohe, USA |
| 1960 | Professor Pier Luigi Nervi, Italy |
| 1961 | Lewis Mumford, USA |
| 1962 | Professor Sven Gottfried Markelius, Sweden |
| 1963 | Lord Holford, ARA, PPTPI, FILA |
| 1964 | E. Maxwell Fry, CBE |
| 1965 | Professor Kenzo Tange, Japan |
| 1966 | Ove Arup, CBE, MICE, MIStructE |
| 1967 | Sir Nikolaus Pevsner, CBE, FBA, FSA, Hon ARIBA |
| 1968 | Dr Richard Buckminster Fuller, FRSA, Hon AIA, USA |
| 1969 | Jack Antonio Coia, CBE, RSA, AMTPI, FRIAS |
| 1970 | Professor Sir Robert Matthew, CBE, ARSA, FRIAS |
| 1971 | Hubert de Cronin Hastings |
| 1972 | Louis I. Kahn, USA |
| 1973 | Sir Leslie Martin |
| 1974 | Powell & Moya |
| 1975 | Michael Scott, Ireland |
| 1976 | Sir John Summerson, CBE, FBA, FSA |
| 1977 | Sir Denys Lasdun, CBE |
| 1978 | Jørn Utzon, Denmark |
| 1979 | The Office of Charles and Ray Eames, USA |
| 1980 | James Stirling |
| 1981 | Sir Philip Dowson, CBE |
| 1982 | Berthold Lubetkin |
| 1983 | Sir Norman Foster |
| 1984 | Charles Correa, India |
| 1985 | Sir Richard Rogers |
| 1986 | Arata Isozaki, Japan |
| 1987 | Ralph Erskine, CBE |
| 1988 | Richard Meier, USA |
| 1989 | Renzo Piano, Italy |
| 1990 | Aldo van Eyck, The Netherlands |
| 1991 | Colin Stansfield Smith, CBE |
| 1992 | Peter Rice, DIC(IC), MICE |
| 1993 | Giancarlo de Carlo, Italy |
| 1994 | Michael and Patricia Hopkins |
| 1995 | Colin Rowe, USA |
| 1996 | Harry Seidler, Australia |
| 1997 | Tadao Ando, Japan |
| 1998 | Oscar Niemeyer, Brazil |
| 1999 | The City of Barcelona, Spain |
| 2000 | Frank Gehry, USA |
| 2001 | Jean Nouvel, France |
| 2002 | Archigram |
| 2003 | Rafael Moneo, Spain |
| 2004 | Rem Koolhaas, The Netherlands |
| 2005 | Frei Otto, Germany |
| 2006 | Toyo Ito, Japan |
| 2007 | Jacques Herzog and Pierre de Meuron, Switzerland |
| 2008 | Edward Cullinan, CBE |
| 2009 | Álvaro Siza, Portugal |

This list includes honorific tiles at the time of the award and professional but not academic qualifications.

The RIBA is grateful to all the sponsors who make the awards possible.

The *Architects' Journal* is the UK's leading architectural magazine. It has been promoting good architecture since 1895. *AJ* believes that the architectural profession benefits from having a single, pre-eminent and undisputed award for quality design. That is why, throughout its nine-year investment with the RIBA, the *Architects' Journal* has helped the RIBA Stirling Prize to become recognized as the highest achievement in UK architecture by both the profession and the general public.

Crystal CG is an interdisciplinary company that specializes in a wide variety of digital applications. Established in 1995, Crystal CG helps its clients achieve their goals by applying 3D visualization technology to produce creative solutions. Based on its advanced digital technique and committed workforce, Crystal CG has now evolved into a broad-based media company and expanded into such areas as design, digital entertainment, history, culture and education, in addition to architectural representation. Crystal CG is establishing a long-term collaboration with the RIBA to enforce the architectural link between the UK and China.

The Marco Goldschmied Foundation, which promotes research into sustainable architecture and supports environmental and human rights issues and educational initiatives, this year donated the £20,000 prize fund for the RIBA Stirling Prize. In addition, the Foundation made a matching donation to the work of Amnesty International through the Amnesty Arts Fund, to encourage architects to join artists, writers and performers in supporting Amnesty's work. The Foundation also continued its twelve-year-long support for the Stephen Lawrence Prize, for which it provides the £5000 prize money and funds a £10,000 Stephen Lawrence Scholarship at the Architectural Association.

# Autodesk

Autodesk provides the tools and technology architects need to bring their ideas to life. From industry-leading design and drafting software to the Revit® platform for building information modelling (BIM), Autodesk offers a robust set of architecture software solutions that helps improve productivity, deliver innovative design ideas and manage change throughout the project life cycle.

## IBSTOCK
building sustainability

Ibstock is the UK's largest brickmaker, and its products provide beauty and protection for many leading buildings. Ibstock has a long association with architecture and especially the RIBA. This partnership has led to sponsorship of many of the local awards schemes run by the RIBA regions. Ibstock's commitment to the architectural profession runs much deeper, however, with support for the RIBA Student Newsletter and RIBA President's Medals, as well as support for international study tours and lecture programmes at many of the leading schools of architecture.

SIV Human Resources Ltd is the leading recruitment agency working within the architectural industry. Having been a proud sponsor of the RIBA Stirling Prize for the last seven years, it believes in supporting architecture through such events as the Stirling Prize Dinner. It has more than seventeen years' experience placing architecture's most talented individuals within the top-performing organizations globally.

## NBS

A good specification is critical to the success of a building project, and an essential, integral part of the design process. For more than thirty-five years, UK architects have turned to National Building Specification master specification systems to produce technically robust, up-to-date project specifications. NBS also offers software for efficient contract administration, online and offline solutions to provide access to technical and regulatory information, and a range of learning services to keep construction professionals' skills and knowledge current. NBS is part of RIBA Enterprises, the commercial arm of the RIBA.

the Rooflight Company

## THE CROWN ESTATE

The Crown Estate is proud to sponsor the Crown Estate Conservation Award. Now in its twelfth year, this award is presented for the best work that demonstrates the successful restoration and/or conservation of an architecturally significant building. The Crown Estate manages a large and uniquely diverse portfolio of land and buildings across the UK. One of its primary concerns is to make historic buildings suitable for today's users.

The Rooflight Company is sponsor of the Manser Medal, awarded for the best one-off house or housing designed by an architect in the UK. The prize is named after Michael Manser, former President of the RIBA, who is renowned for his own steel-and-glass housing designs. The Rooflight Company has built an outstanding reputation for innovation and design quality, and proudly sponsors the Manser Medal as part of its continuing commitment to supporting excellence in architectural design.

The Commission for Architecture and the Built Environment (CABE) is sponsor of the Public Space Award. CABE is the government's adviser on architecture, urban design and public space. The Public Space Award demonstrates that public spaces are as important as housing, schools, offices or any other buildings because the public use such spaces far more than they do buildings. We know that the public see the value in quality spaces and the difference they can make to their lives. The aim of the award is to encourage dialogue and co-operation across professions and to recognize the important role of landscape architects and urban designers in the process of creating places.

The Sorrell Foundation was set up in 1999 to inspire creativity in young people and to improve quality of life through good design. In its third year, the RIBA Sorrell Foundation Schools Award continues to raise further the standard of design in all new primary- and secondary-school buildings and to reward excellence in school architecture.

RIBA Award plaques are produced and donated by the Lead Sheet Association (LSA). The LSA is the primary independent body involved in the promotion and development of the use of rolled-lead sheet. The LSA is proud to have been associated with the RIBA Awards since 1989.

Cosentino, the leading surfaces provider from Spain, sponsors the RIBA Lubetkin Prize. ECO® by Cosentino is a revolutionary new decorative recycled surface material composed of 75 per cent recycled materials, including glass from 65 million bottles and ceramic from 50,000 tiles, as well as granulated glass from consumer recycling; salvaged mirrors and windows; porcelain from china, tiles, sinks and toilets; and crystallized ashes from industrial furnaces. The materials are bonded together with an eco-resin. The launch of ECO® by Cosentino sets an unprecedented standard for the green building and sustainable-design industries, and completes a portfolio of products that offers a unique surface for every consumer need.

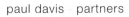 

The RIBA would like to thank all the awards judges, who give freely of their time and whose reports form the basis of much of the text of this book.

The RIBA also thanks the photographers whose work is published in this book (credits appear in the individual entries or on p. 270) and who agreed to waive copyright fees for the reproduction of their work in connection with the RIBA's promotion of the awards.

## PICTURE CREDITS

Photography/illustration credits are provided on page for all award-winning projects. Other images in this book have been reproduced courtesy of the following copyright holders:

Georg Aerni: 220; Iwan Baan: 45; Richard Bryant – Arcaid: 17, 84 top, 85 top; Charles Barclay Architects: 83 bottom; Tim Crocker/ Housing Design Awards: 243; Mitsumasa Fujitsuka: 221; Fernando Guerra – VIEW: 209, 210, 212–13, 216, 217; José Hevia: 219; Paul McMullin: 84 bottom; Rob Parrish: 83 top; Christian Richters – VIEW: 224, 225; Philippe Ruault: 222; Tim Soar: 85 bottom; Rauno Träskelin: 223

Tony Chapman is Head of Awards at the Royal Institute of British Architects. He has been, in vaguely chronological order, a bookseller, librarian, actor, playwright, theatre director, TV researcher/director/producer and architectural bureaucrat. While at the BBC he made a number of programmes about architecture and planning, including the Modernists' riposte to Prince Charles's *A Vision of Britain* with then RIBA President Max Hutchinson. He was thus considered by the RIBA to be a safe pair of hands to run its press office and latterly its awards programme, which includes, as well as the RIBA Awards and Stirling Prize, the RIBA Lubetkin Prize, the European Contemporary Architecture Prize and the Royal Gold Medal.